META MEDICAL ETHICS:
THE PHILOSOPHICAL FOUNDATIONS OF BIOETHICS

BOSTON STUDIES IN THE PHILOSOPHY OF SCIENCE

VOLUME 171

META MEDICAL ETHICS:

The Philosophical Foundations of Bioethics

Edited by

MICHAEL A. GRODIN

Boston University School of Public Health **and**
School of Medicine, and College of Liberal Arts

KLUWER ACADEMIC PUBLISHERS

DORDRECHT / BOSTON / LONDON

A C.I.P. Catalogue record for this book is available from the Library of Congress

ISBN 1-4020-0252-1
Transferred to Digital Print 2001

Published by Kluwer Academic Publishers,
P.O. Box 17, 3300 AA Dordrecht, The Netherlands.

Kluwer Academic Publishers incorporates
the publishing programmes of
D. Reidel, Martinus Nijhoff, Dr W. Junk and MTP Press.

Sold and distributed in the U.S.A. and Canada
by Kluwer Academic Publishers,
101 Philip Drive, Norwell, MA 02061, U.S.A.

In all other countries, sold and distributed
by Kluwer Academic Publishers Group,
P.O. Box 322, 3300 AH Dordrecht, The Netherlands.

Printed on acid-free paper

For Nancy, Joshua, and Leah

TABLE OF CONTENTS

CONTRIBUTORS ix

PREFACE xi

MICHAEL GRODIN / Introduction: The Historical and Philosophical Roots of Bioethics 1

RAYMOND DEVETTERE / The Principled Approach: Principles, Rules and Actions 27

ROBERT TRUOG / Commentary 49

THOMAS SHANNON / The Communitarian Perspective: Autonomy and the Common Good 61

RALPH POTTER / Commentary 77

GEORGE ANNAS / The Dominance of American Law (and Market Values) over American Bioethics 83

JOHN PARIS / Commentary 97

MARTHA MONTELLO / Medical Stories: Narrative and Phenomenological Approaches 109

LACHLAN FORROW / Commentary 125

MARGARET FARLEY / North American Bioethics: The Feminist Critique 131

ADRIENNE ASCH / Commentary 149

ALFRED TAUBER / From the Self to the Other: Building a Philosophy of Medicine 157

ALLEN SPEIGHT / Commentary 197

INDEX 203

CONTRIBUTORS

George Annas, J.D., M.P.H.
Edward R. Utley Professor of Health Law
Chair, Health Law Department
Boston University Schools of Medicine and Public Health

Adrienne Asch, M.S., Ph.D.
Henry R. Luce Professor of Biology, Ethics and the Politics of Human Reproduction
Wellesley College

Raymond Devettere, Ph.D.
Professor of Philosophy
Emmanuel College
Lecturer in Health Care Ethics
Boston College

Margaret A. Farley, Ph.D.
Gilbert L. Stark Professor of Christian Ethics
Yale Divinity School

Lachlan Forrow, M.D.
Coordinator of Ethics Teaching
Instructor
Division of Medical Ethics
Harvard Medical School

Michael A. Grodin, M.D., FAAP
Professor of Health Law, Pediatrics, Socio-Medical Sciences and Community Medicine
Adjunct Professor of Philosophy
Director, Program in Bioethics
Boston University Schools of Medicine, Public Health and College of Liberal Arts

Martha Montello, M.A., Ph.D.
Instructor Social Medicine
Division of Medical Ethics
Harvard Medical School

John Paris, Ph.D., S.J.
Walsch Professor of Bioethics
Department of Theology
Boston College

Ralph Potter, Th.D.
Professor of Social Ethics
Harvard Divinity School

Thomas Shannon, Ph.D.
Professor of Religion and Social Ethics
Worcester Polytechnical Institute

Allen Speight, Ph.D.
Assistant Professor of Philosophy and The Humanities
Boston University

Alfred I. Tauber, M.D.
Professor of Philosophy, Medicine and Pathology
Director, Center for the Philosophy and History of Science
Boston University

Robert Truog, M.D.
Associate Professor of Anesthesia and Pediatrics
Harvard Medical School
Associate Director
Multi-Disciplinary Intensive Care Unit
Children's Hospital

PREFACE

This anthology is the culmination of some 20 years of interest in the field of bioethics. I began my studies in the philosophy of science while at the Massachusetts Institute of Technology in 1970. My interest then, as now, continues to be the complex interrelationship between science and the humanities. While grounded in philosophy and molecular biology, I yearned for a more applied realm for exploration and integration of the value laden nature of science in the public policy arena. After receiving my medical degree from the Albert Einstein College of Medicine, I continued my work in medical ethics focusing primarily on the ethics of human experimentation, newborn and reproductive technologies, and human genetics. As I completed my clinical training at the University of California at Los Angeles and at Harvard, I had the opportunity to use philosophical ethics in an attempt to understand, frame and resolve moral dilemmas in clinical practice. As a professor of medical ethics at Boston University for the past decade, I have taught bioethics at the undergraduate, graduate and post doctoral levels. Over these years I have become increasingly frustrated by the state of contemporary bioethics.

Medicine continues to serve as an interesting paradigm for philosophers to explore novel theories about life, death, mind, suffering and meaning. Philosophy, however, has not served medicine quite so well as a source of knowledge and discipline to resolve the contemporary moral dilemmas found in health care. In some sense the growing frustration and ambivalence has stemmed from inadequate and inappropriate expectations on behalf of both philosophers and physicians.

Philosophers and scientists have a long history and tradition of interchange. Philosophy and medicine have had a more narrow but equally extensive history and tradition. Bioethics, as a formalized applied discipline, has only existed for about 25 years. As the field has matured it has become increasingly clear that there has been inadequate attention to the historical context and deeper philosophical grounding of the discipline and thus the need for a Meta Medical Ethics.

Despite the initial grounding of bioethics in theological discourse, philosophical analysis rapidly took over as the dominant paradigm. Some have argued that law and public policy have supplanted normative ethics. Further critiques of bioethics have come from virtue-based, phenomenological, narrative and feminist approaches. As the field of bioethics matures it becomes increasingly vital to re-examine its theoretical foundations: What is bioethics? How is medical ethics distinct from bioethics, professional ethics or applied ethics? What are its goals? What are its theoretical assumptions? What is its scope? Is it a unique discipline? Must medical ethics be grounded in clinical experience? How can ethical inquiry inform medicine's theory and practices? How can medicine serve as a paradigm for philosophical exploration? Must one have a definition of medicine before one can have a medical ethic? Does medicine have a unique or demarcating body of knowledge, methodology or philosophy?

These are a few of the troubling questions which have received inadequate attention and which this volume attempts to address. The essays and responses are derived from a colloquium entitled "Meta-Medical Ethics: The Foundations of American Bioethics" held on February 7, 1994 at Boston University under the auspices of the Boston University Center for the Philosophy and History of Science and the Law Medicine and Ethic Program of the Boston University Schools of Medicine and Public Health. The colloquium was generously supported by Alfred Tauber, Robert Cohen, Charles Griswold, Jon Westling, George Annas and Robert Meenan. This Symposium included a distinguished faculty of humanists, philosophers, theologians, physicians, lawyers, and scientists. Each speaker and respondent brought his or her own history and tradition to the discourse. The resultant essays offer a rich agenda for future dialogue. The strengths and weaknesses of each critique are identified and the nature and scope of the future agenda explored.

One of the originally scheduled respondents for this colloquium was to have been Professor Jay Healey, Professor and Head of the Division of Humanistic Studies of the University of Connecticut, School of Medicine. Jay was 46 years old when, on September 5, 1993, he died of a pancreatic cancer that had been diagnosed six weeks earlier. He was a gifted scholar, teacher, colleague and friend. He would have been happy to see this colloquium come to fruition.

This volume would not have been completed had it not been for several key individuals. I would like to thank Annie Kuipers and the editorial staff of Kluwer Academic Publishers. Marilyn Ricciardelli provided administrative support. Lauran Brown contributed secretarial assistance and George Leighton provided formatting expertise and indexing for desktop publishing.

Chris Hager added editorial criticism. Alexandra Klickstein and Kathy Bozzuti meticulously read the entire manuscript and provided invaluable and insightful comments as well as superb copyediting. I thank the other members of the Law Medicine and Ethics Program, George Annas, Leonard Glantz, and Wendy Mariner. They are the very best of scholars, critics, teachers, and friends and my work and life has been enriched by our long association. Finally I thank my wife Nancy, and children Joshua and Leah for their love, patience, support and unfailing nurturance. They make it all possible.

Michael A. Grodin
Boston
September 1994

MICHAEL A. GRODIN

INTRODUCTION: THE HISTORICAL AND PHILOSOPHICAL ROOTS OF BIOETHICS

Bioethics has existed as a specialized field of inquiry for only twenty-five to thirty years. In that time scholarly discourse has increased in quantity and quality. Some claim that bioethics has "saved" philosophical ethics from the obscurity of abstraction by giving it contemporary relevance (Toulmin, 1973). Others see bioethics as a central core for the rejuvenation, revitalization and reconstruction of philosophy (Englehardt, 1986). These authors have found in the framing, understanding and resolving of bioethical and medical problems a successful cross-fertilization of the disciplines of health and philosophy. In fact, the claim has been made that medicine has done much more for philosophy by providing concrete paradigms to explore classical and contemporary philosophical and ethical problems, than philosophy has done for medical practice.

Several authors either decry the paucity of analytic scholarship or suggest that bioethical inquiry lacks a significant philosophical grounding or methodology (Brody, 1988). Critics of applied ethics claim that the field will become bankrupt unless it pays further attention to ethical theory and philosophical foundations. It is argued that if the interrelationship between philosophy and medicine in applied bioethics is not to be doomed, it will, at minimum, require significant analytic re-evaluation to help conceptualize, frame, illuminate or resolve real problems in the real world. Such different perceptions of bioethics suggest there is disagreement not only about what bioethics can do and how to do it, but about the very definition of bioethics. As the field of bioethics matures, it becomes increasingly vital to re-examine its theoretical grounding. What is bioethics? How is medical ethics distinct from bioethics, professional ethics or applied ethics? What are the goals of bioethics? What are its theoretical assumptions? What is its scope? Is it a unique discipline? Must medical ethics be grounded in clinical experience? How can ethical inquiry inform medicine's theory and practice? Can medicine serve as a paradigm for philosophical exploration? If so how? Must one have a definition of medicine before one can have a medical ethic? Does medicine have a unique or demarcated body of knowledge, methodology or philosophy?

This chapter explores the historical and philosophical roots of the present day debate surrounding the nature, scope, limits and grounding of bioethics. The history of both medicine and ethics is reviewed to demonstrate the

M. A. Grodin (ed.), Meta Medical Ethics, 1–26.

complex interrelationships and interface between disciplines. Although there is an increasing literature addressing the agenda of medical ethics, its scope, ends and means, there has been insufficient exploration of the fundamental methodological issues associated with bioethics. This chapter attempts to clarify what bioethics does and does not claim. The goal is to identify common ground on which the ends and methods of bioethics can be debated fruitfully, instead of allowing particular disagreements to undermine the benefits of bioethics. The interrelationship of philosophy, theology, public policy and ethics has made substantial ground. However, if bioethics is to grow and flourish, it is necessary to have realistic expectations to guard against frustrations and to seek fruitful common ground. There must be a serious exploration into the grounding philosophy of medicine, the sources of quandary and the determinants or meaning of success and failure.

I. HISTORY OF BIOETHICS

A. Antiquity

The history of bioethics can be dated from the Hippocratic Oath in the Fourth Century B.C.E. The Oath laid out a broad set of principles of Greek medical ethics. The Oath, however, was an esoteric document written under Pythagorean aestheticism, which did not reflect the common practices of the day. The document has injunctions against abortion, euthanasia, and surgery, as well as strict provisions regarding sexual conduct and confidentiality. Further, the Hippocratic Oath reflects the male-dominated nature of ancient medicine. Medicine could only be taught from father to son, or from teacher to student, exclusively within this male profession. Other medical ethical writings from the Hippocratic period, such as *On Decorum* and *The Physician*, deal primarily with etiquette. Additional value-laden ethical discourses during the fourth and fifth centuries B.C.E. can be found in the writings of Plato and Aristotle. Both philosophers were concerned not only with the ethics of the practice of medicine, but particularly with the character and virtue of the physician (Carrick, 1985).

B. Middle Ages

Medical ethics during the middle ages made a significant shift from the philosophical traditions of Greek medicine in an attempt to universalize the ethical principles noted by Hippocrates. Physicians were seen as religious men. Christian writers such as St. Thomas Aquinas in the thirteenth century, Jewish writers such as Moses Maimonides, of the twelfth century, as well as

Muslim writers, all saw the practice of medicine as the highest ideal. The goal of medicine was to serve the sick under God. In this sense the Oath of Hippocrates was cleansed of its paganism and placed in the context of monotheism and religion. Medical ethics during the middle ages became a blend of religious and virtue-based ethics universalized to medical practice.

C. 19th Century

Modern codes of ethics began with the works of the British physician Thomas Percival. His 1803 monograph, *Medical Ethics*, is the first modern code of medical ethics. Then, in 1948, the first American Medical Association (AMA) code, a cautious legalistic noncommittal document focusing almost exclusively on physicians and their medical practices, was written. Each subsequent version of this code became shorter and less normative. There is no note of the patient's concerns within the AMA code nor does the physician have a specific societal accountability or obligation. Physicians in these early codes are treated as craftsmen and businessmen.

D. Early 20th Century

As the 20th century began, discoveries in bacteriology, physiology, and pathology led to a more scientific based medicine. This progression was formalized in 1910 when the Flexner Report on medical education in the United States and Canada called for the formalization of medical education. Hospitals also began their transformation from asylums to modern technology-oriented institutions.

The medical ethics of the early 1900's remained physician dominated and served the internal needs of the medical profession. In the 1930's, the American Medical Association justified opposition to group practice and national health insurance by appealing to this physician-defined medical ethic. The AMA claimed that "medical economics has always rested on fundamental medical ethics." Principles of medical ethics, it was claimed, should be left entirely to medical practitioners.

E. Mid-20th Century

Modern medical ethics had its initial grounding in theological discourse. In the 1940's and early 50's, Catholic theologians such as Charles McFadden and Edwin Healey began to write on medical ethics primarily in theological journals, on such issues as tubal pregnancy, maternal life, and abortion.

During this time, the Nuremberg "Doctors" Trial of 1946-47 revealed the horrifying details of Nazi physician involvement in human experimentation, eugenic sterilization, murder and genocide. The promulgation of the ten-point "Nuremberg Code" on the ethical permissibility of human experimentation marks a watershed in the history of medical ethics. Though the code only addressed nontherapeutic research on adult prisoners, its insistence on the voluntary informed consent of all human subjects marked a dramatic shift away from sole dependence on physicians and scientists for the protection of human subjects. The use of international law to hold physicians accountable for war crimes and crimes against humanity set the stage for a universal modern medical ethics (Annas, 1992).

The first significant U.S. document of modern medical ethics, and the dividing point between a physician-based medical etiquette and modern day medical ethics, was the seminal book written by Protestant theologian Joseph Fletcher in 1954 entitled, *Morals and Medicine* (Fletcher, 1954). Its attention to the patient's perspective separates this book from previous works. Fletcher developed a situation ethics which explored the ethics of euthanasia and reproduction, not from the perspective of the physician or Catholic dogma, but rather by examining the moral agency of the individual patient. Fletcher's work emphasized the importance of freely-exercised patient choice based in knowledge. Fletcher discussed contraception and sterilization, not as unnatural acts, but as acts enhancing choice. Until the 1950's, the ethics of clinical practice were considered solely within the domain of the medical profession. Fletcher argued that medical practice was not exclusively technical in nature, but normative as well and thus within the realm of patient choice.

As the general medical practice of the day moved out of the home and hospital and into the clinic, there was a de-personalization of the medical encounter coupled with advancing technology which provided for the changing nature and scope of both medical practice and medical ethics (Toulmin, 1988).

F. Contemporary Bioethics

By the 1960's a new field of "bioethics" had emerged. Bioethics in its infancy focused primarily on issues surrounding human experimentation. Expositions of contemporary research being conducted without consent and a resurgence of interest in the Nuremberg Code and the Doctors' Trial of 1947 created the framework for a reassessment of medical ethics. The 1960's saw a better educated public. The civil rights, consumer, women's, and disability movements empowered the public. The 1960's also saw a decline in shared communal values and a general distrust of authority and institutions epitomized by opposition to the Vietnam War. This anti-paternalism movement had a powerful impact on health care. Medicine was criticized for increased specialization, fragmentation, institutionalization, paternalism and de-personalization (Pellegrino, 1992).

A seminal article in the history of medical ethics appeared in 1966 by Dr. Henry Beecher (Beecher, 1966). The article, which was published in the prestigious *New England Journal of Medicine,* was an indictment of the ethics of medical researchers. Beecher cited twenty-two examples of medical researchers who had conducted unethical human experimentation endangering the health or life of their subjects. He did much of his work at Boston University's Law-Medicine Institute, formed in 1955. Public and professional outcry ensued, as did calls for specific ethical guidelines for the conduct of medical research. The U.S. Public Health Service, through the National Institutes of Health, implemented more formal and rigorous procedures for the protection of human subjects. The protection of human subjects would no longer be left solely to individual researchers but would be enhanced through independent outside regulations and monitoring. During this early period, however, scientists were still relied upon as the source of protection; monitoring remained a review process conducted by peer scientists. Lay oversight and informed consent were not widely discussed.

The 1978 federal Belmont Report: Ethical Principles and Guidelines for the Protection of Human Subjects of Research, identified three ethical principles to guide clinical research; beneficence, autonomy and justice. This report began to be viewed as providing a valid paradigm for general medical ethics. There was an increasing recognition of and concern for the exploitation of vulnerable populations such as the incarcerated, the poor, the minorities, the handicapped and the mentally retarded, who were most frequently the subjects of research (Rothman, 1990). The 1960's saw a remarkable proliferation of new and powerful technologies. Medicine had to grapple with ethical questions surrounding the advent of organ transplantation, kidney dialysis, ventilators, contraceptives and legal, safe and effective abortions. The establishment of Medicare and Medicaid in 1965 further increased the publics' accessibility to these technological advances.

The late 60's and early 70's saw a powerful patients' rights movement develop as a repudiation of the medical paternalism of the past. This autonomy interest would be protected through the doctrine of informed consent. During this time, bioethics explored the sanctity and quality of life and analyzed the termination of life supports in the elderly and newborns. Increasing concerns focused on the manipulation of nature through DNA technologies. Decision-making at the medical and public health levels was explored through the use of ethics committees, institutional review boards and discussions surrounding the ethics of the allocation of scarce health care resources.

The next milestone book in the intellectual history of medical ethics, *The Patient as Person*, was written by another theologian, Paul Ramsey, in 1970 (Ramsey, 1970). Medical ethics in the 1970's concentrated on issues at the beginning and end of life. There was increasing concern about definitions of life and death, personhood, abortion, and the foregoing of life-sustaining treatment. The advent of prenatal diagnosis and genetic testing in the late 60's contributed to a shift from abstract, purely intellectual concerns to more practical applications and implications of medical ethics. Physicians became increasingly concerned that medical ethics have a practical focus; principles had to lead to rules and a clear delineation of physician roles and responsibilities.

During the 1970's, organizations and centers dedicated to the study of medical ethics issues began to be established, i.e., the Hastings Center (1969), The Kennedy Institute of Bioethics (1971), the Society for Health and Human Values (1971), and the Boston University Center for Law and Health Sciences (1972). Through the 70's there was an increasing interest in academic courses, professional societies, journals, court cases and legislative action as well as federal commissions dealing with medical ethics.

In the 1980's, there was a shift of focus in ethics from the micro issues of the doctor-patient relationship to the new economics of health care. This resulted in an increasing concern about questions of distributive justice and allocation at the macro level. Concerns about health care costs and access grew in importance. During this period there was globalized attention to medical ethics, with a shift away from parochial, Anglo-American views to increasingly international concerns. The Council of International Organizations of Medical Sciences and the World Health Organization promulgated guidelines and international standards for drug trials and human experimentation. Europe became increasingly interested through the "Green Movement" in a broader bioethics and which included global environmental concerns. Interest in medical ethics also began in Asia, especially Japan. In the U.S., the 1980's saw the framing of philosophical problems shift from governmental bodies back to universities and centers where there was a proliferation of work on applying ethical principles and abstract twentieth century moral philosophical standards to medical ethics problems.

By the late 1980's and early 1990's, writers began to describe and note an increasing gap between the concrete and practical concerns of particular doctors and patients, and the philosophical and abstract theoretical medical ethics frequently found in the bioethics literature. Critics argued that preoccupation with philosophical analysis was too general and theoretical to be of value in practical clinical ethics. Philosophical analysis was felt to be too rationalistic and removed from the lives of persons. And thus, in the 1990's, there began a widespread and formalized critique of contemporary bioethics. This critique took many forms including a resurgence of interest in theology. A backlash against principlism resulted in even broader criticism using communitarian ethics, virtue-based ethics, casuistry, narrative and interpretive ethics as well as hermeneutical and phenomenological approaches. Bioethicists became interested in the work of social scientists and anthropologists, the ethics of care, as well as feminist and Marxist approaches.

II. DEMARCATIONS IN BIOETHICS

A. Bioethics Vs. Medical Ethics

The definitions of and distinctions between bioethics and medical ethics remain obscure. Both are forms of applied ethics. For the purposes of this discussion, ethics will be defined as a branch of philosophy, which through formal and systematic analysis, attempts to critically examine human conduct focusing on the rightness and wrongness, good or harm of actions. Normative ethics addresses the nature and justification of universalizable principles to judge what should or ought be done. Classical ethics defined the aim of ethical inquiry as the formation of good character, while modern ethics focuses on the making of good moral decisions. Bioethics is a broad term which incorporates an applied ethical inquiry into all situations where biology affects human affairs. These affairs may be medical, such as genetics or health care practice, or nonmedical, such as animal rights or ecology (Pellegrino, 1993; Clouser, 1978).

Medical ethics is a narrower term referring to applied ethics in the medical realm. In this sense, medical ethics is a sub-field of bioethics. Its primary topics have focused on goals of medicine such as the diagnosis and treatment of disease, health promotion and disease prevention, the relief of pain and suffering, and the care of the ill. Medical ethics is primarily focused within a medical context. Whether the fields of medical ethics or bioethics require a new conceptualization of classic normative ethics remains an area of significant disagreement (Clouser, 1978).

B. Professional Ethics Vs. Medical Ethics

Medical ethics deals with ethical issues and inquiry within the fields of medicine and public health. Professional ethics is a branch of ethics which focuses on professional responsibility and conduct. Medical professional ethics focuses on the conduct of physicians or other health care professionals in a professional setting. The ethics of the professions may be seen as more practical, realistic and responsive to the problems of physicians. Professional ethics may also consider the virtues and character of physicians themselves (Jonsen, 1982; Jonsen, 1992).

C. Clinical Medical Ethics Vs. Philosophical Medical Ethics

Clinical ethics seeks answers to moral dilemmas within the context of active clinical practice. Problems arise in the application of medical ethics to the practice of clinical medicine. Does medical ethics merely apply principles and provide nonprescriptive values, or does it propose specific normative policy recommendations? (Thomasma, 1980). It is claimed that for medical ethics to apply to clinical problems, it must be grounded in a philosophy of medicine. Such a philosophy of medicine must be versed in the clinical practice of medicine, must have practical aims, and the ethical discourse must fit into the context of treating patients (Thomasma, 1980).

Some claim that for clinical ethics to be of value it must address the philosophy of medicine with its epistemology, concepts of health and disease, history, views of people, and values. Others claim that clinical ethics must seek less abstract philosophical methodologies and focus on casuistic clinical case paradigms which facilitate analysis of specific cases in specific circumstances (Drane, 1990). Others counter that philosophical ethics and ethical theory can be of value in applied ethics as long as one recognizes his or her limitations and acknowledges that there is no single "right" answer. Problems associated with the relationship of philosophical to clinical medical ethics relate to uncertainty, the lack of empiric facts, value disagreements, and problems with framing, structuring and identifying the sources of disagreement in an attempt to analyze and resolve moral dilemmas (Noble, 1982; Macklin, 1989).

Practical clinical ethics looks for approaches that can help with specific cases. It may, however, be incorrect to assume that there is a rational justification for clinical ethical decision-making based on such foundationalism as autonomy, unity and rationality. The path from fundamental norms to principles, rules, and facts, may not reflect the nature of clinical decision-making (Hoffmaster, 1989). Some authors claim that clinical ethics must address moral problems in the real world which are complex, dynamic and evolving. Philosophical ethics may impose a view of morality on the real world, rather than construct morality **from** the real world (Thomasma, 1980).

Other writers argue that medicine is a moral enterprise, governed by normative rules (Cassell, 1976). But normative ethics may be relative. Nonetheless, it is necessary to clarify the frame of ethical discourse, prioritize values, and understand the complex problems practitioners face in critical application to specific clinical cases. Bioethics, it is claimed, also focuses on beliefs, values, and norms, which are basic to society and its cultural tradition (Fox, 1984).

Some have argued that philosophical normative ethics alone cannot really be helpful to the health care profession in formulating a true medical ethic. Ethical principles may stem from values professed in a culture, and because our culture is pluralistic, some have claimed that universal principles are neither possible nor desirable (McIntyre, 1975).

A broader conceptualization of clinical ethics acknowledges the cross-cultural and medical anthropological aspects of clinical issues (Liebman, 1990). In order to understand medical systems, one must grasp the nosology, ideology and modes of diagnosis within a culture. Clinical ethics must concern itself with the characteristics of medical professionals and patients. Illness construction is part of a broader social and cultural epidemiology and applied anthropology, which are found both in the clinical and public health settings. Clinical ethics must understand the economics and politics of health care and pay attention to the particular pluralistic needs of a society. Attention to non-Western medical systems is also necessary. Thus, clinical ethics must be cross-cultural and multi-cultural in its perspective, rather than ethnocentric in its value judgments.

Clinical ethics must be interested in public disclosure, community privacy, and other notions broader than individual privacy. Clinical ethics should recognize that health care providers form a small part of health care delivery. Ninety percent of health care delivery falls outside of the classical doctor-patient relationship. Lay nonprofessionals and families form the core of diagnosis and treatment of most illness (Kleinman, 1980).

Clinical ethics should also appreciate assumptions and biases in the culture of medicine itself with its hospitals, medical specialties, bureaucracies, reimbursement mechanisms, hierarchies, referral patterns and technological imperatives. The cultural background of practitioners, their social status, religious beliefs, and the history of their peoples, will also form the needed anthropological substrate for understanding cultural settings and folk beliefs in the delivery of care (Christakis, 1992).

Even the mode of knowing may vary, in that modern Western medicine is based on research, whereas non-Western traditions may be grounded in texts and tradition. Western societies often stress individual rights, privacy and self-determination, while non-Western societies are much more focused on relationships within society and communities. Clinical ethics within non-Western societies is most concerned with dialogue, negotiation, and conformity. These tensions create a significant challenge for the interrelationship of philosophical ethics to clinical ethics on a global scale.

There is a wide diversity of argument concerning the commonality of methodologies, roles, and functions of clinical medical ethics as distinct from philosophical medical ethics. A tension exits surrounding the question of whether clinical medical ethics can impose universal norms or whether it must create norms for specific situations. Philosophical medical ethics, also concerned by this tension, may ask whether constructed principles can apply to specific cases.

III. SOURCES OF BIOETHICS

A. Theology

Theology has a long and rich tradition of contributing to medical ethics (Gustafson, 1975). Religious stories have informed bioethical discourse surrounding finitude and validity. The theological ethos of the medical profession is grounded in self-sacrifice, care, compassion and the good Samaritan. Theology has also had a history of concern for the value of life, the lived life and quality of life (Pellegrino, 1981).

Theology may be considered a critical reflection on the ultimate causes and meanings of human experience. That reflection, however, is qualified by a belief in God in which reason is enlightened by faith, revelation or religious experience (MacQuarrie, 1980). Theology may justify acts using moral argument. Theology can resolve ultimate disagreements among moral theories and moral arguments by demanding a sense of moral obligation (MacQuarrie, 1980). Religion, which may be seen as applied theology, prescribes the beliefs, rituals, and norms of conduct that arise from acceptance or experience of the transcendental power or powers outside man that sustain him and require certain things of him (MacQuarrie, 1980). Ultimately, religion and theology are based in faith and/or a revealed source, even in the context of natural law.

Religion can be said to be fundamentally involved in questions of health, disease and medicine. Religious traditions are concerned about free will, human nature, social conduct and suffering (Campbell, 1990). Religious traditions have historically been interested in questions of life and death, respect for dying and for the body. Religions have framed questions of medicine surrounding vulnerable populations, and looked at notions of sanctity of life, human stewardship, neighborly love and spirituality. Religious traditions have had a long and important role and voice in questions of equity, health care, and justice.

The modern separation of church and state and the compartmentalization or even secularization of contemporary medical ethics is foreign to historical notions of medicine and medical ethics. Prior to 1900, morality in medicine included a person's religious convictions about right or wrong behavior. The moral physician was one who had attributes of human behavior and judgments which reflected the religious ideals of the community (Burns, 1977). In the United States, Christianity often formed the basis for the ethics of most American physicians. In this sense the ideal physician was the ideal Christian physician and thus religion and medicine were historically linked. It is thus not surprising that the early foundational books in medical ethics were written by the Protestant theologians Joseph Fletcher and Paul Ramsey. Jewish theologians such as Jacobovitz, Feldman, Bleich and Rosner, and Catholic theologians such as McCormick and Kearn have also written extensively on religious medical ethics. This early interest in approaching medical ethics from a theological perspective began to decline in the 1970's. Theologians and schools of theology seemed to move away from their preoccupation with health and medicine to issues of race, urban poverty and world peace (Callahan, 1990). Through the 1970's, medical issues became more mainstream, and as religious and theological arguments declined, the courts, legislators and professional societies increasingly explored areas of medical ethics in a search for a common secular framework. The ultimate secularization of medical ethics came in the form of national commissions set up by the Federal government. In 1978, the federally-funded Belmont Report on human experimentation identified the universal secular ethical principles of beneficence, autonomy and justice. These ethical principles served as the foundation for the principle-based medical ethics of the 80's and 90's.

Medical ethics became increasingly alienated from its religious roots. In turn, religion began to either retreat from medical issues, or when addressing medical issues saw its role as pertaining only to its own religious communities. The 1990's have seen a resurgence of interest in the area of religious medical ethics. Some of this has focused on recapturing the practical wisdom of faith traditions in dealing with medical problems. Secular medical ethics has also recognized that religious and theological traditions have historically been more open and successful in responding to medical concerns about such problems as meaning and suffering. Religion has thus contributed not only to the theoretical discourse, but also to the applied clinical aspects of medical ethics.

The secularization of medical ethics claimed that religion was only focused on private matters and could not be generalized to broader populations. Theologians responded in their own communities. Religions conceptualized man as created in the image of God. This sanctification led to a focus on the commonalties and the equality of humanity. Religious traditions maintain a concern about self-sacrifice as a means to attain a common good. They have thus provided a framework for medical ethics which is not based in freedom, autonomy, justice or individual choice, but rather in obligation, responsibility, community and a shared view of the common good. Religious traditions focus on the narrative casuistic structure of peoples lives. These religiously informed life stories are a rich source of medical ethics.

B. Philosophy

Philosophy is a critical reflection on the ultimate causes, meanings, truths and logical connectedness of human experience and fundamental knowledge and ideas (Woodhouse, 1994). Philosophical discourse is rational and reasoned. Insofar as medical ethics is a form of ethics, it must be located within philosophy. It is important to understand the philosophical structure and nature of medical ethics itself.

Medical ethics is not merely an analytic activity. While contemporary philosophy has been preoccupied with an analysis of the language and propositions of thought, medical ethics has been preoccupied with the formulation and application of ethical theories to medical problems. If medical ethics is to extend beyond such analytical realms, it must be concerned about grounding medical ethics in the human condition with its experience and values (Pellegrino, 1986). A fundamental question of the philosophy of medicine is whether a foundation exists for medical ethics which will be coherent, comprehensive and independent of medicine, or whether medical ethics must instead be imbedded in medicine itself. This question is critical for framing and understanding modern medical dilemmas, for if there is no foundational philosophical basis for medical ethics, then medicine will be seen as an arbitrary craft with no justification for determining right from wrong actions. Therefore, medicine will need a grounding in the nature of medicine and the nature of the doctor-patient relationship.

Many have attempted to foresee what form and structure a philosophy of medicine will take. The philosophy of medicine is a field with epistemological, logical, conceptual and theoretical elements (Lindahl, 1990). The grounding of bioethics may thus be seen as an analysis of questions surrounding the method, logic and conceptual foundations of medicine. This study may occur in therapeutic, diagnostic and palliative realms (Caplan, 1992). Another fundamental question for the philosophy of medicine is whether it exists as an independent entity. Some have argued that the philosophy of medicine is a sub-discipline of either the philosophy of science, especially the philosophy of biology, the philosophy of mind, or moral philosophy. The philosophy of science deals with the nature of science and "the nature of theories and laws, the logic of explanations and predictions, the analysis of models, paradigms and metaphors, the analysis of theoretical change over time, and the explication of key concepts" (Caplan, 1992). The philosophy of science applied to medicine would include "the analysis of the methods, assumptions and goals of medical activities and the examination of the ontological foundations of medical research, nosology and practice" (Caplan, 1992). Key concerns are the interrelationship of the philosophy of medicine to medical sociology, and medical history. The philosophy of medicine is also concerned with the role of theories and paradigms. The philosophy of science equally deals with questions of testability, verifiability, and falsifiability of theories, claims and hypotheses.

The content of a philosophy of medicine is rooted in the question how and what does medicine know, and how does it know it? Does it require a canon of knowledge, and does it need to have a specific set of problems that defines its boundaries? A philosophy of medicine has great significance in its relationship to problems of the philosophy of science. A philosophy of medicine is necessary as a foundation of bioethics in that one cannot answer questions of ethics without some presumption about what medicine is and is supposed to do (Englehardt, 1980; Pellegrino, 1981). Further, a philosophy of medicine is needed to contribute to the analysis of problems in medicine itself. Specific problems, such as the concepts of pain and suffering and goals of medicine, must be grounded in a philosophy. Do ideas, values, and assumptions about medicine form a particular epistemic conceptualization about medicine's theory and practice? Pellegrino asks in what sense does a philosophy *of* medicine exist? Is it distinct from philosophy *and* medicine or a philosophy *in* medicine? (Pellegrino, 1986). Medicine, it is claimed, must be unique, demarcated, and distinct in its discipline.

It is clear that both philosophy *and* medicine exist. Physicians use the philosophy of formal logic as part of medical practice when making clinical diagnoses and logical inferences about prognosis and therapy. Philosophers may also use medicine as part of their philosophical exploits. For example, the philosophy of mind may use the neurosciences as part of its discourse.

There is also philosophy *in* medicine. In this regard, philosophy is used to study medicine, as in the fields of medical ethics and bioethics. The question, however, remains as to whether there is a unique philosophy *of* medicine. Such a philosophy *of* medicine will have a well defined view of the nature and theory of medicine. But, in what sense does medicine have a unified theory with its own methodology and way of knowing?

Topics of philosophy *and* medicine and of philosophy *in* medicine might include causality, personhood, the mind-body problem, the logic of medical decisions, and medicine's values and presuppositions. Issues in the philosophy *of* medicine, however, must be distinct from other philosophies and different from medicine itself. In this sense, questions of the philosophy of medicine will relate to what medicine is conceptually and ontologically. Other questions in the philosophy *of* medicine include: What defines health, disease, illness, and normality? What is the nature of clinical judgment, knowledge and causality? What is medicine? What shapes medicine? What does medicine know? How does it know it? And on what basis does it make such inferences?

Many of the issues of the philosophy *of* medicine may be shared with the philosophy of science. These issues might relate to questions of verifiability, validity, falsifiability and the nature of evidence. Many of the issues of the philosophy of medicine may also be shared with the philosophy of mind. These include such questions as the nature of mind and body. A philosophy of medicine or *the* philosophy of medicine, however, will attempt to understand a unified theory of all of medicine which should explain human and biological phenomena (Pellegrino, 1986).

C. Law And Public Policy

The history of medical ethics began in theological discourse and was followed by codes of ethics rooted in historical and sociological inquiry. As the patients' rights movement took center stage in the 1960's, empowerment and privacy became crucial to bioethics debate. Philosophical ethics rapidly moved to the arena of law and public policy.

Increasingly, medical-ethical discourse is found in the courts and legislatures. Serious and significant ethical dilemmas require clear rules and standards. Law is distinct from ethics and theology in that it has different goals, methods and functions. The law, as minimalist, sets the minimum level for acceptability of action within society. Law tends to focus on rights, autonomy and individual freedoms. The source of the law may not be universal but rather formulated by the ruling class. Laws are jurisdictional and are thus both time and space specific. It can be argued that laws are relativistic in that they only apply to specific jurisdictions. Laws ultimately are enforced by government and attempt to maintain social order and adjudicate conflict.

The formulation of specific laws and enforceable regulations regarding social conduct often rely on substantive standards in the area of medical ethics. Courts and legislatures have been called on to address such questions as the definition of death. It was necessary for very practical reasons (such as when to bury a body) to have clear and specific legal definitions rather than philosophical or theological-based notions. Similarly, evaluation of abortion laws required legal consideration of the constitutional right to privacy and defining states' interests in the life of the fetus beyond merely addressing the scientific knowledge of biology and reproduction.

Hospitals and medical institutions also need clear standards for caring for patients (Gustafson, 1990). Hospital policies are informed by or embedded in ethical argument, but specific guidelines are necessary to deal with the socio-political and economic aspects of institutional concerns.

The trend toward using the Federal government as a forum for discourse on medical ethics began in the early 70's (Hanna, 1993). The first federally-sponsored exploration into the field of medical ethics came in the area of human experimentation. The National Commission for the Protection of Human Subjects of Biomedical and Behavioral Research functioned from 1974 to 1978. During that period it issued ten reports. These reports explored the framework and foundation for the ethics of human experimentation and the protection of human subjects in biomedical and behavioral research. As previously discussed, the National Commission identified three fundamental ethical principles to guide human experimentation: justice, respect for persons and beneficence. These principles were embodied in federal regulations. Although the members of the commission began from diverse philosophical and religious backgrounds, there was consensus regarding these secular principles (Toulmin, 1981).

The successful work of the National Commission paved the way for the President's Commission for the Study of Ethical Problems in Medicine and Biomedical and Behavioral Research. This commission functioned from 1980 to 1983 and issued ten reports on topics such as defining death, the protection of human subjects in research, whistle-blowing, genetic screening and counseling, deciding to forgo life-sustaining treatment, splicing life, and securing access to health care. The most influential policy reports were narrow in focus and had clear and specific recommendations, especially the ones on defining death and deciding to forgo life-sustaining treatment. Indeed, a major consensus was obtained in these areas and recommendations were subsequently put into public policy and laws: The Uniform Definition of Death Act, and living will and health care proxy legislation.

Other national commissions were organized but met with much less success. A Biomedical Ethics Advisory Committee was to be established between 1988 and 1990 to continue the work that the President's Commission had done and offer insight on law, policy and Federal regulations to congressional discourse on biomedical ethical issues. This commission never formally acted because its commissioners and constituency were mired in abortion politics. The committee's proposed explorations into fetal research, human genetics, genetic engineering and AIDS created political controversies which could not be resolved.

A similarly frustrating Federal attempt to formulate medical ethics came with the Ethics Advisory Board of the Department of Health Education and Welfare (now the Department of Health and Human Services). The Ethics Advisory Board was established to study the ethics of experimentation on human embryos and *in vitro* fertilization research. Because of abortion politics, this Advisory Board dissolved in 1980 and was not reconstituted. Because no ethics advisory board existed after 1980, no funded proposals in these areas could be authorized by the Federal government. The 1993 re-authorization of National Institutes of Health budget allowed for an ad hoc institution of an Ethics Advisory Board, but only to review proposals where funding was withheld or withdrawn on ethical grounds.

Other Federal commissions have attempted to deal with specific problems and have met with equally difficult political constraints. A fetal tissue transplantation research panel was convened by the National Institutes of Health in 1988. It issued a report recommending procedures for such research, but no action was taken on that report because of the Reagan/Bush Administration's political opposition to its conclusion. President Clinton adopted their recommendations in 1993.

National organizations have also attempted to address medical ethics problems in the public policy forum with varying success. The Office of Technology Assessment, established in 1972 , issued reports on gene therapy. The Institute of Medicine, established in 1970-71 under a charter of the National Academy of Science, issued reports on the ethics of health care. The National Center for Human Genome Research established a specific program to explore the Ethical, Legal and Social Implications of the Human Genome Project in 1989.

All these Federal commissions and national organizations have met with varying success. The greatest success has occurred when there was a narrow, clear and specific problem that required regulation and law. When these groups have grappled with broad agendas without specific tasks, or with politically-sensitive topics, they have either been unable to agree on recommendations, or their recommendations have been largely ignored by lawmakers. To this date, U.S. Supreme Court opinions on abortion and treatment refusal have been more important in shaping public policy in bioethics than any commissions or organizations.

IV. APPROACHES AND CRITIQUES IN MEDICAL BIOETHICS

Much of philosophical medical ethics has been grounded in a principle-based approach. This approach views rules and actions as based on principles of biomedical ethics such as respect for persons, beneficence and justice. Principlism has served as a major force, not only in philosophical theoretical medical ethics, but also in clinical applied medical ethics (Beauchamp & Childress, 1991). Increasingly, however, there has been serious criticism of the principle-based approach. These critiques are based in communitarian ethics, virtue-based ethics, casuistry, narrative and interpretative approaches, hermeneutic and phenomenological approaches, ethics of care, and feminist and Marxist approaches.

A. Principles

Most of the philosophical medical ethics theories in the last twenty years have been analytic in nature. They use principles focusing on theories, methods and techniques to create a rationalist, deductive and formalistic approach to medical ethics, in an attempt to reduce the complexities of medical dilemmas. This philosophically positivist and reductionist approach has classically looked at either rules or principles from a deontological, contractarian, or Neo-Kantian perspective, or has been teleological consequentialist, or utilitarian in its analysis.

The process has often been one of identifying what principles are at stake or in conflict and then by rational argument, establishing which principles should take precedence. In Western medical ethics, autonomy has most often received priority and is often seen as a trump card for other principles. Much of this stems from secular humanist Western liberalism with its emphasis on autonomy as a protection against paternalistic behavior. Beneficence, nonmaleficence and justice are seen as subservient to the principle of autonomy (Callahan, 1984).

There has been a great deal of criticism of this principled approach in the last five years. Writers have noted the problem of applying general philosophical principles to specific cases. Principles may not be a guide to action but rather a collection of considerations when dealing with moral problems (Clouser & Gert, 1990). Moreover, a principle-based approach often neglects specific moral claims of medicine which aim to benefit the patient. Principles must also be applied through derivative second order rules or practices. There are also difficulties between conflicting principles.

B. Communitarian Ethics

A communitarian ethic focuses on notions of obligation and duty rather than focusing on individuals and autonomy. Such an ethic deals with communities and is concerned with reciprocity and solidarity. Social and cultural elements of morality take precedent over rights and autonomy. This communitarian approach is seen as particularly fruitful in looking at chronic diseases; the acute care examples most often used in a principle-based approach seem less relevant. With chronic diseases, patients find themselves in a social and cultural framework and web of services and needs. Communitarian ethics is concerned with community interdependence and obligations (Loewy, 1991), as well as kindness, empathy, caring, devotion, generosity, altruism, sacrifice and love (Fox & Swayze, 1984).

C. Virtue

Virtue-based ethics have always played a central role in medical ethics dating back to the periods of Hippocrates, Plato and Aristotle. Such ethics emphasize living a good life and becoming a good person through the development of virtuous characteristics (Pellegrino, Thomasma, 1993). Virtue-based ethics, in fact, dominated bioethics until the early 60's. Interest in virtue-based ethics has resurged today as one looks at the character of the individuals who are involved in the medical encounter. Virtue theory does not, however, provide sufficiently clear directives to guide specific action. Nonetheless, virtues do play a major role in the moral life and a full accounting of medical ethics must not exclude notions of character and virtue (McIntyre, 1988; McIntyre, 1990; Drane, 1988).

D. Casuistry

The focus on applied clinical ethics has caused a revival of interest in the field of casuistry as a method and mode for resolving specific clinical medical ethics problems. Casuistry is concerned with the cross-cultural dimensions of actual experiences of patients, families, and care givers from different backgrounds (Jonsen, 1988; Jonsen, 1991). Casuistry assumes that there are paradigm cases about which we can all agree regarding the right or wrong resolution. Casuistry claims that we can agree on these paradigm cases even though we may agree for different reasons or from different positions (Toulmin, 1981). The task of a casuistic approach is to create or find these paradigm cases and see how these cases are the same or different from other paradigm cases or categories of paradigms. The primary moral task is to understand dissimilarity or differences of paradigmatic cases in terms of morally relevant distinctions. Casuistry is a reasoning by analogy. It matters less what principles the paradigm case represents than that we agree on the outcome.

Casuistry does seem to fit well with and be similar to the methodology of clinical medicine in that clinicians also deal with specific cases and paradigms. The interpretation of moral issues using reasoning based on paradigms and analogies can lead to conclusions about particular cases.

The criticism of casuistry comes from the lack of consensus on certain principles or paradigm cases. Casuistry is a product of the Middle Ages, during which there was a much greater consensus on certain principles such as the common belief in God, the destiny of human kind and the totality of life (Arras, 1991). But consensus does not exist in the twentieth century, at least not in a pluralistic society such as the United States. Thus, people may disagree about what constitutes a paradigm case and how one can determine if the cases at hand are similar or different enough to resolve paradigmatically. If nothing else, however, casuistry has revealed how case interpretation is a form of analogical reasoning. Casuistry is an alternative to the principle-based approach which describes a narrative of illness as the principle way of knowing in medicine. Disease is not seen as an entity but a chronological organization of events in an illness narrative (Hunter, 1989).

E. Narrative And Interpretative Bioethics

Another critique of medical ethics as it is applied to clinical ethics comes from narrative and interpretative ethics. It is claimed that clinical ethics is not a pure science but rather an activity focusing on interpretation. This interpretation may take the form of interpretation of texts or clinical interpretation of the hermeneutics of medicine (Leder, 1990). The narrative or interpretative approach looks at the ill person, the clinical signs and symptoms, and attempts to understand the meaning of the underlying disease. Authors have noted that patients present themselves with a variety of texts. The patient's illness as lived is an experiential text; their history is a narrative text; and the physical exam is an instrumental and diagnostic text. This narrative and interpretive critique thus focuses on the living experience of the patient (Hartson, 1990; Walter, 1987).

Bioethics is seen as fundamentally an interpretive enterprise, rather than one of discovery or invention. As such, there is a need for practical interpreters and for critical discernment (Geertz, 1973). The critical activity of bioethics identifies a method that sorts out the structure, significance and context of inferences and makes sense of them (Geertz, 1973; Hoffmaster, 1992).

A further application of this narrative approach looks at applied ethics from the situational or contextual approach. In this sense, ethnographic studies are more responsive to health care (Hoffmaster, 1992, 1985). The narrative promotes a renewed interest in history, politics and tradition (Locke, 1990). This methodology may be hermeneutical, linking scientific, clinical and narrative histories (Ricoeur, 1978).

The narrative approach acknowledges that we are all members of a moral community which has worldviews and values shaped by our stories (Gustafson, 1990). Descriptive evidence in medicine may have its roots in a system of medical education which teaches its own construction of narrative. Narratives are not arguments but rather part of the context of clinical practice. Narratives are also evident within structures of institutions, in the motivations of patients and families, and in how technological developments are understood. Narrative stories are seen as biographical developments which frame social, cultural and historical concepts (Donnelly, 1988; Poirer, 1990; Brody, 1988; Reich, 1987).

F. The Ethics Of Care And Feminist Critiques

The ethics of care is seen as a critique of the justice-rights approach. The ethics of care deals with contacts, relationships and responsiveness (Carse, 1991; Glover, 1992; Gould, 1983).

Feminist ethics has identified the gender-specific patterns of sexist oppression which are imbedded in society (Sherwin, 1992). The feminist critique in medical ethics notes that women compose the majority of patients, the majority of nurses and social workers and an increasing number of physicians that practice medicine (Sherwin, 1992). That notwithstanding, women and children comprise a great majority of the poor in the United

States. It is noted that working women's wages are two-thirds of similarly situated men's wages worldwide, yet women comprise half of the global population and one-third of the paid labor force. Despite these numbers, however, women receive only one-tenth of the world income and own less than one percent of the world's property (Sherwin, 1992).

Feminism sensitizes society to the physical and sexual exploitation of women. Women's lives (particularly their reproductive lives) are controlled by social and political systems that seem to be pervasively repressive (Sherwin, 1992). Feminist ethics notes that these systems are controlled by men, who dominate the courts, legislatures, churches and medical societies.

Bioethics too, is seen as dominated by white, upper class and privileged men, who focus on principles of justice, privacy and rights. Whether focusing on autonomy, as does secular humanist ethics, or on rights in the law, informed consent becomes a dominant interest within medical ethics. Feminists note, however, that these principles of autonomy and informed consent can only be realized when hierarchical modes of oppression are eliminated (Sherwin, 1992).

Women find the focus on justice, privacy and rights in arguments within medical ethics to be isolating and alienating (Gilligan, 1982). Feminist perspectives look toward commitment not confrontation, and try to understand medical problems within a web of family and social systems, not in isolation. This leads feminists to reject principlism because of its abstract individualist, rule-oriented nature, that ignores relationships and discounts the fact that the rules perpetuate injustice. Feminist ethics looks for wholeness and integration, partnership and interdependencies, mutual support and community. Feminist ethics understands medicine as a network of care (Gilligan, 1980; Noddings, 1984; Holmes, 1992; Sherwin, 1992).

Nursing has traditionally been dominated by women and has been critical of the atomized and isolating autonomy/rights approach of medical ethics. Nursing ethics in contra-distinction to medical ethics often deals with an ethics of care, commitment to caring and preserving relationships through focusing on families. The feminist perspective looks at medical ethics through the social cross-cultural dimensions of moral life, family, friends, and caretakers.

G. Other Critiques Of Medical Ethics

There are a wide variety of other critiques of medical ethics which identify and explore different theories and interests. The following is a short list of trends in that philosophical analysis.

Several bioethicists have drawn on hermeneutical and phenomenological approaches to look at the nature of ethical discourse in medicine (Heidegger, 1962; Kuhn, 1962; Polany, 1969; Ricoeur, 1965; Gadaamer, 1970; Merleau-Ponty, 1962; Foucault, 1973). Much of this hermeneutical exploration has come out of the work of social scientists and anthropologists dealing with specific descriptions of patients (Kleinman, 1988; Kleinman, 1980; Good, 1981; Marshall, 1992).

Marxism approaches medical ethics from the standpoint of power, oppression and hierarchy. Medical ethics is found to represent upper middle class values. Professional views do not necessarily reflect local community views. In accordance with Marxism, public ethics must be considered at the grass roots of health care decisions.

A secular humanist critique of medical ethics notes that there are pluralistic values in our society. Secular humanism attempts to set ethical analyses, rules and values that allow for due process to protect each others' values and to diminish harm to others (Englehardt, 1976).

A medical ethics of beneficence in trust has focused on the nature of the doctor-patient relationship as critical and foundational to medical ethics. Physicians must act to benefit patients in terms of the patient's good as understood by the patient (Pellegrino, 1988).

Contractual obligation has been proposed as the foundation of a medical ethics that views the doctor-patient relationship as a contract. That contract recognizes mutual obligations, and therefore decisions are made to mutually satisfy both parties (Veatch, 1981).

Trust and personhood grounds the assertion that doctor-patient relationship has a moral character based on trust and physician responsiveness. This conceptualization of medical ethics focuses on the unique aspects found in the personhood of a patient (Zaner, 1988).

A medical ethics focused on covenant and fidelity recognizes the prophetic aspects of the interrelationship of a patient and a physician. The medical encounter is a human encounter with sacred dimensions (May, 1983; Gustafson, 1990).

V. CONCLUSION

This critical review of the history, philosophical grounding and context of bioethics suggests an evolving discipline. Despite powerful critiques of contemporary bioethics, it is necessary to reexamine the nature and scope of medical ethical discourse. Each approach and critique uses a different methodology and starts from a different grounding as it conceptualizes the goals of medical ethics. This explains why no one can define adequately who is a "bioethicist" and what training they should have. A comprehensive understanding of the nature, scope and grounding of medical ethics and its critiques will facilitate a more formal and integrated discipline.

If medical ethics is to reach its full and rich potential, there is the vital need for a meta-medical ethics. Bioethics has grown from infancy through adolescent rebellion to an early stage of maturity. It is time to integrate the critiques of medical ethics and begin to form a fully mature philosophically-based bioethics.

Boston University

REFERENCES

Annas, G., Grodin, M. (1992). *The Nazi Doctors and the Nuremberg Code: Human Rights in Human Experimentation*. New York: Oxford University Press.

Annas, G. (1993). *Standard of Care: The Law of American Bioethics*. New York: Oxford University Press.

Arras, J. (1991). Getting Down to Cases: The Revival of Casuistry in Bioethics. *Journal of Medicine and Philosophy* 16:29-5.

Beauchamp, T., Childress, J. (1991). *Principles of Biomedical Ethics* 3rd ed. New York: Oxford University Press.

Beecher, H. (1966). Ethics in Clinical Research. *New England Journal of Medicine* 274:1354-1360.

Brody, B. (1990). Quality of Scholarship in Bioethics. *Journal of Medicine and Philosophy* 15:161-178.

Brody, H. (1988). *Stories of Sickness*. New Haven: Yale University Press.

Burns, C. (1977). American Medical Ethics Some Historical Roots. *Philosophical Medical Ethics: Its Nature and Significance*. Eds. Spickers, Engelhardt: Reidel 21-26.

Callahan, D. (1984). Autonomy as a Moral Good, Not a Moral Obsession. *Hastings Center Report* 14(5):40-42.

Cambell, C. (1990). The Moral Meaning of Religion for Bioethics. *Bulletin of the Pan American Health Organization* 24(4):386-392.

Caplan, A. (1992). Does the Philosophy of Medicine Exist? *Theoretical Medicine* 13:67-77.

Carrick, P. (1985). *Medical Ethics in Antiquity Philosophical Perspectives on Abortion and Euthanasia*. Dordrecht D. Reidel Publishing Co.

Carse, A. (1991). The Voice of Care: Implications for Bioethical Education. *Journal of Medicine and Philosophy* 16:5-28.

Carson, R. (1990). Interpretive Bioethics: The Way of Discernment. *Theoretical Medicine* 11:51-59.

Cassell, E. (1976). Moral Thought in Clinical Practice: Applying the Abstract to the Usual. *Science, Ethics and Medicine*. Eds. Engelhardt, H. T. and Callahan, D. New York: Hastings on Hudson.

Christakis, N. (1992). Ethics Are Local: Engaging Cross Cultural Variation in the Ethics for Clinical Research. *Social Science Medicine* 35(9): 1079-1091.

Clouser, K.D. (1978). *Encyclopedia of Bioethics*. New York: Free Press 115-161.

Clouser, K.D., Gert, B. (1990). A Critique of Principalism. *Journal of Medicine and Philosophy* 15: 219-236.

Donnelly, W. (1988). Writing the Medical Record: Transforming Story Into Chronicle. *Journal of American Medical Association* 260: 823-825.

Drane, J. (1988). *Becoming a Good Doctor*. Kansas City: Sheed & Ward.

Drane, J. (1990). *Bulletin of the Pan American Health Organization* 24(4).

Engelhardt, H.T. (1980). Erdee Philosophy of Medicine. *A Guide to the Culture of Science Technology and Medicine*. Ed. Durbin, P. New York: Free Press. pp. 364-461.

Engelhardt, H.T. (1986). *Foundations of Bioethics*. New York: Oxford University Press. pp. 3-16.

Fletcher, J. (1954). *Morals and Medicine; The Moral Problems of: The Patient's Right to Know the Truth, Contraception, Artificial Insemination, Sterilization, Euthanasia, Procreation*. New Jersey: Princeton University Press.

Foucault, Michael (1973). *The Birth of the Clinic: An Archeology of Medical Perception*. New York: Vintage Books.

Fox, R., Swayze J. (1984). Medical Morality Is Not Bioethics: Medical Ethics in China and the United States. *Milbank Memorial Fund Quarterly, Health in Society* 52:336.

Gadamer, H. (1970). *Truth and Method*. London: Sheer and Wood.

Geertz, C. (1973). *The Interpretation of Cultures*. New York: Basic Books.

Gilligan, C. (1982). *In a Different Voice*. Cambridge, MA: Harvard University Press.

Glover, J. (1992). Gender in Bioethics: Theory and Practice an Introduction. *Theoretical Medicine* 13:293-294.

Good, B. and Del Vecchio, Good, M. (1981). The Meaning of Symptoms: A Cultural Hermeneutic Model of Clinical Practice in the *Relevance of Social Sciences for Medicine*. Eds. Eisenberg, L., Kleinman, A.. Dordrecht: D. Reidel. pp. 165-196.

Gould, C. (1983). *Beyond Domination: New Perspectives on Women in Philosophy*. Totwa, New Jersey: Rowman and Littlefield.

Gustafson, T. (1975). *The Contribution of Theology to Medical Ethics*. Milwaukee: Marquette University Press.

Gustafson, J. (1990). Moral Discourse About Medicine: A Variety of Forms. *Journal of Medicine and Philosophy* 15:125-142.

Hanna, K., Cook-Deegan R., Nishimi R. (1993). Finding a Forum for Bioethics in U.S. Public Policy. *Politics and the Life Science* 12(2):202-219.

Heidegger, (1962). *Being and Time*. New York: Harper & Rowe.

Hoffmaster, B. (1989). Philosophical Ethics and Practical Ethics: Never the Twain Shall Meet. *Clinical Ethics, Theory and Practice*. Eds. Hoffmaster, B., Freedman, B., & Fraser, G. New Jersey: Humana Press.

Hoffmaster, B. (1990). Morality and the Social Sciences in *Social Science Perspectives on Medical Ethics*. Ed. Weisz, G. Philadelphia: University of Pennsylvania Press.

Hoffmaster, B. (1992). Can Ethnography Save the Life of Medical Ethics, *Social Science and Medicine* 35(12):1421-1431.

Holmes, H. and Purdy, L., Eds. (1992). *Feminist Perspectives in Medical Ethics*. Bloomington, Indiana: Indiana University Press.

Hunter, K. (1989). A Science of Individuals: Medicine and Casuistry. *Journal of Medicine and Philosophy* 14:193-212.

Jonsen, A. & Toulmin, S. (1988). *The Abuse of Casuistry: The History of Moral Reasoning.* Berkeley, California: University of California Press.

Jonsen, A. (1991). Casuistry as Methodology and Clinical Ethics. *Theoretical Medicine* 12:295-307.

Jonsen, A., Siegler, M., Winslade W. (1992). *Clinical Ethics: A Practical Approach to Ethical Decisions in Clinical Medicine.* 3rd Edition. New York: McGraw Hill, Inc.

Kleinman, A. (1980). *Patients and Healers in the Context of Culture: an Exploration in Borderline Between Anthropology, Medicine and Psychiatry.* Berkeley: University of California Press.

Kleinman, A. (1988). *Illness Narratives: Suffering, Healing and the Human Condition.* New York: Basic Books.

Kuhn, T. (1962). *The Structure of Scientific Revolutions.* Chicago: University of Chicago Press.

Leder, D. (1990). Clinical Interpretation: The Hermeneutics of Medicine. *Theoretical Medicine* 11:9-24.

Lieban R. (1990). Medical Anthropology and the Comparative Study of Medical Ethics. *Social Science Perspectives in Medical Ethics.* Ed. Weisz, G. Philadelphia: University of Pennsylvania Press pp. 221-239.

Lindahl, B. (1990). Editorial *Theoretical Medicine* 11:1-3.

Lock, J. (1990). Some Aspects of Medical Hermeneutics: The Role of Dialectic and Narrative *Theoretical Medicine* 11:41-49.

Loewy, E. (1991). *Suffering And the Beneficent Community: Beyond Libertarianism.* Albany: State University Press of New York.

MacIntyre, A. (1975). How Virtues Become Vices: Values, Medicine and the Social Context. *Evaluation and Explanation in the Biomedical Sciences.* Eds. Englelhardt, H.T., Spickers, Dordrecht. Boston: D. Reidel.

MacIntyre, A. (1988). *After Virtue.* Indianapolis, Indiana: University of Notre Dame Press.

MacIntyre, A. (1990). *Three Rival Versions of Moral Enquiry.* Indianapolis, Indiana: University of Notre Dame Press.

Macklin, R. (1989). Ethical Theory and Applied Ethics a Reply to Skeptics in Clinical Ethics: Theory and Practice. Eds. Hoffmaster B., Freedman B., Fraser G. Clifton, New Jersey: Humana Press pp. 101-124.

MacQuarrie J. (1980). God in Experience and Argument in Experience, Reason and God. Studies in Philosophy and History of Philosophy Vol. 8. Ed. Long, E. Washington D.C.: Catholic University Press p. 37.

Marshall, P. (1992). Anthropology and Bioethics. *Medical Anthropology Quarterly.* 6(1):49-73.

May, W. (1983). *The Physician's Covenant: Images of the Healer in Medical Ethics.* Philadelphia: The Westminster Press.

Merleau-Ponty, N. (1962). *Phenomenology of Perception.* London: Routledge and Kegan.

Noddings, N. (1984). *Caring: A Feminist Approach to Ethics and Moral Education.* Berkeley: University of California Press.

Pellegrino, E., Thomasma, D. (1981). *A Philosophical Basis of Medical Practice Toward a Philosophy in Ethics of the Healing Professions.* New York: Oxford University Press.

Pellegrino, E. (1986). Philosophy of Medicine: Towards a Definition. *Journal of Medicine and Philosophy* 11:9-16.

Pellegrino, E., Thomasma, D. (1988). *For the Patient's Good: The Restoration of Beneficence in Health Care.* New York: Oxford University Press.

Pellegrino, E. (1993). Letter Journal of the American Medical Association 270(5):518.

Pellegrino, E. (1993). The Metamorphosis of Medical Ethics: A Thirty Year Retrospective. The Journal of the American Medical Association 269(9):1158-1162.

Pellegrino, E., Thomasma, D. (1993). *Virtues in Medical Practice* New York, Oxford University Press.

Poirer, S., Brauner, D. (1990). The Voices of the Medical Record. *Theoretical Medicine* 11(1):29-40.

Polanyi, N. (1969). *Knowing and Being.* University of Chicago Press.

Ramsey, P. (1970). *The Patient as Person: Explorations in Medical Ethics.* New Haven: New Haven Yale University Press.

Reich, W. (1987). Caring for Life in the First of It: Moral Dilemmas for Perinatal and Neonatal Ethics. *Seminars in Perinatalology* 11(3):279-287.

Ricoeur, P. (1965). *Freedom and Nature*. Evanston, Illinois: Northwestern University Press.

Ricoeur, P. (1978). The Narrative Function. In *Semeia* 13:179-202.

Rothman, D. (1990). Human Experimentation and the Origins of Bioethics in the United States. In *Social Science Prerequisites on Medical Ethics* eds. Weisz, G., Dordrecht, Kluwer Academic Publishers, pp. 181-201.

Sherwin, S. (1992). *No Longer Patient: Feminist Ethics in Health Care.* Philadelphia: Temple University Press.

Thomasma, D. (1980). A philosophy of a clinically based medical ethics. *Journal of Medical Ethics* 6(4):190-196.

Thomasma, D. (1980). The Possibility of a Normative Medical Ethics. *The Journal of Medicine and Philosophy* 5(3):249-259.

Thomasma, D., Pellegrino, E. (1981). Philosophy of Medicine as the Source of Medical Ethics. *Meta-Medicine* Vol. 2. pp. 5-11.

Toulmin, S. (1973). How Medicine Saved the Life of Ethics. *Perspectives in Biology and Medicine* 25(4):736-750.

Toulmin, S. (1981). The Tyranny of Principles. *Hastings Center Report* 11:6.

Toulmin, S. (1988). *Medical Ethics in its American Context.* A Historical Survey. Callahan, D., Dunstan, GR., eds. Biomedical Ethics: An Anglo-American Dialogue. New York: New York Academy of Sciences 7-15.

Vance, R. (1985). Medicine as a Dependent Tradition: Historical and Ethical Reflections. *Perspectives in Biology and Medicine* 28(2):283-302.

Veatch, R. (1981). *A Theory of Medical Ethics.* New York: Basic Books.

Veatch, R. (1989). *Cross Cultural Perspectives in Medical Ethics: Readings.* Boston, Massachusetts: Jones & Bartlett.

Woodhouse, M. (1994). *A Preface to Philosophy.* Belmont, CA: Wadsworth Publishing Co.

Zaner, R. (1988). *Ethics and the Clinical Encounter*. Englewood Cliffs, NJ: Prentice Hall.

RAYMOND J. DEVETTERE

THE PRINCIPLED APPROACH: PRINCIPLES, RULES, AND ACTIONS

One model of ethics has dominated health care in the United States for over twenty years -- applied normative ethics. According to this model, the ethicist relies on general norms, usually principles and rules, to determine what actions are right and what actions are wrong. This model of applied normative ethics, sometimes called "principlism," is now widely challenged.

Challenges to the use of normative principles and rules are not unique to health care ethics. Criticisms of foundations, theory, impartiality, objectivity, neutrality, in short, of any kind of claim that we can judge or evaluate individual human behavior from a general and disengaged perspective are now widespread in moral philosophy. According to the most radical version of this critique, general and impartial moral norms or principles simply do not exist, and any theory supporting such principles and rules is suspect.

The major criticisms of "principlism" in health care ethics are by now well known. Principles and rules often fail to fit complex situations where moral guidance is most needed. Principles and rules often conflict, though there is no methodology for resolving the conflict. Principles and rules sometimes produce unacceptable moral judgments, and no justification exists for making exceptions. Applying principles and rules to particular situations makes moral reasoning appear deductive and axiomatic, and criticisms of ethics so conceived are as old as moral philosophy itself. Principles and rules apply primarily to actions, hence intentions, habits, circumstances and feelings are neglected. Principles and rules originate, overtly or covertly, in metaphysics, but many reject metaphysics as meaningless or as something that must be "overcome." Principles and rules are related to and defended by ethical theories, but the world of ethical theory is composed of competing and incompatible theories. Moreover, the anti-theory movement in ethics challenges the very idea of ethical theory.

Before looking more closely at principles and rules, it is well to note that the word "principle" has had two different meanings in ethics. First, the word "principle" has sometimes designated what is the beginning or the source of the ethical theory itself. Principles so understood are founding or originative principles, and they are not derived from, nor defended by, moral theories. Rather, moral theories are derived from, and defended by founding principles. Second, the word "principle" has also designated a norm for a standard used to make particular moral judgments about right and wrong. Principles are

M. A. Grodin (ed.), Meta Medical Ethics, 27–47.

thus normative or "action-guides," and they are derived from, or at least defended by, moral theories.

The two meanings of principle are easily detectable in most accounts of ethics. In Kant, for example, the founding principle is the autonomy or freedom of the will. "The *autonomy* of the will is the sole principle of all moral laws and of the duties conforming to them..." (Kant, 1956 at 33). From this founding principle, Kantderives the supreme and first principle of morality -- the categorical imperative: "Therefore, if freedom of the will is presupposed, morality (together with its principle) follows by merely analyzing the concept of freedom" (Kant, 1981 at 49). And from the first principle of morality -- the categorical imperative -- the more precise norms of behavior are derived in a simple way: any maxim is considered a normative rule of behavior if we can will it to be universal. The set of maxims or rules so derived provides us with the substantive rules of the moral law. Examples of these universal moral maxims or rules might include "Do not commit suicide" and "Keep your promises."

The same two meanings of principle occur in Mill's utilitarianism. His founding principle is the claim that the ultimate end we desire is an "existence exempt as far as possible from pain, and as rich as possible in enjoyments" (Mill, 1987 at 22). No proof can be given for this "greatest happiness principle" because "questions of ultimate ends are not amenable to direct proof" (Mill, 1987 of 22). We cannot give any reasons why pleasure and freedom from pain for everybody is the ultimate end we desire except to point out that this is indeed what each person desires.

The greatest happiness principle "is necessarily also the standard of morality" (Mill, 1987 at 22). That is, actions are right if they tend to promote happiness, and wrong if they produce the reverse of happiness. This primary moral principle, however, does not directly guide our actions. It can be applied to conduct only through secondary principles and rules. "Whatever we adopt as the fundamental principle of morality, we require subordinate principles to apply it by...[and] gravely to argue as if no such secondary principles could be had...is as high a pitch, I think, as absurdity has ever reached in philosophical controversy" (Mill, 1987 at 36).

This essay will focus on principles in the second sense, that is, on normative principles applied, either directly or through the mediation of rules derived from them, to particular moral problems. Three points will be argued. First, normative principles and rules in ethics have a long history. Second, the criticisms now directed against principles and rules are more relevant to the widespread misuse of principles and rules in health care ethics rather than to principles and rules themselves. Third, principles and rules, rightly understood and appropriately employed, play an important role in ethics.

THE LONG HISTORY OF PRINCIPLES AND RULES

Principles and rules were not new notions invented by the founding fathers and mothers of bioethics in mid-twentieth century. Nor were they invented by seminal modern ethical theorists, most notably Bentham and Kant, who were heavily influenced by the roles of principles in modern science and philosophy. The use of principles and rules in ethics did not begin in the shadow of Newton's *Principia Mathematica* nor Descartes' *Principles of Philosophy* and *Rules for the Direction of the Mind*, but dates from the very beginning of the discipline. If we reject principles and rules, we are not simply rejecting the rule deontology of Kant or the rule utilitarianism of Mill, but something with a much longer history in the religious and ethical traditions of our culture.

The religious ethics inherited in the traditions of Judaism, Christianity, and Islam are moralities of divine law. Moralities are thus conceived as very similar in structure to the contemporary rule-governed morality we find in applied normative ethics. The founding principle is God's will or reason, and the normative principles and rules are God's commandments and laws.

Greek ethics also relied on principles and rules, at first unobtrusively, then more explicitly. At a time when no sharp distinction was made between private and political behavior, the laws of society often functioned as moral rules. Perhaps the most dramatic illustration of this was the argument Socrates (c. 469-399 BCE) made after his trial. Although he insisted that his conviction and death sentence were not deserved, morally, he argued that the trial was legitimate according to Athenian law and thus his moral obligation was to accept the verdict and the death sentence (Plato, 1982 at 50A-54E).

In his last work, Plato (c. 427-347 BCE) argued: "It is really necessary for men to make themselves laws and to live according to laws, or else to differ not at all from the most savage of beasts" (Plato, 1984 at 874E). Plato's remark echoes the classical theme: the purpose of laws is moral. Law guides us to the goal of morality -- the good life. Without it, most of us would flounder and live like animals. We need rules to become virtuous.

Aristotle (c. 384-322 BCE) clearly stated his founding principle. Ethics and politics are about deliberate actions, and the originative principles of deliberate actions are the goals we pursue. "The principles of our actions are the goals of our actions" (Aristotle, 1982 at 1140b16). The goals of action are what is good for the agent, and "...hence it has been rightly said that all things aim at the good" (Aristotle, 1982 at 1094a2). The founding principle of Aristotle's ethics, indeed of all Greek (Aristotle, 1982 at 1094a2) ethics with the notable exception of the Cyrenaics, was something taken as an indisputable fact: in the last analysis, what each of us seeks in life is what is truly good for ourselves, that is, our happiness (Annas, 1993). This ancient founding principle of morality may yet have relevance for health care ethics (Devettere, 1993).

Do principles in the second sense, the normative sense, also occur in Aristotle's writings? Are there normative principles and rules serving as guides for morally right action? Or is Aristotle's ethics an ethics of particular judgment and discernment based on a kind of immediate perception of what will achieve our happiness, that is, of what is the right thing to do? The questions are important because critics of theory and "principlism" in ethics today appeal to Aristotle's "practical wisdom" and moral deliberation as an alternative to a morality of principles and rules. A closer look at Aristotle's ethics, however, reveals that normative principles and rules played an integral role.

First, Aristotle embraced the general Greek idea that ethics is a part of politics, and thus ethics is integrated with the customs and laws of society (Aristotle, 1982 at 1094b1). The fact that Aristotle called his study of ethics "politics" and not "ethics" (Aristotle, 1989 at 1094b11), is a reminder that he considered ethics an aspect of politics.

Second, Aristotle was careful to note that not every feeling or action can be subjected to "practical wisdom" and moral deliberation. There is no need to deliberate about some actions -- they are always wrong. Such is the case, he claimed, with the feelings of spite, shamelessness, and envy, and with the actions of adultery, theft, and homicide. Concerning these feelings and actions, there is no role for practical reasoning or prudence about circumstances, intentions, or exceptions, and no deliberation about a virtuous mean between the extremes of excess and defect (Aristotle, 1982 at 1107a9-26). These feelings and actions are immoral by definition. Although Aristotle did not speak of rules forbidding them, his determination that they are always wrong is analogous to a claim that they are forbidden by rules.

Third, when things are not wrong by definition, then we must engage in deliberation. This deliberation, however, is not solely a deliberation about particulars. Aristotle's *phronesis*, or moral deliberation, also considers the general or the universal (the *kathkolou*) (Aristotle, 1982 at 1141b15-24); it is not an exclusively particular judgment.

Fourth, in some places, Aristotle actually did recommend an explicit rule-governed morality. Faced with the tragedy of a defective infant, a situation of great interest in current clinical ethics, Aristotle did not leave it to the parents and physician to decide whether to treat or not to treat. Instead he advised: "let there be a law that no deformed child shall be brought up..." (Aristotle, 1990 at 1335b20). In a moral philosophy where ethics and politics are two sides of the same enterprise, such a law is equivalent to the moral rule: "Do not treat or nourish defective infants; let them die."

A generation after Aristotle's death in 322, Zeno (c. 342-270 BCE) elaborated what appears to be the first explicit philosophical doctrine of principles and rules in ethics. Although many of his writings were lost, we know that the doctrine of principles and rules existed from the beginning of Stoicism, the philosophical school he founded, because it was the subject of great controversy. Most early Stoics advocated an ethics of both principles and rules, but Ariston, a student of Zeno, argued that we needed only the principles to guide our actions. Orthodox Stoics considered him a maverick and continued to argue for both rules and principles.

The controversy haunted Stoicism for years. Centuries after Ariston, the Roman Stoic Seneca (c. 4 BCE-65 CE) was still arguing against him. Seneca insisted on rules to complement the more general principles, and his remarks provide us with a clear picture of how the orthodox Greek and Latin Stoics conceived of principles and rules. Their conception is remarkably similar to the way many understand principles and rules in medical ethics today. Arguing against Ariston and in favor of both principles and rules, Seneca wrote:

> *What is the difference between the principles of philosophy and the rules, other than the fact that the former are general rules, the latter specific? Each presents rules, the principles in a general way, the rules in a particular way... (Seneca, 1987 at 422).*

What are the Stoic principles? Unfortunately, there is no canonical list. Seneca acknowledges that justice is one of the Stoic's principles by telling us that we cannot violate justice in order to bring about good consequences (Seneca, 1987 at 422). It is not difficult to discern other general moral principles at work in Stoicism. For example, the Stoics were the first people we know of to teach that all human beings are fundamentally equal because they are citizens of the world, and not merely of a city-state or of an empire. Stoics insisted that the free man and the slave, the citizen and the foreigner, were equally human. This explains why they advocated treating our enemies well, even loving them. And this recognition of shared humanity suggests a moral principle familiar to many of us today: respect for persons.

It is important to note that Stoicism was both an ethic of principles and rules, and an ethic of virtue. Today, some proponents of virtue ethics feel compelled to reject the idea of principles and rules when they reject modern rule-based moral theories. Stoicism reminds us, however, that an explicit doctrine of principles and rules is not incompatible with virtue ethics and, in fact, can play an important role in it.

The Stoics were not the only ancient ethicists to appeal to an explicit doctrine of normative principles and rules. Cicero (c. 106-43 BCE) described his task as formulating the rules (*praecepta*) of duty each of us should follow to achieve a good and happy life, and he suggested a good life is unimaginable without them (Cicero, 1985 at II, ii, 7). Moreover, Cicero was apparently the author who advanced the idea of "natural law" into the Latin literature on ethics and jurisprudence. The earlier Greek Stoics had insisted that right action was action "according to nature," but Cicero's translations of them sometimes expanded the phrase to read "according to the law of nature." And Cicero often translated the key Stoic concept of reason (*logos*) not as *ratio* but as *lex*, that is, not as "reason" but as "law." Thus the Stoic idea of acting according to nature was transformed into acting according to the law of nature.

The transformation is more significant than it might first seem. The Greeks had always sharply distinguished between nature and law. Nature was simply given, laws were established by reason. Nature did not teach us laws, reason established them. Cicero obliterated this distinction: "The highest reason implanted in nature is law, which commands what ought to be done, and forbids the opposite" (Cicero, 1977b at I, v, 18). If law is implanted in nature, it is something already given, and the task of reason will be to discover rather than to establish it.

Cicero's move introduced an ambiguity that has haunted legal and moral philosophy for centuries: does human reason establish the rules and laws governing human conduct or does nature teach them to us? The great effort by scholars to organize civil law in the sixth century left the ambiguity unresolved. Justinian's *Institutes* (533), one of the most important books of law ever written, held that civil law derives *both* from the natural law (*jus naturale*) which "nature teaches all the animals" *and* from the law of the people (*jus gentium*) which "the natural reason shared by all people establishes" (Justinian, 1987 at 37). Debates about the respective roles of reason and nature in legal and moral philosophy continue to this day.

Needless to say, Cicero's introduction of a "law of nature" into ethics reinforced a rule-governed approach to morality. Ethical reasoning must now conform to a pre-established norm, the natural law. And the natural law is not something we can modify. It is "an eternal and immutable law binding all peoples at all times" and "God is the author, promulgator, and judge of this law" (Cicero, 1977a at III, xxii).

Jonsen and Toulmin have noted that Cicero developed the first extended set of moral cases, and therefore contributed much to the beginnings of what became known as casuistry. "The third book of the *De Officiis* is the cradle of casuistry" (Jonsen, 1988 at 83). And indeed it is, for there Cicero did present a series of practical cases that became classics in the literature of moral philosophy and theology for centuries. If we look carefully at Cicero's cases, however, we can see how more than casuistry is at work -- he relied on natural law and rules to resolve the cases.

Cicero's cases are examples of an apparent conflict between what is good for us and what is morally right. The apparent clash arises because ethics is the seeking of what is good for us, but sometimes it seems that what is good for us is not morally right.

For example, Cicero cites a case where civil authorities ordered a property owner to tear down part of his building. The owner then sold the building without telling the buyer about the demolition order. Was the owner morally obliged to disclose this? It would not be in his self-interest to reveal the demolition order, but remaining silent about it does not seem right. Hence the conflict between what is good for him and what is morally right.

In this particular case, the seller did not reveal the demolition order and the buyer sought judicial relief when he discovered it after the sale. The judge ruled against the original owner and, Cicero tells us, his decision established the precedent whereby disclosure of defects was henceforth required at the time of sale.

This certainly is an example of casuistry because the case became a paradigmatic example for similar future cases. But Cicero's commentary on the case reveals something deeper than casuistry-- he tells us that the judgment was prompted by law, the *lex naturae*, the law of nature. Cicero acknowledged that customs had become so depraved that many would not have considered the failure to disclose the demolition order as unethical, and that neither statutory law nor civic duty (*jus civilis*) required disclosure, but he insisted that the law of nature (the *lex naturae*) did require disclosure (Cicero, 1975 at III xvii). Thus the judge, who had no civil law to guide him, did not simply decide what was reasonable and right. Rather, in the absence of statutory law and civic duty, he applied a more fundamental law to the case -- the law of nature.

Another of Cicero's cases involved the moral dilemmas arising in friendship. If my friend needs my help, I should offer it, but the help he needs may not be the right thing to do. In such cases, says Cicero, we should follow a simple rule (*praeceptum*): friendship should take precedence over honors, riches, pleasures, etc., but never over our duties to country, to our oaths, or to our trustworthiness (Cicero, 1975 at III, x).

In Cicero's casuistry, the supreme moral principle is the law of nature. It is this general law, and the more particular rules derived from it, that are applied to cases of the first instance. Only then do these cases become paradigmatic examples for future cases.

Cicero's insistence on natural law and rules for resolving moral conflicts is noteworthy because his general attitude after studying the different schools of philosophy was that no theory could provide us with certitude. He thought the most you can say for any philosophical truth is that it is "probable." Nonetheless, when it comes to living, he insisted that the uncertainties of theory must be put behind us, and rules to guide action must be developed and followed as if they were certitudes (Cicero, 1975 at II, ii).

The ever practical Cicero, a man of considerable success in business and law as well as politics, thus reminds us of many busy people today. Once clinicians and attorneys begin to read moral philosophy, they become aware of the complicated and apparently endless theoretical disagreements among moral philosophers. Since these practitioners are unwilling to wait for a definitive theory to emerge, they ignore the theoretical differences in moral philosophy, and adopt as certain a cluster of widely accepted normative principles and rules. They then make moral judgments by applying these principles and rules to particular situations.

Several decades after Cicero, the norm of acting "according to the law of nature" appeared for the first time in the Greek literature. The author, Philo of Alexandria (c. 30 BCE-45 CE), apparently developed his concept of the "law of nature" independent of Cicero. His doctrine may well have been the result of a desire to reconcile his Jewish tradition of living according to the Law of the Torah with the Stoic philosophy of living according to nature. It was Philo, more than anyone else, who introduced the "law of nature" into the Greek literature of antiquity (Koester, 1968).

Philo's doctrine of the law of nature included principles and rules. The universal principles (*archetypoi*) of morality are the general laws known to all people from the beginning of time. The more specific rules are the laws in the Torah. They copy or reflect the universal principles. Philo's doctrine thus strikes a now familiar note. Principles are the general moral archetypes known by all and rules are the more precise formulations of these principles.

Both the Ciceronian "interpretative" translation of the *logos* of nature as "law" of nature and the Philonic synthesis of biblical law with the Greek notion of nature contributed significantly to the rule-based moralities in the Greek and Latin Christian Fathers, in Roman and Western law, in the Canon law of the Christian church, and in most subsequent theological and philosophical ethics. So dominant was the idea that morality must be rule-governed that many had trouble even imagining ethics could be anything but some kind of law-like or rule-governed affair. Even when people began to focus on love as central to the good life, they often spoke of it as the "law" of love.

As we have noted, the idea that ethics is rule-governed characterizes the modern deontological and utilitarian approaches typified by Kant and Mill. There are, of course, exceptions in the history of ethics to the adoption of principles and rules in ethics, but they never seriously undermined the religious and philosophical traditions of rule-based normative ethics.

The history of principles and rules is a long one and spans both religious and philosophical traditions. Today that tradition is being challenged, and the criticisms are not groundless, in fact, they are often to the point. It is not so clear, however, whether the problem is the very idea of principles and rules in ethics, or whether it is the misuse of principles and rules. Using principles and rules in an axiomatic and rigid way, or reducing moral reasoning to little more than the application of principles and rules to particular situations, is deserving of criticism. But principles and rules need not be so used and, in fact, are seldom so used by thoughtful ethicists.

THE MISUSE OF PRINCIPLES

Unfortunately, the following caricature is all too widespread in clinical ethics:

> ***The ethics best suited for medicine and health care is applied normative ethics. Applied normative ethics is the formulation and defense of a system of norms -- the principles and rules -- to determine which actions are right and which actions are wrong. The application of these action-guides to various ethical problems allows people to determine the morally right action, and this determination establishes a moral obligation.***

How did it happen that so many believe this is just about all there is to health care ethics? No serious moral philosopher or theologian advocating principles and rules reduces ethics to this -- neither philosophers such as the Stoics, Cicero, Philo, Aquinas, Kant, and Mill, or such bioethicists as Beauchamp, Childress, Veatch, Engelhardt, Brody, Pellegrino and Brock. All claim that normative principles and rules are only one aspect of ethics.

By way of example, consider the widely used text *Principles of Biomedical Ethics* (Beauchamp & Childress, 1989). The authors set forth the now canonical principles of autonomy, beneficence, justice and nonmaleficence. They justify particular moral judgments by rules, and the rules by the more general principles. The focus of their book is applied normative ethics because the principles and rules will be applied to biomedicine. But this is not all they say.

Beauchamp and Childress also claim that moral theories and moral experience are dialectically related. This suggests that theories can illuminate experience and determine what we ought to do, but that experience can test, corroborate, revise and even replace a theory by moving us to seek an alternative. "It seems mistaken," they claim, "to say that ethical theory is not *drawn from* cases but only *applied to* cases" (Beauchamp & Childress, 1989 at 16, authors' emphasis). They insist that their proposed dialectical approach both applies moral principles to cases *and* reformulates the principles in light of cases. They want their principles to play a significant role, but they also maintain the experience in practical problems is "no less important" than the principles (at 16).

Beauchamp and Childress also take care to state that our moral principles and rules are not universal in the strong sense of applying to everyone everywhere. They explicitly say that they do not believe there is only one moral system of universally applicable principles and rules (Beauchamp & Childress, 1989 at 19). They voice suspicion about any view that makes principles and rules binding in an absolute way because moral absolutism disallows discretion which "is essential to the moral life, and an overly rigid adherence to rules can produce moral victims" (Beauchamp & Childress, 1989 at 49).

Another example is Robert Veatch's *A Theory of Medical Ethics* (Veatch, 1981). On the basis of a social contract, Veatch claims reasonable people could agree on a set of moral principles which include beneficence and five additional non-consequentialist principles -- contract keeping, autonomy, justice, honesty, and the avoidance of killing. Since these principles tend to be abstract, more precise moral formulations or rules are needed to guide moral judgments in particular cases. In his contract theory, the rules arise when reasonable people agree to interpret the principles and to make them more specific so they can be applied to specific problems. Moral rules thus play an important role in moral judgment.

Just what is the role of rules in ethics? Any answer to that question, (Veatch, 1981 at 310) he argues, must avoid two extremes. We cannot say that rules are totally useless, but neither can we say, Veatch insists, quoting Judith Shklar, that ethics "holds moral conduct to be a matter of rule following, and moral relationships to consist of duties and rights determined by rules" (at 310). We cannot accept an exclusively rule-governed ethic because "it leaves no room for judgments by lay people or professionals to decide in particular cases that there is an exception or that one rule does not apply because it is not really meant to cover the particular situation." In short, we "must recognize that some case-by-case judgment of what is ethically required is necessary" (Veatch, 1981 at 310).

Where, then, did the widespread idea that ethics is simply, or even mostly, a matter of applying principles and rules to particular cases come from? The sources, I think, are several.

First, although medical ethicists advocating the derivation of principles and rules from the modern utilitarian, deontological, and social contract theories acknowledge that ethics is something more than applying rules to particular situations, they often fail to develop what this "something more" is and how it works. They neglect to explain how we reach a decision or make a judgment when the principles clash, or when the rules conflict, or when the application of a principle or rule leads to an obviously unacceptable moral conclusion. We are told discretion in a particular situation can modify or override principles and rules, but no one has offered a thorough treatment of when and how a moral agent ought to do this. The advocates of principles and rules devote most of their energies to explaining the normative principles and rules and to applying them to particular cases, and thus give the impression that this is the major work done in ethics. But if experience is "no less important than principles," than we also need to know the role our experience plays in making moral decisions and judgments.

Second, many of the textbooks used in courses devoted to medical or health care ethics leave students with the impression that health care ethics is little more than the application of principles and rules to moral dilemmas. The standard format for many of these texts is an opening chapter on the various moral theories, usually utilitarianism, Kantian deontology, social contract, divine law, natural law, and the virtues. The authors are scrupulously fair -- they describe the strengths and weaknesses of each theory. At the end of the chapter the bewildered students are left with a handful of incompatible theories, and a suspicion that disarray exists on the level of ethical theory.

The texts then introduce a set of specific norms for making moral judgments. Although the major ethical theories are incompatible, the textbook reassures the students that they all point to the same basic moral principles or concepts which we can use to guide our behavior. Some examples:

1. Ronald Munson says "...each of the five basic moral theories we have discussed endorses the legitimacy of these principles" (Munson, 1992 at 31). (His principles are autonomy, beneficence, justice, nonmaleficence, and utility.)

2. Beauchamp and Walters say "...most types of general ethical theories would recognize these three ethical principles as valid" (Beauchamp & Walters, 1982 at 26). (Their principles are autonomy, beneficence, and justice.)
3. Mappes and Zembaty say that an examination of the "major normative ethical theories provides the groundwork" for three central concepts in biomedical ethics (autonomy, paternalism, and rights) and six additional principles designed to justify limitations on individual liberty (Mappes and Zembaty, 1991 at 24).
4. Beauchamp and Childress discuss two types of ethical theories -- the utilitarianism of Hume, Bentham, and Mill, and the deontology of Kant. Then they attempt to establish that an ethical theory "provides a framework of principles within which an agent can determine morally appropriate actions" (Beauchamp & Childress, 1989 at 25). Although Mill's *Utilitarianism* contains a strong criticism of Kant's deontology (Mill, 1987 at 12-13), Beauchamp and Childress nonetheless think "some rule-utilitarian and rule-deontological theories (where 'rule' includes principles) converge on the same principles and rules" (Beauchamp & Childress, 1989 at 62).

Hence, once the normative principles and concepts are set forth, students of "applied normative ethics" are left with the impression that the disarray on the theoretical level is of no serious consequence because all the major theories lead to a similar cluster of principles. Students then make the next obvious move when faced with a dilemma: they forget the theories and make the principles central.

Third, an approach based on normative principles applied to particular situations offers what good teachers often seek -- a method, and a simple one at that. Teachers can tell their students, take these principles, derive rules from them, and then apply the principles and rules to particular situations to know what is the right thing to do. Granted, dilemmas will occur, but at least the method is clear. After the chaos of incompatible moral theories, the relative calm of teaching students how to make a moral judgment by applying principles is attractive, and often graded well by instructors looking for consistency in academic exercises far removed from the emotions and conflicts of the clinic.

Fourth, justifying particular moral judgments by principles and rules has enormous appeal to many people. Normative principles offer an anchor in a world where many people no longer find a basis for ethics in traditional sources. As natural law and divine law lost prominence in moral theory, an ethics of principles and rules became an attractive alternative, perhaps even a nostalgic alternative, for those seeking some kind of impartial normative basis for ethics.

Fifth, and perhaps more important than most realize, a number of significant commissions and task forces in our country have repeatedly endorsed a medical ethics of principles and rules. Indeed, the Congress of the United States has mandated the use of moral principles in medical research. The act of Congress establishing the National Commission for the Protection of Human Subjects of Biomedical and Behavioral Research in 1974 directed it to identify the "basic ethical principles" underlying research with human subjects and to develop "guidelines" in accord with these principles and to "apply such guidelines to biomedical and behavioral research" (National Research Act, Public Law No. 93-348).

The eleven members of the Commission dutifully responded by identifying three basic ethical principles for guiding research. Their *Belmont Report* defined a basic ethical principle as a "general judgment that serves as a basic justification for the many particular prescriptions for and evaluations of human actions" (National Commission, 1978 at 4) and identified three such principles: autonomy, beneficence, and justice.

The National Commission's approach thus followed closely a model of ethics advocated by the influential moral philosopher, William Frankena. Frankena thought morality rested on two basic principles, beneficence and justice. Although these principles come from two different moral traditions (beneficence is rooted in the utilitarian tradition and justice in the Kantian tradition), Frankena thought these two principles were "in some sense ultimately consistent" (Frankena, 1973 at 53). Frankena summarized his doctrine of principles and rules as follows:

> *Thus, in such expressions as "the principles of morality"...what is ordinarily referred to may be defined as...the moral action guide that everyone who looks at the world clear-headedly and informedly from that point of view will eventually agree on...In short, our moral discourse...involves the concept of an objectively or absolutely valid moral action-guide, and our moral judgments and decisions claim to be parts or applications of such an action-guide (Frankena, 1976, p.174).*

It is not without interest to note that a member of that National Commission is now critical of its use of principles. Albert Jonsen has recently written:

> *As a Commissioner, I participated in the formulation of that (Belmont) Report. Today I am skeptical of its status as a serious ethical analysis. I*

> *suspect that it is, in effect, a product of American moralism, prompted by the desire of Congressmen and of the public to see the chaotic world of biomedical research reduced to order by clear and unambiguous principles (Jonsen, 1991 at 125).*

The three principles identified in the Belmont Report were widely employed in the institutional review boards which the Commission recommended and the federal regulations soon required. In fact, the federal regulations required "a statement of principles governing the institution in the discharge of its responsibilities for protecting the rights and welfare of human subjects..." (45 CFR 46.103(b)(1), 1981). Members of the institutional review boards frequently, and understandably, continue to apply the three principles proposed by the Commission as they work to satisfy the federal requirements and to protect human subjects in research.

The principles of autonomy, beneficence, and justice seemed to work well in ethical deliberations about research, so it was not surprising that they appeared in the reports of the President's Commission for the Study of Ethical Problems in Medicine and Biomedical and Behavioral Research. This Commission met from 1980 to 1983 and its final report candidly acknowledged that "three basic principles predominated" in its work -- the principles of well-being, respect for self-determination, and equity. And the Commission said it "tried to apply these principles consistently in its various reports" (President's Commission, 1983 at 66).

The principles were used again in the more recent New York State Task Force reports (NY Task Force, 1986, 1987, 1992), in the *Guidelines* published by the Hastings Center (Hastings Center, 1987) and in many other reports and committee statements. Thus their role in health care ethics became increasingly more powerful as time went on.

What was missing, however, from the National Commission and from the President's Commission, from the New York State reports and from the Hastings Center guidelines, and from just about every other report or set of guidelines published since 1972, is any extended treatment of how to determine what is right or wrong when none of the principles apply, or when particular judgments overrule the rules, or when discretion trumps the normativity of the principle. We are told it happens, that no ethic can simply be the axiomatic application of action-guides, that experience and particular moral judgment can override principles and rules, but we are never told how. Hence readers of these reports and guidelines are left with the same idea readers of the textbooks are left with -- ethics is little more than a matter of applying principles.

These are just some of the reasons that help explain why, despite the warnings of the ethicists and moral philosophers who make principles and rules a major component of their approach, the principles and rules have come to play such a dominant and, at times, exclusive role in health care ethics.

What, now, might we do? Given the long history of principles and rules, it may be premature simply to abandon them, especially if the problems may be more with the misuse of principles and rules than with principles and rules themselves. On the other hand, most criticisms of principlism are cogent. Any effort to reduce ethics to an exercise in applying normative action-guides to particular situations in order to determine what is right or wrong must be criticized. But efforts to abandon normative principles and rules altogether are equally questionable. The challenge is to find an appropriate place for principles and rules in health care ethics.

A PLACE FOR PRINCIPLES AND RULES

What is right about principlism is, as Aristotle noted, the claim that ethics includes general features as well as particular deliberations and judgments. What is wrong about principlism is its failure to develop the important aspect of personal deliberation and particular judgment that falls outside the application of principles and rules to particular problems. This failure is what gives the impression that applied normative ethics is a one way process -- the application of normative principles and rules to particular situations so we can determine what is the morally right thing to do. The ethical process also goes in the other direction -- it is the application of personal deliberation and particular judgment to the normative principles and rules so we can determine what substantive norms are morally right and, if they are morally right, how they are to be understood and applied in the particular situation.

Personal deliberation and particular judgments cannot be neglected in the ethics for several reasons. First, the normative principles and rules of medical ethics are generalities that were derived from personal deliberations and particular judgments in the first place. They do not descend from the agreement of rational people looking at the world.

The normative principles and rules of ethics have not always been there, waiting to be discovered by the Stoics, or by Kant and Mill, or by biomedical ethicists. People reflected on their experience, and then generated the principles and rules from their particular moral deliberations and judgments. Our primary experience is with particulars; the general comes later and is abstracted from it. Once general principles are developed, the unfortunate tendency is to forget their origin in collective personal experience and history, and to think they were always there. As soon as the human origin of principles is remembered, it makes no sense to insist that they control all future determinations of what is morally right or wrong.

Second, principles and rules are necessarily general and dated, and hence never precisely fit the particular situation. They must be constantly interpreted and reformed, and this is done by subjecting them to particular moral judgments. Moreover, normative principles should be ignored whenever applying them damages the good they were designed to protect. Even Kant, an ardent supporter of universal principles and rules in ethics, knew this. At the end of his life, he continued to insist that suicide is always against the moral law, but he also wondered whether we could say it was immoral for a man, realizing he was going mad, to commit suicide lest he in his madness harm others (Kant, 1988 at 84-85). And Augustine, a theologian who does not enjoy the reputation of laxity in morality, especially in sexual matters, insisted adultery was always against God's law, but wondered whether a woman who slept with a rich man for money to pay her husband's debts and free him from death row was really committing adultery (Janssens, 1982 at 42-43).

For moral decisions and judgments not governed by rules we need the moral discernment that Aristotle called "perception." Moral perception is similar to the kind of perception we exercise when we recognize a figure is a triangle (Aristotle, 1982 at 1142a25-30) despite its unusual angles or its placement among other figures. Aristotle also reminded us that moral discernment is similar to clinical discernment. A good clinician knows more than the science; he/she can also sense what is actually happening in complex and ambiguous cases. The physician's clinical reasoning is an interpretation of a particular situation as well as an application of general principles. As only those familiar with geometry can consistently recognize the triangle in different presentations, and as only those familiar with clinical practice can consistently make the right diagnosis, so only those familiar with virtue -- the virtuous -- can consistently recognize the morally right thing to do in different situations.

Good perception in moral matters means much more than knowledge of principles and rules. We must also strive to be aware of what is truly good for our communities as well as for ourselves, of the narratives of each life, of the moral lessons found in literature and in social, cultural and legal traditions, of feelings and hopes, of class and gender biases, and of religious beliefs and personal preferences. The particular judgments generated by this moral perception are, in one sense, actually more normative for actions than are principles and rules because these particular judgments were the origin of the principles and rules in the first place.

It is really not that difficult to think of normative ethics as embracing both principles and rules as well as particular moral judgments embedded in lived narratives. We see the same dialectical configuration in many areas of life. Language is an example. Mastery of the rules of grammar and of the vocabulary are important for mastering a language and, in some cases, extreme violation of the rules will so muddle the language that the intended meaning is lost. But the rules did not precede the language and, when they are established, they do not control it but continue to evolve under pressure from the way people actually use the language.

Languages are first spoken, then written, and only then do the rule makers, the grammarians, arrive. The elegant languages of early Greek and early biblical literature were spoken and written without benefit of explicit rules. Homer and Sophocles, Moses and Isaiah, and so many others all wrote before the first grammars and dictionaries were assembled at Alexandria in the third century. The grammatical principles and rules of classical Greek and biblical Hebrew were extracted from the living languages. Once assembled, the grammars and dictionaries are certainly normative, and we often appeal to them, but they are not what the language is all about. The living language had the first word, and it has the last word because the grammars and dictionaries of living languages continue to evolve.

To understand the interplay of both general and particular normative elements in moral decisions and judgments, we can also learn something from law, especially case law. Despite the controversies in philosophy of law giving rise to the various theoretical positions of natural law, legal positivism, critical legal studies, and legal realism, a general pattern of legal reasoning is evident in the actual development of case law. Edward Levi summarized it thus:

> *Therefore it appears that the kind of reasoning involved in the legal process is one in which the classification changes as the classification is made. The rules change as the rules are applied. More important, the rules arise out of a process which, while comparing fact situations, creates the rules and then applies them... A controversy as to whether the law is certain, unchanging, and expressed in rules, or uncertain, changing, and only a technique for deciding specific cases misses the point. It is both (Levi, 1950 at 203).*

I suggest the same is so in ethics. The particular judgments came first, then the normative principles and rules were developed for guidance. These are applied to future cases, but they change as they are applied. Ethics is thus both rule-governed and case-governed; the cases generate the rules, the rules are applied to future cases, and these cases can modify or overturn the rules.

The principles and rules are more than "rules of thumb," yet less than absolute. The principles and rules of grammar do guide language, and the principles and rules of law do guide judicial determinations. But good language and good case law are much more than applying these rules to particular situations. Language and law are living systems, evolving forms of life, creative practices, and the principles and rules generated by any practice can never completely dominate it. Language and law cannot exist without normative principles and rules applied to particular sentences and cases, but neither can good or bad sentences, or legal decisions be determined simply by the application of principles and rules to particular sentences or cases. As speakers change the rules of language, and judges change the rules of law, so moral agents change the rules of morality.

The thesis argued in this essay is that principles and rules have a place in ethics. Ethics needs a founding principle, a starting point; and that foundation may well be what the Greeks thought it was -- our natural desire not simply to live but to live well, to live a good life. Ethics also needs normative principles and rules, but principles and rules are not the only normative components in ethics. The undeveloped claim of Beauchamp and Childress -- that general principles and particular judgments are dialectically related -- means that particular judgments sometimes determine whether a principle or rule needs to be modified, suspended, or even abandoned. Applied normative ethics is both the application of principles to cases, and the application of cases to principles. The general normative principles and the particular normative judgments are complementary. Focusing on either aspect alone misreads what ethics has always been in the best of both our religious and philosophical traditions. By mistaking a component of moral knowledge for the whole, principlism undermines personal deliberation and judgment, and ultimately morality itself.

Recognizing the historical quality of human existence, and therefore the historical development of our moral norms, makes some uncomfortable, and this discomfort may be the reason why advocates of the principle and rule approach so seldom attempt to develop the normativeness of particular judgments. More likely, however, the reticence to develop the existential, historical, psychological, narrative and social aspects of ethics is the sheer difficulty in doing so. As it is incredibly difficult to explain the ever developing side of language and law pushing beyond the guiding rules of grammar and precedent, so it is equally difficult to explain the ever developing side of ethics as it pushes beyond, and modifies, its normative principles and rules. We know the developments occur, but we do not know just how they happen, and we cannot predict or control them.

To some extent, just as language and law are, to a degree, unpredictable, so is ethics. Odysseus was widely admired as a brilliant example of Homeric virtue for centuries, but his cunning and deceitful way were challenged by the great playwrights, and by Aristotle himself when he twice praises Neoptolemus for defying Odysseus in Sophocles's *Philocetes* (Aristotle, 1982 at 1146a19-22 and 1151b18-23). It is unlikely that Moses or Solomon ever dreamed of a day when polygamy and concubinage would be considered immoral or that Aristotle and St. Paul ever dreamed of a day when slavery would be condemned. And it is unlikely that the Hippocratic physician ever dreamed of time when treatment "of the sick according to my ability and judgment" would give way to the legal and moral requirements of informed consent (Edelstein, 1987 at 6).

This does not mean that ethics is simply social custom, something that changes with the times. But it does mean that the normative principles and rules of ethics are, unlike those of formal systems such as geometry, subject to historical development that cannot be predicted in advance. For now, however, we do the best we can. We try to live well, to make our lives good lives, and for that we need everything that can help us. Ethics requires both the deliberation and judgments of morally sensitive persons in particular situations, and also the general principles and rules. Rarely are either the particular judgments or the general norms alone sufficient for knowing, to the extent it can be known, how to live well. Rigid adherence to moral rules can make moral victims, but so can the tyranny of unfounded particular judgments.

Only in the irresolvable dialectic of particular judgments and general principles do we avoid the destructive aspects of both particularism and principlism in language, in law, and in ethics.

Emmanuel College

REFERENCES

Annas, G.J. (1993). *The Morality of Happiness*. New York: Oxford University Press.

Aristotle (1982). *Nicomachean Ethics*, trans. H. Rackham. Cambridge: Harvard University Press.

Aristotle (1990). *Politics*, trans. H. Rackham. Cambridge: Harvard University Press.

Beauchamp, T. and Childress, J. (1989). *Principles of Biomedical Ethics*. New York: Oxford University Press.

Beauchamp, T. and Walters, L. (1982). *Contemporary Issues in Bioethics*. Belmont, CA: Wadsworth Publishing Company.

Cicero (1975). *De Officiis*, trans. W. Miller. Cambridge: Harvard University Press.

Cicero (1977a). *The Republic*, trans. C. Keyes. Cambridge: Harvard University Press.

Cicero (1977b). *Laws*, trans. C. Keyes. Cambridge: Harvard University Press.

Devettere, R.J. (1993). Happiness and clinical ethics. *Journal of Medicine and Philosophy* 18:71-89.

Edelstein, L. *Ancient Medicine: Selected Papers of Ludwig Edelstein*, eds. O. Temkin and C. Temkin. Baltimore: Johns Hopkins University Press.

Frankena, W. (1973). *Ethics*. Englewood Cliffs, NJ: Prentice-Hall.

Frankena, W. (1976). "the principles of morality." In *Perspectives on Morality*, ed. K. Goodpaster. Notre Dame: University of Notre Dame Press.

Hastings Center (1987). *Guidelines on the Termination of Life-Sustaining Treatment and the Care of the Dying*. Briarcliff Manor, NY: The Hastings Center.

Janssens, L. (1982). Saint Thomas Aquinas and the question of proportionality. *Louvain Studies* 9: 42-43.

Jonsen, A. and Toulmin, S. (1988). *The Abuse of Casuistry*. Berkeley: University of California Press.

Jonsen, A. (1991). American Moralism and the Origin of Bioethics in the United States. *Journal of Medicine and Philosophy* 16: 115-129.

Justinian (1987). *Justinian's Institutes*. Ithaca: Cornell University Press.

Kant, I. (1956). Critique of Practical Reason, trans. L. Beck. New York: MacMillan Publishing Company.

Kant, I. (1981). *Grounding for the Metaphysics of Morals*, trans. J. Ellington. Indianapolis: Hackett Publishing Company.

Kant, I. (1988). The Metaphysics of Morals. In *Kant's Ethical Philosophy*, trans. J. Ellington. Indianapolis: Hackett Publishing Company.

Koester, H. (1968). NOMOS PHYSEOS: The Concept of Natural Law in Greek Thought. In *Religion in Antiquity*, ed. J.Neusner. Leiden: E.J. Brill.

Levi, E. (1950). *An Introduction to Legal Reasoning*. Chicago: University of Chicago Press.

Mappes, T. and Zembaty, J. (1991). *Biomedical Ethics*. NY: McGraw-Hill Book Company.

Mill, J.S. (1987). *Utilitarianism*. Buffalo: Prometheus Books.

Munson, R. (1992). *Intervention and Reflection: Basic Issues in Medical Ethics*. Belmont, CA: Wadsworth Publishing Company.

National Commission (1978). *The Belmont Report: Ethical Principles and Guidelines for the Protection of Human Subjects of Research*. Washington: U.S. Government Printing Office.

New York State Task Force (1986). *Do Not Resuscitate Orders*. New York: New York Task Force on Life and the Law.

New York State Task Force (1987). *Life-Sustaining Treatment: Making Decisions and Appointing a Health Care Agent*. NY: New York State Task Force on Life and the Law.

New York State Task Force (1992). *When Others Must Choose: Deciding for Patients Without Capacity*. New York: New York State Task Force on Life and the Law.

Plato (1984). *Laws*, trans. R.G. Bury. Cambridge: Harvard University Press.

Plato (1982). *Crito*, trans. H.N. Fowler. Cambridge: Harvard University Press.

President's Commission (1983). *Final Report on Studies of the Ethical and Legal Problems in Medicine and Biomedical and Behavioral Research.* Washington: U.S. Government Printing Office.

Seneca (1987). *Letters.* In *The Hellenistic Philosophers,* vol. 2, eds. A.A. Long and D.N. Sedley. Cambridge: Cambridge University Press.

Veatch, R. (1981). *A Theory of Medical Ethics.* New York: Basic Books.

ROBERT D. TRUOG, M.D.

PRINCIPLES, RULES AND ACTIONS: A RESPONSE TO DEVETTERE

The field of bioethics is perhaps most distinguished from other academic endeavors by its multidisciplinary roots and development. In his essay entitled "Principles, Rules, and Actions," Professor Devettere has provided a philosophical perspective on the relationship between the principle-based and case-based approaches to ethical decision-making. As a physician whose practice is primarily devoted to caring for critically ill children, I will reflect upon this analysis from the viewpoint of one who is faced with practical ethical dilemmas on a fairly regular basis. In the eclectic spirit of those who are engaged in bioethics, I will try to apply some insights from this perspective to the conclusions presented by Professor Devettere.

THE ATTRACTION OF PRINCIPLES FOR CLINICIANS

I will depart from the usual academic writing style and employ an autobiographical approach to explore the attraction that ethical principles have for clinicians. Although my own experience is necessarily somewhat idiosyncratic, I believe that my views are to some extent representative of those of many clinicians. For example, like most physicians, my pre-medical education was narrowly focused upon the sciences. My exposure to courses in the humanities was mostly perfunctory and superficial. This emphasis upon science was further reinforced during medical school, where the required courses in ethics were given little weight and were poorly attended. The path toward becoming a "good" doctor was defined almost entirely by the acquisition of scientific knowledge and technical skills. Whatever lipservice was accorded to the development of ethical character and moral judgment was effectively undermined by the attitude of my physician mentors, who consistently reinforced the importance of a detached and rational objectivity. All "ethical" problems could be reduced to "medical" problems, if one only looked at them from the proper perspective.

So it is perhaps not surprising that I shared with my medical school colleagues an almost total disinterest in medical ethics. There were so many more important things to learn. After all, one of the reasons I was attracted to medicine was because it offered the promise of technical mastery and achievement without the ambiguities that plague philosophy and the humanities.

M. A. Grodin (ed.), Meta Medical Ethics, 49–59.

While there were certainly exceptions, I believe that I was typical among my physician colleagues in not appreciating the importance of bioethics until I was almost finished with my residency and fellowship training, several years after completing medical school. Those who teach bioethics to medical students, residents, and fellows know that while these physicians can expound with impressive mastery upon the biochemical bases of obscure diseases, they can rarely articulate anything more than a crude and semi-coherent discussion of the ethical dimensions of their work. In my case, only after I felt confident about my knowledge and technical skills could I really begin to see that the most difficult decisions in medicine are often not what we can do, but what we should do. Only after I was in the position of needing to resolve these ethical dilemmas did I come to appreciate my lack of preparation and knowledge for dealing with them.

During the last month of my medical training I attended the one-week course in medical ethics offered through the Kennedy Institute for Ethics in Washington DC, and I learned to recite the now-famous "Georgetown Mantra" of autonomy, beneficence, maleficence, and justice (Beauchamp & Childress, 1989). Although this approach may seem almost comically simplistic to philosophers, the course had a profound effect on me. For the first time, I perceived that ethical dilemmas could sometimes be resolved through reason and argument, rather than just by personal viewpoint or majority opinion. I am sure that the incredible popularity of the Georgetown course is at least in part related to the fact that it gives clinicians tools with which to solve ethical problems; it makes ethical problems "solvable" in the same way that clinical problems are solvable, through the application of rules and principles.

Armed with the ethical principles expressed by Beauchamp and Childress, ethics took on a new interest for me. Like many other clinicians , I never seriously considered critiquing either the approach or the principles. For one thing, the approach seemed to work very well in solving a wide range of problems. For another, I was unaware of any alternatives. Principlism not only seemed like the best way to approach ethical dilemmas, it appeared to be the only way.

A couple of years later, my interest in ethics led me to pursue graduate studies in philosophy. I learned that there was a lot more to moral philosophy than the four sacred principles, and I had the opportunity to explore the ethereal realm of metaethics. Not only did I begin to see some of the problems with a "principled" approach to moral philosophy, but I became aware of criticisms that arose not from within moral philosophy itself, but from related areas like sociology, psychology, and political philosophy.

Professor Devettere has alluded to some of these problems in his essay. I will expand upon his observations by showing how these issues arise within the context of clinical practice.

THE LIMITATIONS OF PRINCIPLES: A CASE

To illustrate the limitations of the "principled" approach, I will continue on this same autobiographical track and draw from my personal experience as an intensive care clinician and ethicist at Children's Hospital in Boston. We recently cared for an adolescent boy in our intensive care unit who had suffered a tragic accident which had left him with severe brain damage. During the first week of his admission in the intensive care unit, everything possible was done to minimize the degree of ongoing destruction to his brain from the swelling that followed the initial injury. After the first week, it became clear that these efforts had not been successful, and that he was going to have permanent and devastating neurological damage. His parents were practicing Catholics, and they consulted with their priests and fellow parishioners about how to proceed. After many discussions between all involved, the careteam and his family agreed to limit his care to only those measures that would enhance his comfort, and to do nothing for the sole purpose of extending his life. In other words, they continued to provide him with routine nursing care, as well as sedatives and pain-relievers if he appeared to be uncomfortable. They agreed not to resuscitate him in the event of a cardiac arrest, however, and agreed not to reinstitute mechanical ventilation if he should develop respiratory failure from a pneumonia or collapse of his lungs. Several more weeks passed, and the neurologists who were consulting on his care concluded that his chances of ever recovering any degree of consciousness were virtually nil, thereby indicating that he was in a persistent vegetative state. His caregivers informed his parents that the families of patients who are in a persistent vegetative state sometimes choose to discontinue the administration of "artificial" feedings, where "artificial" is defined as feedings which are given either through a tube passed from the nose into the stomach or through a tube placed directly through the abdominal wall into the stomach. After further discussion with their religious advisors, the parents of this boy asked the careteam if they would discontinue his tube feedings. They knew that if this was done, he would die of dehydration within several days or weeks. Since artificial feedings had never before been discontinued on any patient at Children's Hospital, the careteam decided to ask the hospital's Ethics Advisory Committee for a recommendation. The Committee met first with the doctors and nurses who cared for the patient, then with the boy's parents and their priest, and finally in closed session among themselves.

The Committee ultimately recommended that the wishes of the parents should be respected, and that the artificial feedings should be discontinued. The deliberations that led to this conclusion could be analyzed in many ways. In retrospect, it could be said that the Committee applied established principles of bioethics and deduced an acceptable conclusion. The ethical line of reasoning that was finally outlined in the written recommendation was as follows:

1. Competent adults have a virtually unlimited right to refuse unwanted medical therapy.
2. Artificial feedings are a medical therapy.
3. Therefore, competent adults may refuse artificial feedings.
4. If a patient is incompetent, decisions should be made by an appropriate surrogate, in accordance with the patient's previously expressed wishes, if known.
5. Parents are the appropriate decision-makers for incompetent minors, provided they are not acting against their child's best interest.
6. Since this patient was almost certainly never going to regain consciousness, discontinuation of artificial feedings would not be contrary to his best interest.
7. Therefore, his parents should not be disqualified as surrogates on the basis of this request.
8. Therefore, his parents may choose on his behalf to have artificial feedings discontinued.

This rather sterile analysis of the dilemma in no way mirrored the actual deliberations of the Committee, however. Among the issues considered by the Committee were:

1. What is the symbolic importance of "feeding," in the context of caring for the sick and disabled? How is a decision to discontinue feedings different from a decision to discontinue other medical therapies, like antibiotics or mechanical ventilation?
2. Would discontinuing feedings in this case be a first step down a slippery slope? Would this decision make us less reluctant to terminate feedings on individuals with lesser degrees of neurologic

injury, on the assumption that life is no longer in their "best interest?"

3. Do the lives of permanently unconscious patients have any value? Do we have any obligations to these patients? Do they have any rights?
4. Would this be killing? Even though the discontinuation of feeds is an act of omission rather than commission, the death of the patient is the inevitable result of the action. Would this violate our moral prohibitions against killing?
5. Would this practice erode the morale of the doctors and nurses who must be involved? Would they find it difficult to participate in a care-plan which is explicitly focused upon bringing about the death of the patient?
6. Even if discontinuing feeding is acceptable, why should we put the family through more pain by forcing his death to occur over several days or weeks? Once the decision has been made to let him die, why not kill him, and end the suffering of both the patient and family quickly and painlessly?
7. How should the economic burden of caring for a patient in a persistent vegetative state be factored into the decision?

Although the Committee did eventually agree on the recommendation to accede to the family's wishes and withdraw artificial feedings, there was no agreement among the Committee members as to the ethical justification for this decision. Some felt the decision was justified by the principle of double effect, and viewed his death as a foreseen but unintended side effect of discontinuing his feedings. Others saw this justification as sophistry, and felt that discontinuing his feeding was just a socially acceptable way to kill him. Still others believed that since he was permanently unconscious, he was "as good as dead" already. And finally, others were persuaded primarily by economic concerns.

The lesson that I drew from my experience with this case is that while ethical principles often function well in a *post hoc* explanation of the conclusions that are reached, they play little role in the actual deliberations that precede and lead to the conclusions, especially in cases that are difficult and at the margins of accepted practice. A similar conclusion was reached by Jonsen and Toulmin out of their experience with the National Commission for the Protection of Human Subjects in the 1970s (Jonsen & Toulmin, 1988). This is also in accord with the views of Professor Devettere, who concluded that in these types of cases, the particular judgments are "actually more normative for actions than are the principles and rules, because these particular judgments were the origin of the principles and rules in the first place" (Jonsen & Toulmin, 1988 at 26).

What Is Ethical "Reasoning"?

I personally agree with the views of Professor Devettere, but I think that there are at least two aspects of his analysis that deserve closer scrutiny. First, he adopts a metaethical view that requires a dialectical relationship between considered moral judgments and ethical principles. This view has become quite popular recently, and it is probably the predominant metaethical paradigm among bioethicists today. John Rawls has contributed to the attractiveness of this view in his popularization of the process of "reflective equilibrium," whereby an iteration between considered moral judgments and ethical principles leads to actions and judgments that reflect a stable moral equilibrium (Rawls, 1971). If the casuist's reference to "paradigmatic case" is replaced by the term "considered moral judgment," and if the defender of principlism acknowledges that the principles are not foundational and non-exceptionable, but are only prima facie and revisable, then the apparent chasm between these two approaches to bioethics closes, and the differences between them evaporate.

Two features of this approach still need a great deal of further thought, however. First, not enough has been said about what it is that defines a "considered moral judgment" or a "paradigmatic case." What are the necessary features that allow them to function as anchors at one end of the dialectic continuum between cases and principles? What would be wrong with a "considered moral judgment" that condoned the act of murdering one person to obtain organs that would save the lives of five other persons, each of whom is dying with terminal organ failure? Such a judgment could be in "reflective equilibrium" with the principles of at least one school of moral philosophy (i.e., consequentialism). What is lacking is a theoretical foundation for ruling in or ruling out certain judgments as being either "considered" or "paradigmatic."

Second, more needs to be said about the status of principles within this formulation of ethical reasoning. Are they merely "summary statements" of a variety of "considered judgments"? Are they best described as "rules-of-thumb"? Or do they have normative force that transcends their summary functions? The principles of physics provide an interesting analogy. The "principle" of F=MA (force equals mass times acceleration), for example, is more than just a summary statement of a number of experimental observations. It is more than just a "rule-of-thumb" about how we might in general expect objects to act when subjected to an external force. We believe that F=MA conveys something that is "true" about the world, and that the principle transcends the observations that support it. Nevertheless, F=MA is not foundational, it is not unexceptionable. We have learned that at the margins of space, time, and velocity, this "principle" of physics is not the best description of reality.

Although the "principles" of physics and ethics seem to share many characteristics, there are important differences as well. For instance, the exceptions to F=MA are all established by principles that are more fundamental to physics than even this classical equation. In other words, it is the even more general empirical and mathematical principles of physics that serve to prove the exceptions to less foundational principles like F=MA. In ethics, the reverse seems to be the case. As we move from the level of principle to the more foundational level of ethical theory, our uncertainty increases rather than diminishes. Unlike with physics, appeal to more fundamental levels of generality leads to greater uncertainty rather than to clarification and greater confidence.

Despite these problems, the "dialectical" or "reflective equilibrium" model has become very attractive to applied ethicists. Professor Devettere gives the impression, however, that this is the way all good moral philosophers have always conceived of the relationship between general theory, principles, and particular judgments. "No serious moral philosopher or theologian advocating principles and rules reduces ethics to (deductive reasoning from principles)." He goes on to say that "The normative principles and rules of ethics have not always been there, waiting to be discovered by the Stoics, or by Kant and Mill, or by biomedical ethicists. People reflected on their experience, and then generated the principles and rules from their particular moral deliberations and judgments" (See Devettere at 35, 41).

Despite these assertions about the uniform acceptance of the dialectical model, I find it hard to believe that Kant saw the categorical imperative as being in a dialectical relationship with the moral judgments of everyday life, thereby accepting the implication that particular judgments might have the power to alter rules of morality that he believed were dictated by the logic of reason. Similarly, those who ascribe to religious traditions do not see the principles of morality as primae facie, as being in reflective equilibrium with everyday moral judgments. It was this relativism that many people found so disturbing about the "situation ethics" developed by the late bioethicist Joseph Fletcher. The idea that the Ten Commandments could be revised to the Nine Commandments or the Eleven Commandments by moral deliberation is not generally accepted (to say the least) by those who ascribe to religious traditions.

Indeed, one of the secrets of the success of Beauchamp's and Childress' textbook is their promulgation of four "foundational" principles of bioethics. For me personally, and for many of my medical colleagues, the attraction of the Georgetown approach was that it provided a structure and a process for dealing with ethical dilemmas. Beauchamp and Childress taught us how to break down ethical dilemmas into four categories (respect for patient autonomy, duties of beneficence and nonmaleficence, and considerations of justice), and then to reach a conclusion based upon the relative merits of the competing considerations that emerge from this analysis.

Although Professor Devettere implies that Beauchamp and Childress never intended their four principles to be seen as foundational, a close reading of each successive edition of their textbook reveals that in fact there has been a progression in their thought, and that the earlier versions do seem to recommend a deductive method for applying their principles to the resolution of specific cases. Although the more recent editions of the book are clear that the principles should be seen as non-foundational and revisable, I would argue that the success of their approach among practicing doctors and nurses has been to some degree dependent upon these principles being misinterpreted as unexceptional truths, that is, as a secular equivalent of the Ten Commandments. In other words, while I personally agree with the metaethic outlined by Professor Devettere, I would emphasize that we should not underestimate the extent to which the "dialectical" view would be perceived as radical and even disturbing by many clinicians and non-academicians.

There is also a second, and I believe much more important, question raised by Professor Devettere's comments. If good ethical decision-making is not just reasoning from principles, then what is it? Professor Devettere writes that "The undeveloped claim of Beauchamp and Childress - the claim that general principles and particular judgments are dialectically related - means that particular judgments sometimes determine whether a principle or rule needs to be modified, suspended, or even abandoned" (See Devettere at 44). Professor Devettere seems to imply that if the normative weight of particular judgments was more widely acknowledged and recognized, then the misuse of principles and principle-driven decision-making would disappear. The problem with this view, I believe, is that we know almost nothing about what justifies particular moral judgments when they are not justified by deductive reasoning from principles. As illustrated in the case described above, the ethical reasoning that was written into the Ethics Advisory Committee's conclusions was primarily a *post hoc* device for justifying the conclusions of the Committee to the patient's family and caregivers; they were of little relevance to the deliberation process itself. Describing just exactly what factors were relevant to the deliberations, however, is not easy. Several metaphors have been developed to shed light on the process, but I believe all of them are somewhat off of the mark.

Professor Devettere notes that Aristotle believed that moral perception is similar to the kind of perception we exercise when we recognize a figure is a triangle, despite its unusual angles or its placement among other figures. Another metaphor claims that moral discernment is similar to clinical discernment. "A good clinician knows more than the science; she can also sense what is actually happening in complex and ambiguous cases. As only those familiar with geometry can consistently recognize the triangle in different presentations, and as only those familiar with clinical practice can consistently make the right diagnosis, so only those familiar with virtue - the virtuous - can consistently recognize the morally right thing to do in different situations" (See Devettere at 42). The problem with both of these analogies, it seems to me, is that in both geometry and clinical medicine we have independent means for assessing the perceptiveness of the observer. We can objectively state whether one observer of triangles is better than another, simply by seeing who gets it right most often. There is no ambiguity at all over the definition of a triangle, although some triangles may be harder to spot than others. Similarly, even though it may be difficult to specify exactly what it is that makes one clinician better than another, in the final analysis we have very clear criteria for determining which clinicians are superior to others, simply by seeing who gets the diagnosis right most often. We have no such independent method for assessing the moral "wisdom" of the virtuous person. Indeed, it is uncertainty about what is to count as moral "correctness" that is at the root of the problem.

Devettere makes two further analogies to moral reasoning. First, he makes an analogy between moral reasoning and legal reasoning. Both tend to reason from "paradigmatic cases" or "considered moral judgments" toward decisions about progressively more difficult cases. Jonsen and Toulmin have referred to this process of extrapolation as "moral triangulation." So far so good. The problem, however, is that this only tells us that reasoning in ethics is very similar to reasoning in law. This analogy does not shed any light on what goes into these forms of reasoning. It does not illuminate the qualities that contribute to excellent forms of reasoning as opposed to inferior forms of reasoning. If the decision-making process around ethical dilemmas is mysterious, so is the decision-making process around difficult legal cases.

Next, Professor Devettere advances an analogy between the development of language in a society and the development of ethical reasoning around difficult cases. With regard to language, he notes that "…the rules did not precede the language and, when they are established, they do not control it but continue to evolve under pressure from the way people actually use the language." (See Devettere at 43). He goes on to suggest that the development of ethical reasoning in response to new dilemmas may be very much like the development of languages. I believe that he is probably right, but I find this insight disturbing nonetheless. If I were to learn, for example, that in one hundred years it will become perfectly acceptable to dangle a modifier, I would be much less concerned than if I were to learn that in one hundred years we will no longer regard it as wrong to lie or to steal.

In other words, the "undeveloped claim" of Beauchamp and Childress is undeveloped in their textbook and in the philosophical literature more generally because the nature of ethical reasoning seems to be fundamentally quite mysterious. As Professor Devettere acknowledges, perhaps "…the reticence to develop the existential, historical, psychological, narrative and social aspects of ethics is the sheer difficulty in doing so. As it is incredibly difficult to explain the ever developing side of language and law pushing beyond the guiding rules of grammar and precedent, it is equally difficult to explain the ever developing side of ethics as it pushes beyond, and modifies, its normative principles and rules. We know the developments occur, but we do not know just how they happen, and we cannot predict or control them" (See Devettere at 44).

Where does all of this leave us? I agree with Professor Devettere that the principles of ethics are not foundational or non-exceptionable, and that they must be revised within the ongoing process of seeking a reflective equilibrium with our considered moral judgments. I do not think that Professor Devettere fully acknowledges, however, just how radical this view is within the historical context of moral reasoning, both religious and secular. I also do not believe that he sufficiently emphasizes the way in which principles have come to play a proxy role in justifying our ethical decision-making. Since the deliberations that underlie our ethical judgments are so complex and mysterious, we often adopt ethical principles as a way of rationalizing our decisions on a *post hoc* basis, without fully owning up to the fact that we are unable to articulate the underlying factors that are in actuality determinative in shaping our moral judgments. Rather than being helpful deductive tools, I believe that the principles of ethics may function most importantly as signposts along the road, reminding us to take account of certain values, such as respect for persons and considerations of justice, that we might otherwise overlook. If nothing else, recognition of these points may serve to make us more humble in the way we view our own ethical judgments, and help us to acknowledge that our justifications for decisions may be more tenuous than they seem. In the end, all we may be able to say, as Professor Devettere notes, is that "We try to live well, to make our lives good lives, and... For now, do the best we can" (See Devettere at 45).

Harvard Medical School

REFERENCES

Beauchamp, T. L., and Childress, J. F. (1989). *Principles of Biomedical Ethics*. 3rd ed. New York: Oxford University Press.

Jonsen, A. R., and Toulmin, S. (1988). *The Abuse of Casuistry*. Los Angeles: University of California Press.

Rawls, J. (1971). *A Theory of Justice*. Cambridge: Harvard University Press.

THOMAS A. SHANNON

THE COMMUNITARIAN PERSPECTIVE: AUTONOMY AND THE COMMON GOOD

In this essay I will consider the issue of autonomy in relation to the common good. In the first part of the presentation I will concentrate on autonomy by giving an overview of what I consider its salient features and its application to two cases. In the second part I will consider the common good in relation to autonomy.

I. AUTONOMY AND ITS CONTEXTS

A. Autonomy

Together with respect for persons, justice and beneficence, autonomy has been a major workhorse in bioethical analysis over the last several decades. From issues like abortion to euthanasia, advance directives to artificial reproduction, we have relied almost exclusively on autonomy as the cornerstone of ethical analysis. Let any challenge to personal freedom or private decision-making be made and almost immediately, in the wonderful phrase of Art Caplan, the "autonomy drum begins banging." Think, for example how autonomy functions as the main line of defense against any attempts to qualify or regulate access to or use of reproductive technologies, including, but not limited to, artificial insemination, IVF, surrogate motherhood, and abortion. Autonomy has had a profound impact on the practice of medicine and on how medical ethics as a discipline has developed.

The issue of autonomy was highlighted in a dramatic way in the play and later the movie *Whose Life Is It?*, the tragic story of a young and competent man who wishes to end his life because he will remain a quadriplegic. The story of Dax, the victim of severe burns over almost his entire body, is another widely documented case of a competent patient refusing life saving treatment. Both cases were resolved by the continuation of treatment and by cries of outrage because of such blatant overrides of autonomous judgments.

This should be no surprise, for autonomy is the "All American" value. Almost from conception we have had drummed into us the message that we must be the master of our fate, the captain of our ship, the one to forge our own destiny with our own hands and that we are the one solely responsible for our own fate. The myth of the self-made person has taken strong root in our culture.

M. A. Grodin (ed.), Meta Medical Ethics, 61–76.

And to be sure there is a very positive dimension to that myth. It is clearly the source of creativity, energy, and initiative. Americans do have a strong sense of responsibility and that has spurred us to action, to seize our destiny, to realize that the future is of our making. The new world is a world of opportunity, a world of improvement, a world of possibility.

B. Two Case Studies

Let me present two cases in which autonomy structures major elements of decision-making in medical ethics. First, I will consider some ethical issues in guardianship of the elderly. Then I will consider some issues in artificial reproduction. Analysis of the issues will follow later.

1. Adult Protective Services

I begin with some comments in an essay entitled "Ethical Issues in Adult Protective Services" by Jane Boyajian.

Privacy is defined here as the right to make one's own decisions and decide what is in one's best interests. We would all agree to this. But what is interesting and relevant are the conclusions drawn from this principle. Privacy involves respecting the decision of another, leaving them alone and free from interference. Finally, it means letting people "live according to a lifestyle others find repulsive, even harmful, without interference from others. Potentially vulnerable adults can refuse social services which caseworkers believe will improve their quality of life" (Boyajian at 2-6).

Another issue raised in the article is what the author calls an obligation in a democratic society to promote autonomy over protection and intervention. The issue here is a critical one, because there has been a history of paternalistic abuse of the elderly, the mentally ill, and others with diminished competence. One needs to remember that to assert a priority is not to establish that such a priority actually exists.

A third issue raised in this article is professional conduct. The author states that "the first step in promoting an ethically responsible professional practice is separating personal values from professional assessments...Personal considerations have no place in professional decision-making" (Boyajian at 2-6). The comment raises, but does not resolve, issues related personal values and professional ethics.

2. Artificial Reproduction

Let me now turn to some issues raised with respect to artificial reproduction. The area of human reproduction presents a very focused area of tension between the wishes of the individual and social norms, restraints, and resources.

Legally the issue came into clear focus with the 1968 Supreme Court decision in *Griswald v. Connecticut.* The court determined that the State had no business involving itself in a couple's decision of whether or not to have a child. Another dimension was added in the 1973 *Roe v. Wade* case which decriminalized all state abortion laws. The basis of this decision was that the right of privacy was broad enough to encompass a woman's decision to abort.

Such control over one's body as the basis for the validation of surrogacy is highlighted by Lori Andrews in her book, *Between Strangers*. She notes her and others' surprise at some women's opposition to surrogacy, particularly since it was women who argued for and supported the control of women's bodies by women. Such a qualification of autonomy, by prohibiting surrogacy, could open the door to other forms of reproductive regulation. Thus, she argues, autonomy forms a strong defense against bodily intrusions.

II. BEYOND AUTONOMY: A RETURN TO THE COMMON GOOD

A. A Critique of Autonomy

1. Shortcomings in the Myth of Autonomy

As powerful and positive as is the myth of autonomy, there is a downside to it. I argue that the foundations of it are false. There are no self-made people. No one of us starts from square one in anything. At birth we are given a language, a culture, education, socialization, and all manner of skills. We are born into a community which to some extent nourishes us and gives us the foundation on which we build. How far we take that is indeed, to a large extent, up to us, but we must not forget that we began in a community that formed us and gifted us.

It is also the case that we, as a culture, have taken the concept of individualism about as far as it can go. We understand autonomy to be a situation in which I am so individual, so idiosyncratic that I, and only I, can know what I think, what I feel, and what is good for me. We seem to have taken the philosophy of individualism to its logical conclusion and affirmed that indeed we are all islands, apart from each other. Very little, if anything, unites us. What we share is our separateness, not our common goods and destiny. Many in our culture no longer assume that parents know what is good for their children, that teachers know what is good for students, that spouses know what is good for each other, that physicians know what is good for patients.

Perhaps this degree of the emphasis on autonomy and individualism is symbolized by the most common expression of contemporary relations: the contract. A relation frequently consists only of what is expressly specified by the terms of the contract. If it is not expressly stated, then we do not have to do it, nor should there be any expectation of our doing it. Perhaps the most interesting form of this is the pre-nuptial contract. No longer is it for better or worse or richer or poorer but rather for "x percent" of actual and anticipated income, together with wages lost because of time invested in the relationship instead of one's career. The marriage contract has replaced the marriage covenant because of the priority of autonomy over the community.

This cultural situation has left us quite alone with few, if any, to know our interests, what is good for us, or what might help us to mature as a healthy member of our society.

The consequence of the recent dominance of autonomy, located in a rapidly increasing technological arena, has been a profound isolation of the individual from the family and the community. The rights of the individual or the autonomous choices of the individual are essentially trumps that the individual can use either to demand or to reject relations. But such relations are a function of autonomous choice, not a consequence of living in community. The autonomous individual stands in final and total judgment of all that impacts him or her.

The immediate shortcoming of this position is manifestly clear and most problematic when the patient is unable to speak on his or her own behalf, i.e., when comatose, unconscious, or in some other way incompetent. Resolutions of this situation rang from advance directives of one sort or another, trying to specify the patient's best interests, or substituting judgment of what the patient would do if he or she knew of this situation for the judgment that the patient needs to make but cannot. All of these are ways to preserve autonomy by replicating the patient's autonomy in situations in which the exercise of autonomy is impossible. They are based on the perception that incompetence is not a disqualification for the exercise of autonomy. One retains one's rights and the right to exercise these rights in such a condition of incompetence.

However, a soft underbelly of autonomy is beginning to be revealed. We are beginning to recognize that some requests or demands made by autonomous individuals can be problematic. The fact that someone chooses a therapy does not automatically qualify one for that therapy. The fact that one chooses a therapy does not mean that the therapy will be successful. The fact that one rejects a therapy, does not mean that such a decision was an appropriate one. And even the fact that one has the right to make an autonomous decision does not mean that the impact on others or the community should not be taken into account.

We are beginning to recognize that the social impact of individual, autonomous choices has profound significance. One such area of impact is the cost of health care. The sum of autonomous choices in medical care is staggering. Not all do -- or even can -- receive the same medical therapy, even though needs may be similar. The shortage of organs for transplantation continually brings this problem to public awareness. Yet another area is the increasingly strident debate over euthanasia -- whether done in an individual act, or with the assistance of a physician. Finally, given that health insurance in America is largely private and to a large degree contingent on one's employment, we find autonomy confronting a rather insurmountable corporate barrier.

The upshot of all this is that autonomy, though an important and critical value in our society and the practice of medicine, is proving itself inadequate to help us resolve critical social issues. In particular, our over-reliance on autonomy has seduced us into thinking problems such as the ones described above are individual problems and can be resolved on the individual level. Our captivation by autonomy has also led us to think of the individual as an isolated being, complete in his or her own self. In this view, the community is frequently seen as an obstacle -- if not an outright barrier -- preventing the individual from achieving his or her desires or goals. However, some, myself included, say that America at the present time is living proof of the falseness of the claim that individual choices to promote one's own good lead to the good of all.

2. The Paternalistic Response

Questioning autonomy typically leads to cries of paternalism and violations of liberty. Paternalism -- either doing something for someone without their requesting it or not cooperating with someone when they request our help -- has gotten quite bad press, particularly in our country, and particularly in the helping professions. The professionals in these areas actually thought they had some good ideas about how to help people and tried to put them into practice. The doctrine of informed consent was a strong and appropriate protest to inappropriate and unwarranted interventions into people's lives, bodies, and value systems.

There certainly were and are abuses of paternalism. Much reform and creativity in various fields -- education, medical training, the arts -- were stifled because a certain group knew how to do it and what all the students needed. Much personal growth was thwarted because parents and educators had certain goals in mind to which individuals had to conform for their own good. People have been prevented from following their interests because what they wanted to do was too dangerous, too risky, too new, perhaps too exciting. And so initiative was stopped.

But now, as I have indicated, autonomy holds sway and almost any intervention to help someone -- even when they need it -- falls under the suspicion or condemnation of paternalism. We have almost worked ourselves into a position in which we think that we as humans share nothing in common, that we have no common values, needs, aspirations, or goods. In the interest of promoting autonomy, we have talked ourselves into a denial of any commonality of interests with the consequence that practically any intervention is an invasion of individual privacy.

James Q. Wilson, in his recent book *The Moral Sense*, asks the interesting question: "Are we prepared for the possibility that by behaving as if no moral judgments were possible, we may create a world that more and more resembles our diminished moral expectations: We must be careful of what we think we are, because we may become that" (Wilson, 1993).

3. *Response to Autonomy in Adult Protective Services*

In my earlier comments about adult protective services I presented several issues derived from autonomy, including the right to lead a repulsive lifestyle, the right to refuse medications, and professional ethics. Let me make some comments about those issues.

I would think that in adult protective services, many of the individuals, while moderately autonomous, also need a lot of protection. Perhaps that's why this area is referred to as protective services. I think one can promote and respect autonomy while still providing appropriate and adequate levels of service. The issue is not to do for others what they can and ought to do for themselves. It is to recognize that providing help and assistance are not automatically violations of autonomy. Instead of thinking in terms of rights of autonomy and prohibitions against paternalism, instead of thinking in a conflict model, why not think in terms of a cooperative or collaborative model in which both the patient and guardian work toward mutually desired goals. Shifting the model will not resolve conflicts -- and conflicts there will surely be -- but a shift in frame of reference will help rethink strategies we use to achieve our goals.

I should think we want professionals with strong values and beliefs. And I should think we would want the value-laden professionals to bring the best of their values to bear on the resolution of a case. Of course we don't want someone coming in and taking over and telling us to put sweaters on because they know we're cold. But if someone is not formed and developed in a value context, that person isn't going to be very good at recognizing anyone else's values. Also someone who has a strong value perspective in their own professional life is going to recognize a conflict of values and is going to be sensitive to the problems in particular situations. We might disagree about the solutions and resolutions, but at least we will know what the debate is about: it's about the ethical response to a human being in need, and not some technical debate about procedures.

I find the statement that someone has the right to lead a repulsive lifestyle rather appalling. This is the conclusion to which we have been lead by an exaggerated sense of autonomy and privacy: individuals have the right to lead repulsive lifestyles while we stand by and applaud such exercises of autonomy. This is particularly ironic when medications that could help that person by resolving elements of a depression that might be causing the lifestyle are available. This is not an argument for simply going in and taking over someone's life. It is an argument that when we can figure out why someone is leading a basically destructive lifestyle and can intervene in a moderate way through medication, autonomy may fall to beneficence. Why continue to let someone harm themselves to the point of either causing irreversible physical damage so they are permanently bedridden, or cause themselves to become incompetent and then, and only then, provide the appropriate medication? I genuinely think that the good of intervention in cases like these accomplishes more good than harm.

One of the first cases described to me when I began to work in bioethics was of a woman who was severely depressed. While depressed she always refused medicine, because she would forget to take her medicine, she always refused the medicine. But when she had been taking the medicine, she always consented to it. The way the case was resolved was that the team decided the person who chose the medication and lived without depression, was her better self, and so they assumed she would always want her medicine. That solution makes sense to me. The good to be achieved and the harm to be avoided, particularly in the areas of physical and mental illness, seems to me to outweigh the harm done through a modest violation of autonomy.

4. *Autonomy and Artificial Reproduction*

Even though we live in a culture which generally supports almost unlimited reproductive rights, there are proposals which argue that access to the new reproductive technologies be qualified. For example, some propose that only married heterosexual couples should have access to IVF. Others argue that commercial surrogacy, in particular, should be prohibited altogether. Such suggestions are, at least prima facie, violations of autonomy and a restraint of an individual's reproductive freedom. Are there justifications for apparent restrictions such as these?

A critical dimension of autonomy is freedom. If one does not have the capacity to choose or to remain constant in one's choices, then one can hardly be thought of as free. Yet freedom is somewhat of a confusing reality, particularly in our culture.

Freedom has certainly played a major part in the establishment of our nation. The Bill of Rights, in particular, is an ongoing, living testimony to some of our most cherished freedoms. Yet there are debates about those freedoms: Does free speech include the right to destroy the flag? can song lyrics be censored? can a woman's reproductive decisions be qualified? All of these raise profound issues about one of our most treasured gifts.

One of the critical ethical dimensions of freedom in our culture is our seeming equation of freedom with the capacity to choose. That is, freedom consists in either the face of a choice or the capacity to choose and the protection of freedom consists in protecting choice. Such a position suggests that what is chosen is not central to the ethical analysis. If one couples this with our primarily procedural legal system, guaranteeing the capacity for choice discharges our ethical and legal duty.

Such a position on freedom is important because it ensures that a critical capacity will be safeguarded from unwarranted intrusions or interferences. Autonomy is at the core capacity to be ourselves. The protection of freedom of choice ensures the protection of a core element of that autonomy. Yet I am uncomfortable with that position. It is reminiscent of Bentham's position that there is no moral difference between playing push-pin and doing philosophy. What is morally relevant is reduced to what one has chosen instead of whatever value, or lack thereof, might be associated with either choice.

To some extent we need to at least consider the value of what is being chosen. Not to do so would be to accept a position of total value neutrality or to assume that all realities are of the same value. Either position fails to discriminate where discrimination is indicated. A richer concept of freedom would incorporate the value of what is chosen. Such a position is derivative from the medieval philosopher Scotus who argued that the essence of freedom was not merely the capacity to choose but rather adherence to the good that one chooses.

Such a position automatically raises profound concerns in our culture -- what is the good and who defines it, for example. Nonetheless, there is an element in this perspective that we need to reincorporate into our ethical analysis. That is the recognition that the fact that something is chosen neither ends the ethical discussion, nor makes that choice worthwhile. While we need to protect the procedural dimension of freedom, we also need to evaluate what we choose, lest we fall into an ethical or cultural indifference.

Minimally, then, I argue that the fact of being chosen does not ethically ensure that reality's worthwhileness or that all objects of choice are thereby ethically valuable. Assumedly, one would choose something because of a value in that reality and this would be done after some comparison. Thus choices are value-laden though such values can be argued about. Additionally, one could be asked to justify and/or defend one's choice.

Such a position does not require that there be a test of values either by an institution or individuals. Rather it seeks to acknowledge that choices convey values and that their worthwhileness can and ought be debated. Additionally, while it is also clear that an object increases or decreases in value in relation to its desirability to me, such objects have a meaning and value in themselves, a pre-moral goodness or badness that is then factored into the moral decision. Thus, choice occurs within a context that is already value-laden, though the reality of choice further articulates those values.

This perspective does not seek an end to reproductive rights. Rather it seeks to examine those rights in relation to the good they hope to actualize and the overall significance of that good. While not all will agree on the same goods or the same priority of goods, at least the debate will be moved to the values at stake. At some point, a discussion such as this is necessary to move us beyond the procedural conundrums in which we find ourselves.

B. A Reconsideration of the Common Good

Considerations of the common good have fallen by the wayside in the last several decades in mainstream discussions of social and political ethics. In part this has been because, as Bellah phrases it, "American culture has focused relentlessly on the idea that individuals are self-interest maximizers and that private accumulation and private pleasures are the only measurable public goods" (Bellah, 1991 at 50). Another dimension of this is shift from the family's being child-centered to its being adult-centered (Bella, 1991 at 46). This shift reflects a priority of personal fulfillment over the good of family members and an understanding of the family as a locus for individual fulfillment over development of an identity through social interactions. Downplay of the common good is also reflected in our reliance on cost-benefit analysis for social decision-making. What is given priority here is social efficiency and a neglect of the externalities that follow from such decisions. Finally, we continue to hear the rhetoric that the government and our institutions are the enemy of the individual. While the Reagan mantra of "Get Government off our backs," is not as frequently invoked, the sentiment remains alive, particularly in many of the critiques of the Clinton health proposal.

What we seem to have forgotten is that "even autonomy depends on a particular kind of institutional structure and is not an escape from institutions altogether" (Bellah, 1991 at 12). We have further forgotten that autonomy is "only one virtue among others and that without such virtues as responsibility, and care, ...autonomy itself becomes... an empty form without substance" (Bellah, 1991 at 12).

As a way of responding to the issues raised thus far, I want to propose a reconsideration of the common good as a critical component of personal and social decision-making. In doing this, I want to recognize two caveats. First, I want to affirm, following the wisdom of Joseph Pieper, that it is "definitely not possible to define the *bonum commune*, in this sense, with any comprehensiveness and finality" (Piper, 1989 at 65). Thus I do not conceive of the common good as a type of institutional or repressive Procrustean bed with which to trim excesses of autonomy. Second, again following Pieper, "the 'good of a commonwealth' includes the inborn human talents, qualities and potentials, and part of the *justitia distributiva* is the obligation to protect, preserve, and foster these capacities" (Pieper, 1989 at 66). The positive contribution of the concept of the common good is, as I see it and as I understand how it is located in the Catholic social ethic, to encourage and enhance participation in the community so that individual action will benefit both.

1. The Common Good

a. The Lure Of Nostalgia

In discussing the common good, a double nostalgia must be resisted and ultimately rejected. One version is American and is derived from a vision of rural or small town America as seen through the idealization of the founding of our Republic or in the paintings of Norman Rockwell. Another version is papal and longs for the idealized Middle Ages.

> *At one period there existed a social order which, though by no means perfect in every respect, corresponded nevertheless in a certain measure to right reason according to the needs and conditions of the times. That this order has long since perished is not due to the fact that it was incapable of development and adaptation to changing needs and circumstances, but rather to the wrongdoing of men. Men were hardened in excessive self-love and refused to extend that order, as was their duty, to the increasing numbers of the people; or else, deceived by the attractions of false liberty and other errors, they grew impatient of every restraint and endeavored to throw off all authority (Pius XI at 64).*

To be sure there are virtues to be admired and emulated in such visions but our world is, to a large degree, industrialized and urban. Our problems, though they may be similar to those of past generations, cannot rely on the solutions of our forbears for our times and social context are quite different.

b. A Constructive Reconsideration of the Common Good

Following the lines of thought developed by Michael and Kenneth Himes in their book Fullness of Faith: The Public Significance of Theology, I would like to present some constructive proposals for reconsidering application of the common good in our situation.

2. The Encyclical Tradition

In Roman Catholic social theory, from which I derive my perspective, the concept of the common good has a rich, varied history. In *Rerum Novarum*, the 1891 encyclical by Leo XIII that began the modern tradition of Catholic social thought, Leo defines the common good as that for the sake of which civil society exists and "is concerned with the interests of all in general, and with the individual interests in their due place and proportion" (Leo XIII, 1992 at 33). More specifically Pius IX, in *Quadragesimo Anno*, stated that "Those goods should be sufficient to supply all needs and an honest livelihood, and to uplift men to that higher level of prosperity and culture which, provided it be used with prudence, is not only no hindrance but is of singular help to virtue" (Pius IX, 1992 at 59). Both of these conceptions of the common good derived from such a society was "self-evidently substantive, objectively knowable, and indivisible" (McCann, 1987 at 164). While such a perspective is overly optimistic at best and epistemologically naive at worst, nonetheless such a concern for the good of society and all of its members stays at the heart of the encyclical tradition.

John XXIII began a shift from such an hierarchical and static vision of society and the common good by identifying the foundation of the common good as the human person who has rights obligations flowing from his or her nature (John XXIII, 1992 at 132). This moved the focus from the structure of society to the person and used the concepts of rights to ensure the protection and enhancement of the individual in society and the concept of obligation to guarantee that the person actively participate in the development of society. Such thinking led John to a vision of the common good which did not stop at national boundaries but also included "the entire human family."

The Second Vatican Council, in its pastoral constitution *The Church in the Modern World*, continued this line of thought by recognizing that "the concrete demands of this common good are constantly changing as time goes on." This important document recognizes that the common good is a dynamic concept and one which must be responsive to the changing needs of human society.

The American Catholic Bishops continued this line of thinking in their Pastoral Letter "Economic Justice for All." The bishops say, for example, that "human dignity, realized in community with others and with the whole of God's creation, is the norm against which every social institution must be measured" (USCC, 1992 at 584). Again they affirm that "[t]he common bond of humanity that links all persons is the source of our belief that the country can attain a renewed public moral vision" (USCC, 1992 at 584). And finally, the bishops state that *"The dignity of the human person, realized in community with others, is the criterion against which all aspects of economic life must be measured"* (USCC, 1992 at 584).

The bishops then use this perspective to develop a vision of social justice that "implies that persons have an obligation to be active and productive participants in the life of society and that society has a duty to enable them to participate in this way" (USCC, 1992 at 595). Here they follow Pius XI who said "It is of the very essence of social justice to demand from each individual all that is necessary for the common good" (USCC at 595). Thus the bishops envision justice as a means through which the person achieves the perfection of his or her self through participating in the well being of society. In the perspective of the bishops, then, the core of justice is the establishment of "minimum levels of participation in the life of the human community for all persons" (USCC, 1992 at 595), rather than establishing zones of privacy whereby individuals attempt to seek their private good independent of the community.

This orientation presents a vision of justice and the common good that is not quite in the mainstream of American libertarian theory. The bishops recognize this and argue that the next phase of the American experiment needs to be securing for this vision of social-justice-as-participation the same status as the other rights we currently celebrate. The significant difference is that the bishops' vision orients the person to their role in the community, whereas our traditional vision focuses on the autonomous individual.

3. *Re-fashioning the Common Good*

This emphasis on community, social justice, and human dignity realized in community leads to a certain shaping of an understanding of the common good which has a different emphasis than in the past. This shift looks to freedom, equality and participation as core elements. I will touch on each of these in relation to the encyclical tradition as well as independant of it.

As I noted earlier, the American experience of freedom in general is "freedom from". And typically, what we most desire to be free from is coercion, particularly any institutional coercion. While that perspective has contributed significantly to advances in our society, the question of the object of our freedom remains undeveloped in our society. Thus we need to focus on what I call "freedom for". This is the issue of the significance and value of our choices. Minimally we need to recognize that choices are not value-neutral. Though sometimes what we do is whimsical, most of the time our choices reflect preferences and priorities with respect to some goods we wish to achieve. We also need to reconsider the reigning assumption that the fact of my choosing an option makes that option worthwhile or free from critique. As I say this, I hear the autonomy drum beginning to beat in the background. But I think we need to seriously consider the values behind the choices we make. For, while the choices are undeniably ours and ours alone to make, some are harmful to ourselves and society. To say this is not to give free reign to censorship or invite a new wave of Puritanism. Rather it is to recognize that what we choose has a significant effect on who we become, and who we become has a powerful effect on what society becomes. Perhaps rather than prohibit actions, we need to begin to model appropriate behavior to show the positive consequences that can accrue for ourselves and society.

Equality resonates strongly within our culture and vast social and personal energy has been spent in achieving greater degrees of equality for all citizens. Yet we face a dual danger now with respect to equality. First, some may think that equal means same or identical and attempt to locate criteria for equality on quantitative measures. Second, others may identify equality with freedom from all norms in the name of idiosyncrasy or autonomy.

The social norm of equality of persons is derived from our common dignity and value as persons. Such dignity "need[s] to be incarnated in social policies and practices" (Himes, 1993 at 41). Most critically this means that we must strike the proper balance between a false uniformity and a destructive utilitarian individualism. We must recognize the value and uniqueness of each person and the wealth of riches they bring but must also remember that our origin and development as persons is communal. To seek equality for oneself is also to affirm the same for my neighbor.

The emphasis on participation in society as a means of achieving the common good is a traditional theme in the encyclical tradition being reiterated in a different context. Formerly participation meant living out the duties of one's state in life. These duties were derived and defined from the hierarchical society in which one lived and found one's purpose. Thus participation was mainly passive and culturally proscribed.

Participation now reflects self-determination both through individual choices concerning, for example, one's lifestyle or career, and through participation in the development of the community. Participation is individual and social, political and economic. Michael and Kenneth Himes state well the implications of this re-imaged pluralism.

> *This call for active participation implies subsidiarity and pluralism. What is needed for healthy social life is that an abundance of human associations and groups be allowed to flourish so that persons will be able to find a wide array of institutions that give form and structure to participatory community in the various realms of human existence.*

> *Furthermore, the bias is toward the grassroots in deciding at what level decision-making should occur in an organized group. This is to insure that even a well-meaning paternalism does not eviscerate the participation of people in the life of the community (Himes, 1992 at 36).*

III. CONCLUSIONS

Michael and Kenneth Himes argue that, according to the communitarian perspective, liberalism has failed in five significant ways:

1. it has led to the decline of civic virtue, the practices encouraged by what has been called the tradition of republicanism or civic republicanism;
2. liberalism fosters a political community that speaks of an individual citizen's right but downplays civic duties;
3. there has been a disappearance of public space where common life can occur;
4. there is a marked lack of participation in the political activities necessary for democracy to flourish;
5. endemic to liberalism is a failure to acknowledge that social life is constitutive of the human person resulting in the neglect of important social institutions (Himes, 1993 at 36).

Embedded in such a critique, of course, are other assumptions about society and the human person. The assumptions and values derivative from them have formed the basis of my critique of autonomy and my suggestions for a different social agenda. Yet I want my comments to reflect an appreciation for and commitment to a rightful freedom, equal regard, and broad participation in the way we organize society (Himes, 1993 at 42). I want to re-introduce the concept of the common good, not to serve as a repression of individual or communal aspirations, but rather to invite us to re-conceptualize our society and the good we need to share in common so that such a society can be viable.

Here I follow Dennis McCann's suggestion that the concept of the common good must be procedural, not substantive; partial, not universal; consensus-based, not hierarchically imposed. Broad social participation in such a quest can check efforts of power blocks who attempt to impose their vision of the good on others. Conflict is not eliminated here but is seen as part of a larger process of the definition of self and community rather than individuals and groups carving out zones of privacy or lifestyle enclaves.

Finally, in the words of Michael and Kenneth Himes,

> *The common good must not be seen as so specific in detail that diversity within society is repressed. What must be sought instead is an open, informed, civil discussion by citizens so that consensus on what Murray called the orders of justice, peace and morality in public life might be attained through persuasion, not coercion (Himes, 1993 at 44).*

This essay is an invitation to begin such a discussion.

Worcester Polytechnic Institute

REFERENCES

Bellah, R. (1991). *The Good Society*. New York: Alfred A. Knopf. pp. 12, 46, 50.

Boyajian, J., *Minnesota Adult Protective Services Guide*, pp. 2-6.

The Church in the Modern World, Vatican Council II. (1992). p. 78. In David O'Brien and Thomas A. Shannon, *Catholic Social Thought: A Documentary History*. Maryknoll, New York: Orbis Books. p. 220.

Himes, M.J. and K.R., OFM, (1993). *Fullness of Faith: The Public Significance of Theology*. Paulist Press. pp. 36, 41, 42, 44.

Leo XIII. (1992). *Quadragesimo Anno*, p. 97. In David O'Brien and Thomas A. Shannon, *Catholic Social Thought: A Documentary History*. Maryknoll, NY; Orbis Books p. 64.

Leo XIII. (1992). *Rerum Novarum*, p. 37. In David O'Brien and Thomas A. Shannon, *Catholic Social Thought: A Documentary History*. Orbis Books p. 33.

Leo XIII. *Quadragesimo Anno*, p. 79. *Catholic Social Thought*, p. 59.

McCann, Dennis. "The Good to be Pursued in Common," in Oliver Williams and John Houck, eds., *The Common Good and U.S. Capitalism* (Lanham: University Press, 1987), p. 164.

John XXIII. (1992). *Pacem in Terris*, p. 9, 98. In David O'Brien and Thomas A. Shannon, *Catholic Social Thought*, p. 132, 147.

McCann, D. (1987). pp 164. "The Good to be Pursued in Common." In Oliver Williams and John Houck, eds., *The Common Good and U.S. Capitalism*. Lanham: University Press.

Pieper, J. (1989). *Joseph Pieper: An Anthology*. San Francisco: Ignatius Press. pp. 65, 66. Emphasis in original.

United States Catholic Conference. (1992). *Economic Justice for All*, pp. 25, 27, 71, 584(Italics in original), 595, 596(Italics in original). In *Catholic Social Teaching*.

Wilson, J.Q. (1993). *The Moral Sense*. New York:Free Press. *Social Thought*, p. 220.

RALPH B. POTTER

THE COMMUNITARIAN PERSPECTIVE: A RESPONSE TO SHANNON

In responding to Tom Shannon's essay, our first task should be to remind ourselves that the tension between "autonomy and the common good" is a current expression of an ancient antinomy which reappears in many guises. In other decades and disciplines, it has been framed in terms of the individual versus society, the particular against the universal, the contingent opposed to the necessary.

Our second task, I believe, should be to speculate on why autonomy has come to be the "workhorse" of medical ethical reasoning, the "all-American value." One cannot hope to match the pithy elegance of LaRochefoucald's maxim (#218) holding that "Hypocrisy is the homage vice offers to virtue." But we can propose that "Autonomy is the price we pay for self-control." Self-control, in turn, is the indispensable means of making a highly-differentiated and diverse society such as ours function. Moral restraints must be voluntarily assumed and internalized if we are to have so many moving parts coordinate their actions and sustain high levels of economic and cultural productivity. That high productivity undergirds our expectations of having means at our disposal to live free of economic and cultural poverty. Given the intricate interdependence entailed in the high division of labor that supports our mode of life, a high degree of autonomy must be sustained in order to avoid the astounding costs that would be encountered by systems of motivation relying upon more external incentives, rewards, and inducements.

If you want to profit by the self-control and discipline of self-starting persons who, year after year, get up and go to work, perfect demanding skills, obey the laws of their community and the codes of their profession, raise their families as befits them, take on burdens of participating in voluntary associations, all for their own good reasons, with a minimum degree of external supervision, without waiting to be told what to do next, you will have to expect them to carry over the same expectations of self-determination when circumstances place them in the care of medical services. Subsidiarity needs to be brought down from the realm of political theory to be applied to personal decision-making as well. The autonomy we enjoy provides, on balance, a very good bargain. It serves the common good, even when one can cite bizarre cases of excess at the margins.

Our third undertaking is to give an alternative account of what may be amiss at those margins. It is not autonomy or self-determination that is the

M. A. Grodin (ed.), Meta Medical Ethics, 77–81.

source of difficulties, but the impoverishment of the sense of the self. The self that persons present, to themselves and to the world, seems, in many instances strikingly narrow, fragmented, and shaved down to fit into tiny pockets within society.

I attribute this, in part, to a tardy but laudable assimilation, in wide segments of the population, of the recognition of our *historicity*, that is, the consciousness of our social origin and embeddedness. A century and a half after more advanced thinkers took seriously the shape of selves by particular factors at work in the specific times and places of their formation, the findings of Marx and Freud, Weber and Troeltsch, Mannheim and other practitioners of the sociology of knowledge have percolated into popular consciousness.

It would be unthinkable for me to deny that being a middle-aged WASP male who grew up in the 1940's and 50's has not had an important formative influence. These experiences have formed my way of viewing and describing the world and accounting for the sentiments and behavior I notice in myself and others, as well as the things I fail to notice.

If I *didn't* try to take such realities into account, students and colleagues would quickly remind me of the particularity of my history and the partial quality of the habitual modes of perception which flow from it. I would reply in the same mode to them. And there we are. We can't jump out of our own skins. We are born into small worlds and inherit from them habits of thought, structures of plausibility, moral and aesthetic sensibilities, which seem self-evident until challenged by those we encounter in "the great world" that lies beyond family and school and early communities of socialization.

My fourth point is to draw attention to the reluctance of many persons to come out from the small worlds in which they were first formed. That I take to be a source of the impoverishing narrowness of so many selves. They are stunted by their unwillingness to come out and meet "the generalized other" that, in mirroring back many facets, helps create a self with many sides to it.

Tom Shannon is on the right track in echoing the call for "participation" in society. It is to be noted, however, that the representatives of his own Roman Catholic tradition in America spent over one hundred and fifty years building up a parallel structure of separate institutions, from drill teams to philosophical societies, to guard the faith of the immigrant against the corrosive force of the general culture and still wish to receive special public funding for a large system of parochial schools set apart from the public domain in which a consciousness of the common good is most likely to be engendered by common participation. The example is open to imitation.

In fact, we now see the multiplication of all sorts of enclaves, occupied by selves trimmed down to fit within boundaries defined by religion, race, gender, class, sexual preference, age, occupation, recreation, taste, or level of cultivation. Indeed, we have people choosing to label themselves by the name of their best-known frailty, identifying themselves primarily as members of this or that therapeutic group. Our social world is cut up along many biases. Many persons suppose that they can arrange their existence within self-contained boundaries that will shield them from having to deal with persons who differ in the dimensions they have chosen to make salient in defining their identity.

The dire impact this has upon the doing of ethics is my fifth theme. As people search for safe niches in which to lead a narrowed existence, it is not surprising that we are suffering an outbreak of particularistic "niche ethics." We have types of ethics qualified by the particular sub-cultures from which they spring or the narrow audiences to which they are targeted within a fragmenting public. There are medical ethics qualified by the disciplines with which they are concerned. Business ethics addresses those in a single segment of the economy. Feminist ethics conveys the insights of those who are oppressed. Womanist ethics concentrates on the experience of the fraction of feminists of African-American origins.

Ethics, to be ethics, must have a universalistic grounding and aspiration. It must claim to speak to the condition of *all* persons in order to have a bite upon *any*. Ethical arguments must demonstrate that particular actions and policies function to redistribute benefits and harms. For this there must be an underlying theory, capable of being explicated on demand, of what constitutes a benefit and harm. For this there must be an underlying theory, capable of being explicated on demand, of what constitutes a benefit and harm. That requirement makes philosophers and theologians of us all, at whatever level of profundity we are capable of achieving.

By way of a sixth point, I would note that ethical discussion is inherently controversial. Only the hard cases come up for explicit consideration. The doing of ethics requires a high level of civility. But civility suffers when there is little sharing in the life of "the great society." which has historically been white middle-class males. Civility is that consideration we owe to all persons on the basis of their being fellow citizens, fellow members of the *civil society*, apart from any special bonds of kinship, religion, race, group membership, professional bond, affinity, or whatever. The decline of civility drives people back into their niches, intensifying fragmentation.

Seventh. Moral argument is unspeakably complicated, far beyond mathematical and scientific disciplines that can abstract from messy particulars. One could view the rise of niche ethics as a *simplifying* device resorted to in face of this immense complexity. Simplification, in some form, is always necessary. By my account, ethical debate is always *"truncated."* It is invariably cut short before every potentially relevant consideration has been discussed and dealt with to the perfect satisfaction of all participants. Considerations that might be highly pertinent from certain perspectives are left out of account, dealt with in abbreviated form, or assumed to be "irrelevant" and dismissed as a waste of time. Certain forms of discourse are institutionalized in particular quarters and those who wish to dwell on other points are ruled out of order and often shunned.

There is much more I would like to say about the natural history of ethical argument, how debates begin and end. But let us turn to the question, "What is to be done?" For philosophers, in the face of the foolish tendency to identify oneself with a tiny segment of a special group instead of claiming the full dignity of being a human being, sharing most attributes with all others ever born, I would say that the best response is to go on doing and living ethics in the grand and ancient manner, asking and answering the classic question, "How ought we to live?"

A great deal of practical wisdom has been accumulated on that question by our forbears. Concerns which occupy much of the time of many persons have been tested and found wanting: Fame is fickle. Wealth is instrumental. Sensual pleasures are fleeting. Beauty fades. Power and tyranny are isolating. Bullying engenders reprisal. High position is precarious. Pretension is ludicrous. Fraud brings dishonor.

There are things worthy of respect. Craftsmanship. Honesty. Kindness. Or, in the very short list drawn up by the influential Cambridge Don, G.E. Moore, at the turn of the century: "By far the most valuable things which we know or can imagine, are certain states of consciousness, which may be roughly described as the pleasures of human intercourse and the enjoyment of beautiful objects" [*Principia Ethica* 1903 (Cambridge: Cambridge University Press, 1963) at 188]. Moore's list is a bit short on heroism and service, but we need to see that discussions billed as "ethics" are pushed to this level.

Ethics, which moves back and forth, in both directions, across the territory between our deepest beliefs and our concrete determinations concerning what is to be done, should not be confused with another discipline, useful and demanding in its own right, which might best be called "biolaw." Practitioners of "biolaw" need not blush so deeply if they cannot lay bare the ultimate justifications for our actions, which rest beyond positive legal enactments.

Even when dealing with highly technical questions on a hospital ethics committee we need to make it clear that ethical arguments must finally be grounded in our willingness to embrace a *way of life* able to accommodate the policies we recommend. To carry moral weight we need to live philosophically in the midst of those to whom we speak.

In summary, the most useful check upon autonomy is the reminder of the similar autonomy of other persons. Invoking autonomy gives no privilege of imposing upon others or intruding into *their* sphere of self-determination. That says a lot, because there are, in practice, very few benefits to be gained by insisting upon one's freedom to choose unless, through consideration for others and acknowledgment of a common good, one can engage the other persons' willingness to cooperate with our endeavors. You just can't do much all by yourself. You can, however, undertake to expand that self to recognize your interconnectedness with others. That is my central theme.

My great teacher, James Luther Adams, illustrated the constriction of the sense of self by quoting an epitaph found on an English tombstone: "Here lies John Jones, born a man, died a greengrocer." That shrunkeness is the tragedy we should seek to diminish by refusing to allow ethics to shrivel up into a technical performance.

Harvard Divinity School

proceeds we recommend. To carry moral weight we need to live philosophically in the midst of those to whom we speak.

In summary, the most insistent check upon autonomy is the reminder of the similar autonomy of other persons. Invoking autonomy gives no privilege of imposing upon others or intruding into their sphere of self-determination. That says a lot, because freedom, in practice, very few men are tempted [illegible] by insisting upon their freedom to choose unless, through consultation with others and acknowledgement of a common goal, one can engage the other persons' willingness to cooperate in our endeavors. You can't do much all by yourself. [illegible] concern, however, undertake to expand that self to recognize your interconnectedness with others. That is my central theme.

My great teacher, James Luther Adams, illustrated the contraction of the sense of self by quoting an epitaph found on an English tombstone: "Here lies John Jones, born a man, died a greengrocer." That shrinkage is the tragedy we should seek to diminish by refusing to allow ethics to shrivel up into a technical performance.[*]

[*]Harvard Divinity School

GEORGE J. ANNAS

THE DOMINANCE OF AMERICAN LAW (AND MARKET VALUES) OVER AMERICAN BIOETHICS

American bioethics draws both its strengths and weaknesses from the fact that it is rooted in and dominated by American law (Annas, 1993). Its strengths are derived from the rich tradition of American Constitutional law which itself is founded on concepts of liberty, equality and justice. Its weaknesses stem from the fact that the multicultural American experience is unique in the world, and that its once famous "melting pot" is threatened with cultural fragmentation. This, combined with America's secular humanist liberalism, helps explain why its free market economic system often seems to provide a more coherent value system for its citizens than any other creed.

Historian Arthur M. Schlesinger, Jr. has captured and capsulized the American experience (Schlesinger, 1992). Tocqueville, he notes, observed that immigrants to the United States became transformed into Americans "through the exercise of the political rights and civic responsibilities bestowed on them by the Declaration of Independence and the Constitution." More than a century later in 1944, Gunnar Myrdal of Sweden wrote of Americans, "of all national origins, religions, creeds, and colors" they hold in common "the most explicitly expressed system of general ideals" of any country in the West. In Schlesinger's paraphrase, "the ideals of the essential dignity and equality of all human beings, of inalienable rights to freedom, justice and opportunity." Myrdal had labeled these ideas "the American Creed" and properly observed that in trying to live up to them, "America is continuously struggling for its soul" (Schlesinger, 1992 at 27).

It may be too much to say that American bioethics is engaged in a struggle for the soul of American medicine; but it is not too much to say that the values and ideals of American law, as expressed in the Declaration of Independence and the Constitution, have consistently dominated the ethical discourse concerning both substantive and procedural approaches to medical practice. In this essay I address the dominance of American bioethics by American law, discuss the failure of the major contribution of American bioethics, the ethics committee, to solve ethical problems, and describe how the American marketplace has converted medical ethics into business ethics.

The Dominance of American Bioethics by Law

The Declaration of Independence is the foundational document of the American Revolution and the American experience. At its core is the belief

M. A. Grodin (ed.), Meta Medical Ethics, 83–96.

that all persons are endowed with "certain unalienable rights" including the rights of "life, liberty and the pursuit of happiness" (Willis, 1978). The document which established our government, the U.S. Constitution, was almost immediately amended by adding the Bill of Rights to it. The first ten amendments specify individual rights, such as freedom of speech and freedom of religion, that the government cannot interfere with (at least not unless it can demonstrate a compelling state interest for such interference). Thus it is fair to say that when we discuss Americans we are talking about people with rights; and when we discuss the life and death of Americans, we cannot help but frame the discourse in terms of rights. Rights talk dominates America, and this dominance is inescapable in our country.[1] The major issues in bioethics over the past two decades have involved abortion, care of the dying, and human experimentation. In all of these areas the principles of American law, usually constitutional law, have defined and dominated the debate (Annas, 1989).

The abortion debate, of course, has been primarily a legal, and often a political, debate, at least since the 1973 case of *Roe v. Wade*. *Roe* held that a pregnant woman has a constitutional right to privacy to terminate a pregnancy, and that the state could not prohibit such termination prior to fetal viability. When it looked like *Roe* was going to be overturned in 1989 by *Webster*, I helped organize a group of bioethicists from around the country to file a brief, the first "bioethics brief" ever filed in the U.S. Supreme Court, to argue that *Roe* should not be overturned. The decision to write a bioethics brief was quite controversial because it seemed to some to be putting the field of bioethics into the position of endorsing the morality of abortion. But I thought it was exactly right, because I believe bioethics is a public enterprise that must be involved in national policy. This means that bioethics must be involved in law making. In this regard we must recognize that although law and morality are often treated as if they were the same in America, there are *real* differences. Protecting a woman's legal right to choose to terminate a pre-viable pregnancy tells us nothing about whether her decision to do so in any particular instance is a morally defensible one. The Court split 4 to 4 in *Webster* over whether *Roe* should be overturned saving this question for another day. *Roe* ultimately survived its next test in the 1992 *Casey* decision, although states need now only show that restrictions on abortion do not "unduly burden" a woman's decision (rather than that they are supported by a compelling state interest).[2] The election of President Bill Clinton, and his promise to appoint only those Justices who support *Roe* to the U.S. Supreme Court, makes *Roe* (as modified by *Casey*) secure for the foreseeable future. Abortion remains legal. Although serious moral and ethical problems exist involving indications for abortions, how a decision should be made, and the status of the fetus, these issues have been all but ignored in public discourse because of our focus on the law.

At the other end of life, the right to die discourse has been dominated by law since the 1976 *Quinlan* case (Quinlan, 1976). The question in *Quinlan* was whether and on what basis life-sustaining ventilator treatment could be legally withdrawn from a person in a persistent vegetative state. The court decided that a patient's next of kin or guardian could make such a decision. More than fifty additional appellate court decisions were rendered on this subject until the *Cruzan* case, which was decided by the U.S. Supreme Court in 1990. All but two of these courts came to the same ultimate conclusion as *Quinlan*. The facts of *Cruzan* were substantially identical to *Quinlan,* except that Nancy Cruzan required only a feeding tube to continue to live in her persistent vegetative state. The Court determined that all competent adults have a Constitutional right to liberty to refuse *any* and all medical interventions, including tube feeding. When the person cannot speak for him or herself, it also held that states could condition the exercise of this right on finding "clear and convincing evidence" of the person's wishes regarding treatment refusal (Annas, 1993 at 85-97). After *Cruzan* was decided, a group of bioethicists who were attending the Annual Bioethics Retreat in Lutsen, Minnesota, issued a statement on what *Cruzan* meant for the practice of medicine and for bioethics (Annas, 1990). Again, I thought that response to the law was exactly right, and tried to use consensus ethics to prevent ethics and medical practice from being overwhelmed by legal procedures. Currently the right to die debate has moved into the physician-assisted suicide realm. Not surprisingly, it continues to be dominated by legal concerns, such as passing statutes to prohibit assisted suicide or to provide physicians with legal immunity for actively assisting patients to commit suicide (Annas, 1993).

In terms of human experimentation, I find persuasive Arthur Caplan's statement at a 1989 bioethics conference that "bioethics was born from the ashes of the holocaust" (Caplan, 1989). The holocaust required society to recognize that medicine was incapable of setting its own ethical standards. The law again was central. The Nuremberg Code, enunciated by U.S. judges sitting at Nuremberg at the doctors' trial (the second trial at Nuremberg) remains a foundational document in bioethics (Annas, 1992). The primary authors of that legal document were two U.S. physicians who testified at Nuremberg, Leo Alexander and Andrew Ivy. So at the beginning of bioethics -- there were no "bioethicists" at that time -- it was lawyers and doctors who worked together to develop legal standards of conduct (Annas, 1992 at 121-144). The Nuremberg Code itself later became the primary source for federal regulations (legal rules) developed by the first national bioethics commission, the National Commission for the Protection of Human Subjects of Biomedical and Behavioral Research, a Commission that developed *legal* regulations for the conduct of human experimentation. It is also worth noting that the Commission's primary ethical document, the Belmont Report, centered the regulation of human experimentation on three ethical principles, the first and third of which are fundamental American legal principles: autonomy (liberty), beneficence, and justice (National Commission, 1978). Although the regulation of human experimentation has been dominated by law in the U.S., it should be noted that in the international sphere, international law (like the Nuremberg Code and the International Declaration of Human Rights) is more accurately described as international ethics. This is because there is no court or other enforcement mechanism (other than public opinion) to punish offenders. International law, like ethics, is aspirational rather than mandatory (Grodin, 1993).

More generally, American bioethics has developed as a reaction to medical paternalism whose power and capacity to render patient wishes irrelevant has been intensified by medical technology. The legal reaction to paternalism, including the related civil rights and women's movements, made three major characteristics of contemporary bioethical discourse inevitable: the stress on self-determination; the use of cases; and the use of procedural mechanisms to solve disputes. Self-determination or liberty is, as has been stressed, the fundamental concept enunciated in our Bill of Rights, our Declaration of Independence, and our common law history. The use of case examples parallels the history of the common law itself, which is based on using past judicial decisions (precedents) as a basis for deciding current controversies. Finally, much of the law is concerned with the use of procedural mechanisms to resolve disputes. So, it is almost inevitable that when you get procedural decision making, you get lawyers, because lawyers are experts at procedures. It should also be noted that at least some ethicists see it as reasonable to testify about ethical standards of conduct in court. By testifying in court as to what the proper decision is in a particular case, these ethicists seem to confirm their own belief that law and ethics are the same, or at least that law and ethics set the same standard of conduct.[3]

Nor is it just bioethicists that refer (and defer) to the law. American physicians have a long history of equating ethical obligations with legal obligations. This accounts for the consistent insistence of organized medicine, through groups like the American Medical Association, that if society wants physicians to act in particular ethical ways, such as stopping to help accident victims, it must grant physicians legal immunity for these actions. This insistence on legal immunity pervades and often dominates ethical discourse in medicine. It was at the heart of much of the right to die/right to refuse treatment discussion (in which most cases that came to courts, such as the Karen Quinlan case, were there because physicians who believed treatment termination was ethically appropriate, nonetheless would not act without legal immunity)[4] and continues to dominate the physician-assisted suicide debate, including the referenda in California and Washington. The quest for prospective legal immunity in these cases makes no more sense than it would if heart or brain surgeons refused to operate on patients unless the court gave them prior legal immunity in case anything went wrong in the operation. The AMA also continues to insist that the major problems with medicine are not ethical or financial, but legal; and that legal "reform" of the medical malpractice litigation system is much more important than medical practice or ethical reforms designed to prevent medical malpractice itself (Todd, 1993). One looks in vain for any history of either moral courage or ethical self-policing in American medicine. Instead what one discovers is a consistent pattern of special pleading and self-interest.

This pattern helps explain why the most important ethical development in medicine over the past two decades, informed consent, had to come to medicine through the courts rather than as a self-imposed ethical principle (President's Commission, 1982). Informed consent is, of course, a flat rejection of medical paternalism by requiring physicians to share certain information with patients prior to treating them. It is remarkable that information sharing had to be imposed by law, and that many in the medical profession still view information sharing with patients as either optional or inappropriate. Just as law was needed to counterbalance paternalism, it has also been needed to help bend technology to human purposes by taking informed consent seriously and letting patients decide whether or not to use advanced medical technologies.[5]

It is also no accident that of the two major national commissions on bioethics, the staff director of both was a lawyer, and the chair of one of the two was a lawyer (Annas, 1994). The major products of these Commissions were also legal: federal regulations on human experimentation, and a model state law on brain death. This legal dominance over bioethics is probably inevitable in the United States because we're a pluralistic society made up of at least 110 racial and ethnic groups. Mythologist Joseph Campbell may have put it best: "In America law is what holds us together, there is no other ethos"(Campbell, 1988). And, he could have added, no other bioethics either. Law becomes, of necessity, our lowest common denominator ethics.

Ethics Committees

The ethics committee is the primary American contribution to bioethics, but the ethics committee is incapable of solving ethical problems. Nonetheless, it is understandable that procedural devices are invented when agreement on substantive ethical rules or principles is seen as impossible. Because the ethics committee is so central to American bioethics, it was fitting that a 1992 national conference on The Birth of Bioethics centered on America's most famous (or infamous) ethics committee: the Seattle dialysis patient selection committee (Annas, 1985). Have we learned something in the last 30 years of bioethics that might move us beyond the use of a white middle-class committee making decisions that mirrored their prejudices rather than basing decisions on ethical principles?

One recent piece of evidence from Oregon suggests that we have not. When Oregon decided to "ration procedures rather than patients," it drew up a prioritized list of procedures it would fund for the currently uninsured. One of the procedures was liver transplantation. In Oregon's penultimate ranking, liver transplants for cirrhosis of the liver or biliary tract without mention of alcohol got rated 364. This is a high ranking, and would be funded by Oregon. But alcoholic cirrhosis of the liver ranked only 695. This is near the bottom of the list and would thus never be funded. This was the Seattle dialysis committee all over again: institutionalized discrimination against individuals (not procedures) on the basis of the source of their disease. As in the Seattle experience, when this discrimination was publicly acknowledged it was found intolerable, and Oregon's final list combined all liver transplants into one funded category.

This is not to say, however, that ethics committees can never be helpful in education, retrospective case reviews, policy forums, or even in sorting out problems of health care resource allocation and rationing. In 1983-84, for example, I chaired the multidisciplinary Massachusetts Task Force on Organ Transplantation which had as part of its public mandate making recommendations regarding how human hearts and livers should be rationed in the state (Organ Transplant Task Force, 1984). We studied the market approach, the lottery approach, the physician approach, and the committee approach. We opted for an approach that combined what we thought were the best elements of these approaches. Our goal was to have a selection procedure that was fair, efficient, verifiable and reflective of important social values. Ultimately we recommended that an initial screening process be based exclusively on objective medical criteria designed to measure the probability of a successful transplant -- which the Task Force defined as survival "for at least a number of years" and rehabilitation. This would determine the pool of suitable candidates. Thereafter, individuals from the pool would be selected for the next available organ on a first-come, first-served basis (which we believed was like a natural lottery) (Organ Transplant Task Force at 72-88). This was not a surprising outcome because it is commonsensical and based on fundamental American values.

More surprising, and potentially more useful in an era of cost constraints, is the Task Force's list of ways to try to avoid large shortfalls in the organ supply: (1) make medical eligibility criteria stricter, perhaps by adding a more rigorous quality of life definition; (2) increase the resources devoted to organ procurement; or (3) persuade individuals who need organs *not* to join the pool of candidates. The Task Force's explanation of the third option emphasized autonomy:

> *While most persons medically eligible for a transplant probably would want one, some would not -- at least if they understood all that was involved, including the need for a lifetime commitment to daily immunosuppression medications, and periodic medical monitoring for rejection symptoms. Accordingly, it makes public policy sense to publicize the risks and side effects of transplantation, and to require careful explanations of the procedure be given to prospective patients* ***before*** *they undergo medical screening (Organ Transplant Task Force at 83).*

Although the Task Force's report failed to stem the rising tide of heart and liver transplant programs in Massachusetts, this lesson rings true today and applies equally well to health care rationing in the 1990s: not everyone wants all the wonders of modern medicine, and we respect autonomy by providing the public with full information (and the right to refuse treatment) on all medical procedures.

It seems reasonable to conclude that ethics committees with a clear charge that meet in public and must justify their recommendations in writing can help encourage a responsible public dialogue. On the other hand, institutional ethics committees with vague charges that meet in private may do more harm than good.

Hospital-based institutional ethics committees have been used in a variety of legal cases. In the Karen Quinlan case the New Jersey Supreme Court suggested such an ethics committee to keep disputes out of court by directly granting physicians legal immunity from prosecution for discontinuing treatment on patients in a persistent vegetative state. No other court in the United States has seen fit to delegate its immunity-granting authority to a private entity. Federal regulations in the area of human experimentation rely almost exclusively on committees, usually called Institutional Review Boards or IRBs, that are composed almost exclusively of researchers and meet in private to make important decisions. This includes not only the content of research protocols and consent forms, but sometimes who is a suitable experimental subject as well. Their track record in controversial drug research seems acceptable. But, at least in highly visible and controversial research, IRBs have failed. For example, in the Barney Clark artificial heart case there was a patient (subject) selection committee that functioned almost exactly like the original Seattle dialysis committee to decide who would get the artificial heart. After Barney Clark died, it was said that he was too sick to be a suitable research subject. In the Baby Fay case there was an institutional review board (IRB) that met under emergency conditions to decide whether she should get a baboon heart, even though neither the science nor the ethics were adequately reviewed. And most recently in Pittsburgh, an IRB decided it was acceptable to put a baboon liver into an HIV positive human subject with virtually no understanding of the risks or benefits involved. All of these committees underestimated the risks and overestimated the benefits to these subjects.

My own view is that private, institutional ethics committees (and IRBs) are incapable of preventing discrimination or fostering equality. They are properly described as "institutional," since they are chartered by, appointed by, and work for the institution -- not patients, research subjects, or the community. It is not an overstatement to conclude that bioethics committees exist more to enable physicians to do to patients whatever they want to, even to experiment on them or end their lives, rather than to help or protect patients. This, of course, is not a socially useful or ethical role for ethics committees.

Some would argue that this description fits only dysfunctional ethics committees. Of course, not all members of ethics committees are apologists for their institution or its physicians, and ethics committees can do some good. Ethics committees can serve to help educate the hospital staff about ethics and ethical obligations, can help raise the level of awareness of ethical issues, can help develop hospital policies that protect important patient rights, and can even help promote a dialogue between care givers and patients and their families when communications break down. But ethics committees cannot and should not make decisions in cases involving disputes between patients and their care givers. This is not only because the patient is unlikely to be properly notified and represented, it is also because as currently constituted and run, ethics committees are much more likely to serve as "ethical cover" for their institutions than to actually foster an ethic that can help protect patients by promoting their rights and welfare (Annas, 1991). Most ethics committees were conceived of for the purpose of risk management and keeping controversial cases out of court; as such they are more properly labeled risk management committees. Like bioethics itself, hospital ethics committees are fixated on law and tend to equate ethics with what the law demands.

Far from serving patients by challenging existing paternalistic practices, ethics committees are for the most part born domesticated, convened in secret, and are dominated by physicians who almost always chair the ethics committee and usually make up the dominant professional membership of it (Scheirton, 1992). Of course physician dominance makes no sense if ethics committees are a response to paternalism -- it only makes sense if their function is to protect business as usual. Ethics committees can test themselves on these issues by asking how often, if ever, they take a position against the wishes of the hospital administration or medical staff. A real ethics committee cannot content itself with simply following the law; it must work to *improve* the ethics of the institution and its staff. In this sense it must challenge rather than follow institutional authority when that authority is exercised against the rights and welfare of patients. One may have to be subversive to be ethical in American health care institutions.

Medicine, Money and Ethics

American bioethicists consistently underestimate the influence of money and commercialism in American medicine, and this has put medical ethics at risk of being transformed into business ethics. American medicine runs on massive amounts of money, and with health care expenditures approaching the one trillion dollar mark, economics almost naturally dominates medicine. As Arnold Relman pointed out more than 15 years ago, business ethics threaten to dominate medical ethics (Relman, 1992). More medical technologies, including transplantation, are used as advertising mechanisms to tell the community: We have a full-service hospital (or health plan) or a great hospital on the cutting edge of new technology.

The cosmetic surgery industry is just the most obvious example of medicine selling a product people don't need, but convincing them that they do need it, to make money for the surgeons by increasing their business (Wolfe, 1992). Researchers like Naomi Wolfe, and physicians like Arnold Relman, not the bioethicists, have pointed out the dehumanizing nature of medicine practiced as a profit-maximizing, procedure-maximizing business. It is thus not surprising that rationing by ability to pay has recently been resurrected with new proposals to permit the sale of human organs to the highest bidder. What is surprising is that over the last 30 years of bioethics almost no one in the field has discussed what is perhaps the central ethical flaw in our health care system: the lack of insurance and access to care of 40 million Americans. As Paul Starr has noted, rights in health care have received much more emphasis than the right to health care (Starr, 1982 at 388).

The President's Commission for the Study of Ethical Problems in Medicine and Biomedical and Behavioral Research did perform a study on *Securing Access to Health Care* in 1983. The group, however, could not agree on an ethical framework for universal health care access. This failure helps explain why, when President Clinton's Health Care Task Force included an "Ethics Cluster Group," that group of ethicists was unable to articulate the ethical basis for universal coverage (Dubler, 1993). Like most ethics groups, it was called in late (after the Task Force had started its deliberations), asked to volunteer its time, given no staff or coherent mission, and ultimately simply used to help provide "ethical cover" for an already-agreed upon plan based on managed care and "managed competition." Perhaps not surprisingly, given the failure of U.S. bioethics to deal with either the market or market failures in medicine, the Clinton plan (and its competitors) is driven not by an ethical vision, but by economics. Likewise, virtually all medical professional associations have their own ethics committees. Unfortunately, these almost always act simply as ethical support for the practices their members want to engage in, and these practices are in turn primarily determined by the market rather than any independent ethical analysis of their usefulness. In all of these contexts it is fair to conclude that business ethics has already displaced medical ethics; or perhaps more accurately, medical ethics has failed to displace traditional business ethics.

In her keynote address at the 1992 "Birth of Bioethics" conference, writer Shana Alexander said: "I trust my lawyer more than I trust my doctor." Even though I appreciate her trust of lawyers, it's a terrible sentiment. But I think it's shared. I think that's the only reason Jack Kevorkian can be viewed with anything but horrible distaste. Americans are so afraid of going to the hospital and losing control, especially at the end of life, that many would prefer to be killed at home. People **don't** trust their physicians, and with good reason. Autonomy, even though it's a major American value and a major legal value, is still not taken seriously in the modern hospital.

As we move into the genetics age with the Human Genome Project, the United States government has given a budgetary line to bioethics for the first time: three to five percent of the budget of the Human Genome Project is to go to study the Project's ethical, legal, and social policy implications (ELSI). The question is, why? At a ELSI principal investigators' conference in September 1992, Dr. Elke Jordon of the Human Genome Center greeted the group by saying: ELSI is "absolutely essential to the overall success of the

Human Genome Project…you're playing a key role in this endeavor." What key role? Certainly not to question the wisdom or pace of the project itself. Bioethicists are needed to help provide ethical cover for an expensive and unprecedented project. Scientists and some physicians (even the U.S. Senate) have learned the lesson that we must at least have a cover story that we're doing ethics even though the project itself has as much to do with patents and profits as it has to do with science.

Conclusion

Having argued that bioethics has been dominated by law, that the ethics committees are not a useful contribution, and that bioethicists consistently underestimate market ideology and are thus turning medical ethics into business ethics, what does the future of bioethics look like? I like to be optimistic, but unless we stop focusing on bioethics committees, start taking commercialism much more seriously, and start doing real ethics rather than amateurish law, bioethics will soon die an unmourned death. And we bioethicists would have had a short, happy life.

Bioethics must move beyond law and economics, and be challenging and even subversive. As Arthur Schlesinger has concluded: "The American identity will never be fixed and final; it will always be in the making" (Schlesinger, 1992 at 138). American bioethics should be actively involved in "the making." I also think we should be about fashioning an American bioethics that will rely heavily on law, but move beyond it. As this volume demonstrates, there is considerable sentiment to divide up American bioethics, much the way American society is being divided up. For example, there are calls for a feminist bioethics, an ethnically-sensitive bioethics, a bioethics of class and culture, among other variations. Many of these potential subdivisions, such as virtue-based ethics, communitarian ethics, and feminist ethics actually preceded the development of bioethics. They are also much less rooted in law than contemporary principle-based bioethics. Nonetheless, like obsessive multiculturalism, these movements seek to divide rather than unite us. We have an opportunity to act now, but it will not last forever.

If American bioethics does not get involved in the making of a unifying American bioethics, based on American law, but looking beyond it, I think we can look forward to having the words of T. S. Eliot on our civilization in *The Rock* (which he wrote just before World War II) applied to us: "And the wind shall say here were decent Godless people. Their only monument, the asphalt road and a thousand lost golf balls." When our ancestors look back on bioethics, I hope they have more to say than: "Here were decent people.

Their only monument, the artificial body and the minutes of a thousand bioethics committees."

Boston University

REFERENCES

Annas G.J. (1985). The Playboy, the Prostitute, and the Poet. *American Journal of Public Health* 75:187-89.

Annas G.J. (1989). *The Rights of Patients*. Carbondale, IL: Southern Illinois University Press.

Annas G.J., Arnold B., Aroskar M. et al (1990). Bioethicists' Statement on the U.S. Supreme Court's *Cruzan* Decision. *New England Journal of Medicine* 323:686-687.

Annas G.J. (1991). Ethics Committees; from Ethical Comfort to Ethical Cover. *Hastings Center Reports* May-June pp. 18-20.

Annas G.J. and Grodin M.A., Eds. (1992). *The Nazi Doctors and the Nuremberg Code: Human Rights in Human Experimentation*. New York: Oxford University Press.

Annas G.J. (1993). Physician-Assisted Suicide: Michigan's Temporary Solution. *New England Journal of Medicine* 328:1573-76.

Annas G.J. (1993). *Standard of Care: The Law of American Bioethics*. New York: Oxford University Press.

Annas G.J. (1994). Will the Real Bioethics (Commission) Please Stand Up? *Hastings Center Report* January pp. 19-21.

Campbell J. with Moyers, B. (1988). *The Power of Myth*. New York: Doubleday.

Caplan A. (1989). Keynote address, Holocaust and Bioethics Conference, Minneapolis, MN.

Dubler N. (1993). Working on the Clinton Administration's Health Care Task Force. *Kennedy Institute of Ethics Journal* 3(4):421-31.

Grodin MA, Annas G.J. and Glantz LH (1993). Medicine and Human Rights: A Proposal for International Action, *Hastings Center Report. July pp. 8-12.*

National Commission (1978). *The Belmont Report*, DHEW Pub. No. (OS)78-0012, U.S. Government Printing Office.

Organ Transplant Task Force (1984). *Report of the Task Force on Organ Transplantation*. Boston, MA: Department of Public Health.

President's Commission for the Study of Ethical Problems in Medicine and Biomedical and Behavioral Research (1982). *Making Health Care Decisions*. Washington, DC: U.S. Government Printing Office.

Quinlan J. and Quinlan J. with Battelle, P. (1976). *Karen Ann: The Quinlans Tell their Story*. Garden City, NY: Doubleday.

Relman A.S. (1992). What Market Values are Doing to Medicine. *Atlantic Monthly* March pp. 99-106.

Scheirton L.S. (1992). Determinants of Hospital Ethics Committee Success. H E C Forum 4(6): 342-59.

Schlesinger, Jr. A.M. (1992). *The Disuniting of America: Reflections on a Multicultural Society*. New York: W. W. Norton Co.

Starr P. (1982). *The Social Transformation of American Medicine.* New York: Basic Books pp. 388-92.

Todd J. (1993). Reform of the Health Care System and Professional Liability. *New England Journal of Medicine* 329:1733-35.

Willis G. (1978). *Inventing America: Jefferson's Declaration of Independence.* New York: Vintage Books.

Wolfe N. (1992). *The Beauty Myth.* New York: W. Morrow.

ENDNOTES

1 The dominance of rights talk in America is not, of course, limited to bioethics. It has also been seen as the major flaw in American law by those who believe our established system of rights brings with it intolerable problems of "immunity and domination" that detract from rather than promote a sense of community. See, e.g., Roberto Mangabeira Unger, The Critical Legal Studies Movement, *Harvard Law Review* 96:561-675 (1983). It is probably more accurate to say, however, that the *purpose* of the U.S. community is to protect the rights of its individual members.

2 See Annas, *Standard of Care, Supra* note 1, pp. 47-60. The "bioethics brief" is partially reproduced in *Am. J. Law & Medicine* 15:169-177 (1989). See generally, Symposium Issue: Justice Harry A. Blackmun: The Supreme Court and the Limits of Medical Privacy, *Am. J. of Law & Medicine* 13:153-525 (1987).

3 The commentator on this chapter, Professor John Paris, a Jesuit priest, is one ethicist who has testified many times in court. From both his testimony and his written articles, he seems to agree that the law has supplanted ethics in both theory and practice in the health care setting. At the trial of Paul Brophy, Paris testified regarding his initial discussion with Mr. Brophy's wife, Patricia, about whether she could move her husband out of the hospital to another facility where his wishes would be honored:

> *As I recall, she told me that if she attempted to have him moved, they would get a court order to block it. At this point I said, "Oh, are we in the mess that I think is an absolute bane of medicine today and that is the sheer abdication of responsibility for [to] the law." [Tr. at 2-102; May 23, 1985]*

Later Fr. Paris equated the law and ethics, saying, "The ethical standards that I would want to do are those that probably, you can find in the ruling of the Massachusetts Appeals Court in the *Hier* [Mary Hier] case." [Tr. p. 2-172] See also, Paris JJ & Varga AC, Care of the Hopelessly Ill, *America*, Sept. 22, 1984, at 141-144.

[4] For example, when Karen Quinlan's father, Joseph, finally made the decision to have his daughter removed from the ventilator, her doctor, Dr. Morse, said, "I think you've made the right decision" (p. 116). It was only after he talked to the hospital's lawyer that he and the hospital refused to cooperate with the Quinlans unless they obtained a court order [Quinlan, J. and Quinlan J. (with P. Battelle) *Karen Ann: The Quinlans Tell their Story*, Doubleday, Garden City, New York, 1977, at 121].

[5] Technology's leading historian, Lewis Mumford, has noted, for example, that scientific knowledge has a dark side that only social policy and law is powerful enough to attempt to avoid it. When "not touched by a sense of values [scientific knowledge] works…toward a complete dehumanization of the social order." He continues:

> *The plea that each of the sciences must be permitted to go its own way without control should be immediately rebutted by pointing out that they obviously need a little guidance when their applications in war and industry are so plainly disastrous… (The Lewis Mumford Reader, Miller, ed., 1986, at 220).*

Reliance on the notion of "values," cannot serve in an age which has cheapened that term to come to mean a call for moral relativism at best, and a reflection of personal taste at worst. It is probably because of our current vacuous notion of values that they are touted as potential saviors from the many dehumanizing technologies devised by the minds of men. Values do nothing to slow the pace of "progress" and offer no threat to the technological imperative. Langdon Winner has persuasively argued that we need much more: something with meaning. He has suggested law, with its focus on human *rights*, as essential. Among other things, he has noted that Moses did not come down from the mountain with "Ten Values"; and that the first ten amendments to the Constitution are not called the "Bill of Values" (Winner, L., *The Whale and the Reactor,* 1986 at 163).

JOHN J. PARIS, S.J.

THE DOMINATION OF LAW IN AMERICAN BIOETHICS: A RESPONSE TO ANNAS

> *Because the issue [termination of life-sustaining treatment for incompetent patients] with all its ramifications is fraught with complexity and encompasses the interests of the law, both civil and criminal, medical ethics and social morality, it is not one which is well-suited for resolution in an adversary judicial proceeding. It is the type [of] issue which is more suitably addressed in the legislative forum, where fact finding can be less confined and the viewpoints of all interested institutions and disciplines can be presented and synthesized. In this manner only can the subject be dealt with comprehensively and the interests of all institutions and individuals be properly accommodated.*
>
> *Satz v. Perlmutter, 379 So.2d 359, 360 (Fla., 1980).*

"I trust my lawyer more than I trust my doctor." This comment from Shana Alexander's address at the fall 1992 "Birth of Bioethics" conference in Seattle establishes the theme of George Annas' approach to bioethics. It is law and lawyers, not ethics or physicians that set the tone and the thrust of American bioethics. This aggrandizement of law by a lawyer comes as no surprise. Nor is the diminution of the role of physicians novel to those who have followed Annas' two decades long emphasis on personal liberty and individual rights. Under the rubric of "patient rights" Annas praises the increasing role of the individual in issues ranging from abortion at the beginning of life to termination of medical treatment at its end (Annas, 1993).

While Annas and I share many of the same values and goals, especially on end of life issues, we have not always agreed on the role courts should have in these pressing problems (Annas, 1981; Paris, 1981b). In his view, the law sides with patients to oppose the arbitrary use of power whether by physicians or the government. That is why, he asserts, law, not philosophy or medicine has become primarily responsible for the agenda, development and current state of American bioethics. In all this, Annas would have us believe "American law is dedicated to fostering individual rights, equality, and justice" (Annas, 1993 at 3).

This romanticized, idealized view of the law is starry-eyed at best. It is certainly at odds with Grant Gilmore's insightful description in *The Ages of American Law* of the role law has played in the American experience. There Gilmore quotes as illustrative of the role law has occupied in the American scene Oliver Wendall Holmes' observation that "The first requirement of a

M. A. Grodin (ed.), Meta Medical Ethics, 97–108.

sound body of law, is that it should correspond with the actual demands of the community, whether right or wrong" (Gilmore, 1977 at 49). Holmes' thesis that the law is nothing but a continuing struggle in which the rich and the powerful impose their will on the poor and the weak culminated in his ringing declaration in *Buck v. Bell* (274 U.S. 200, 1927) that "Three generations of imbeciles is enough." That ruling, in which the Supreme Court authorized the sterilization of the feeble-minded Carrie Buck, is proof positive of the limits of Annas' claims for American law.

Without entering the critical legal realists debate on the source and goals of American law, let us examine Annas' thesis that it is the law, not ethics, that dominates bioethics and that it is to law and the legal process that we should turn for protection of individual rights, equality and justice. The thesis is not new, nor is it confined to bioethics. As the Tonya Harding fiasco makes clear, Americans seem unable to resolve their moral and ethical issues other than in the framework of the legal system.

That reality was noted by Alexis deTocquivelle more than a century ago in his now classic study of democracy in America, where he observed that Americans, unlike Europeans, have the strange propensity of transforming moral dilemmas into legal problems as if judges, unlike the rest of mere mortals, possess the insight, understanding and integrity to provide a definitive resolution to questions of the human condition (deTocquivelle, 1990). That hope, as Gabriel Marcel, the great French existentialist philosopher would put it, confuses mystery with problem. That confusion leads us to act as if the complexities of human behavior could be reduced to solvable problems of geometry. Life, however, is not so easily plumbed.

To use the example Professor Annas gives, and one I will assiduously avoid, "It seems natural to Americans that the morality of abortion has been recast as the right of abortion" (Annas, 1993 at 3). Does Professor Annas really believe that the Supreme Court's recasting of the abortion debate (in terms of "rights") in *Roe v. Wade* has tempered, let alone resolved the political debate on abortion? Had George Bush defeated Bill Clinton and had Ruth Bader Ginsberg been Scalia II, is there any doubt as to how the Court would now be ruling on a "woman's right" to choose? It seems to me to be more the composition of the court than the "penumbras and emanations" of the Bill of Rights that determines the outcome of that legal dispute. Or did Dooley misread the real when he observed "Th' Supreme court follows th' iliction returns."

In his praise for the role of law in American bioethics, Professor Annas writes of the brief filed by "Bioethicists for Privacy" in *Webster* and the commentary of a group of bioethicists published in the *New England Journal of Medicine* that "both the brief and the statement were not about what philosophers would term ethics; they were about the state of American law: what it is and what it should be" (Annas, 1993 at 3). This is put forth as if law, not morality, should be the basis of how we behave. The justification George Annas advances for this position: "Ethics has not teeth. You cannot sue unless there is a violation of some legal canon." Here we have the American mind set writ large -- suing is the only thing that counts.

Let us look at some of the leading bioethics cases to see if the courts that have addressed these issues share Professor Annas' perspective on the role of law in American bioethics. In one of the first explorations of the right of a patient to refuse medical treatment, the Massachusetts Supreme Judicial Court noted: "We recognize at the outset that this case presents novel issues of fundamental importance that should not be resolved by mechanical reliance on legal doctrine" (*Saikewicz*, 1977 at 422). The Supreme Judicial Court recognized that such reliance could not provide an adequate framework for probing and understanding the nuanced issues in this case. Instead, as Justice Paul Liacos writing for the Court put it, our task "is furthered by seeking the collective guidance of those in health care, moral ethics, philosophy and other disciplines."

Noting that the law, far from leading, "always lags behind the most advanced thinking in every area," Liacos concluded that in this difficult and demanding area of bioethics, "[The law]" must wait until theologians, and the moral leaders and events have created some common ground, some "consensus" before taking a stand on how we should proceed in such ventures. In the language of jurisprudence, an issue has to be "ripe" before the courts are prepared to rule on the topic.

In *Saikewicz* the court thought it advisable to consider the influence of medical ethics on doctors' decisions when dealing with the terminally ill patient before it undertook to provide its own response to that question. In doing so it turned, perhaps unaware of the primary sources of its analysis, to the long rich four hundred year old tradition of Roman Catholic moral theology on the use of ordinary/extraordinary means of preserving life. That tradition, succinctly encapsulated in Paul Ramsey's now landmark essay "On (Only) Caring for the Dying" (Ramsey, 1970), not the later legal doctrines of informed consent or liberty interests, was the fundamental basis of the Supreme Judicial Court's ruling that the never competent Joseph Saikewicz had a "right" to decline potentially life-prolonging medical treatment.

Despite the Court's expressed statements on the value of the moralists' reflections on these topics, Annas, in a brief submitted on behalf of Concern for Dying to the Supreme Judicial Court in *Brophy v. New England Hospital*, the first case requesting the removal of a feeding tube from a living patient, admonished the Court to banish ethicists, their views and their works from the legal arena, the very place where he claims the bioethical issues should be resolved.

The Supreme Judicial Court rejected that advice. Chief Justice Paul Liacos went out of his way to comment, "We encourage and seek insights and the collective guidance of those in health care, moral ethics, philosophy, and other disciplines" (*Brophy*, 1986 at 429). And in a footnote to that comment, Liacos added, "We have not been disappointed and once again we have been aided by the work of the parties and the Probate judge, and the outstanding briefs filed by the *amici curiae*."

Judge Christopher Armstrong of the Massachusetts Appeals Court, one of the most informed and articulate writers on these issues, in an opinion in the *Earle Spring* case asked what he termed the recurrent and always difficult ethical problem: "To what extent should aggressive medical treatments be administered to preserve life after life itself, for reasons beyond anyone's control, has become irreversibly burdensome?" (*Spring*, 1979 at 846). Armstrong's response is instructive: "The law does not furnish an answer to that question." In his view it leaves the answer to the person involved. The only issue for the courts, he argues, is to protect that right for the incompetent patient.

Let us see how well American courts have played that role under what Professor Annas calls the rubric of "patient rights." The New Jersey Supreme Court has played the most prominent and progressive role in the development of that area of law. It was also, with *Quinlan*, the first court to do so. Its standard, developed in *Quinlan*, *Conroy* and *Jobes,* is that the now incompetent patient's right to decline unwanted medical interventions is to be determined on one of three bases: the prior written or oral statements of the then competent patient, the known values of the patient, or an assessment that the burden of pain would outweigh whatever benefit the patient would receive from the treatment.

While Judge Alan Handler's observation in his dissent in *Conroy* that "pain" does not exhaust the range of human interests and that such a standard would provide no protection for the dignity of a patient in a persistent vegetative state whose prior values were unknown is correct, the New Jersey courts have served fairly well in protecting the interests and rights of incompetent patients.

The Massachusetts Supreme Judicial Court has a more mixed record. While the substantive ruling in *Saikewicz* provides a classical exposition of the ethical issues involved in these cases, the Supreme Judicial Court's "substituted judgment" standard, and even more the procedural requirement of prior court authorization before a life-prolonging treatment may be withdrawn from an incompetent patient have proven problematic.

"Substituted judgment," under which the court is "to don the mental mantle of the incompetent" to determine what it is that the now -- and sometimes always -- incompetent would want, is, at best, in Judge Liacos' own words, "a legal fiction" (Liacos, 1989). If, as in *Saikewicz*, the patient was never capable of a rational thought, how, other than a "best interest" test could we legitimately determine what the patient would want? And how, under any scenario -- save fantasy -- could a court discern, as the Supreme Judicial Court claimed to do more than once -- whether the infant Baby Billy at New England Medical Center would or would not want a Do-Not-Resuscitate Order? (*Custody of a Minor*, 1982).

The response to the Supreme Judicial Court's procedural requirement of court involvement to withdraw life-sustaining treatment from an incompetent patient, despite Professor Annas' pronouncement that *Saikewicz* could readily be reconciled with *Quinlan* (Annas, 1979), was quickly apparent in Massachusetts. Physicians refused to withhold or withdraw potentially life-sustaining medical treatments without the protective security of a court order. *Dinnerstein* and *Spring* are evidence of the disruption of appropriate medical care occasioned by the Massachusetts Supreme Court's intrusion into bioethics.

These disruptions, though, pale in comparison to the damage to patient's rights done by court involvement in New York state. There the Court of Appeals, the state's highest court, in the companion cases of *Eichner* and *Storar* ruled that there must be "clear and convincing" evidence from the once competent patient that he would not want life-prolonging treatment before such interventions could be withheld or withdrawn from a now incompetent patient.

At the time of the *Eichner/Storar* rulings I wrote that the Court of Appeals' opinion in *Storar* "[D]isenfranchised a whole class of people: those without a living will or its equivalent. Under the *Eichner/Storar* standard minors and the vast majority of the population who have never been expressed an opinion on the rights of the dying would have to undergo all treatment for a condition which threatens [their] life" (Paris, 1981a at 1425). George Annas denounced that reading as "absurd." He claimed that the rulings in these cases were confined to the two individuals involved and that any extension of the Court's ruling to include other parties was both "inaccurate" and "wrong" (Annas, 1981).

When in the subsequent *Eulo* case the Court of Appeals cited *Eichner* as the source of its statement that the right to decline treatment is personal and "under existing law in this state could not be exercised by a third party when the patient is unable to do so," Annas dismissed the court's comments as "dictum."

No such escape presented itself when the New York Court of Appeals ruled in *O'Connor v. Westchester County Medical Center* that "clear and convincing proof" of the patient's "firm and settled commitment, while competent" was required before a court could authorize the withholding of life-prolonging treatment from the now incompetent Mary O'Connor. The source cited by the New York court for the ruling was its prior holding in *Storar*. Annas' response: the court was "wrong."

"Unrealistic, unfair, inhuman -- totally unworkable" were the words Judge Stewart F. Hancock, Jr. used in his *O'Connor* concurrence to describe the court's requirement that before treatment could be withheld or withdrawn from a dying incompetent patient there had to be evidence of a "patient's actual intent." As Hancock put it: "Relief depends exclusively upon a showing of a present subjective intent, based upon the patient's past oral or written statement unequivocally expressing her desire not to have artificial life support continued under specific circumstances" (*O'Connor*, 1988 at 614). Where the patient has not done so -- as would be true of children, the never competent, the uninformed, the unreflective and the inarticulate -- Judge Hancock writes, "artificial life support may simply not be withheld or withdrawn under *Storar*." That, of course, is precisely what I had written eight years earlier in the commentary Professor Annas described as "blatantly incorrect."

What is the practical outcome of the New York court's intrusion into bioethics? It is perhaps best summed up by in the observation of Judge Richard Simons in his *O'Connor* dissent that since very few individuals will be able to meet the court's new test, "The right of self-determination is reduced to a hollow promise" (*O'Connor*, 1989 at 616). The "clear and convincing" standard required by *O'Connor*, which Simons labels "unworkable and unwise," will, in his view, produce decisions that "reflect the value choices of the Judge, rather than those of the patient." Such decisions, in his words, "are nothing short of arbitrary intrusions into the personal life of the patient." That outcome I suggest, is not -- and ought not be -- an occasion for rejoicing by those concerned with "patients' rights."

Wrong, unfair, unwise though it might be, the requirement of "clear and convincing evidence" established by the New York Court of Appeals is now the law in that jurisdiction. In the recent *Elbaum* case, Judge Stewart

Hancock, in a concurring opinion, suggested New York's standard was in need of legislative revision. His colleague Justice Joseph Bellacosa upbraided Hancock for "casting clouds of doubt on the reliability" of the state of the law.

The extent of the adverse impact of the New York "law" on patients' rights is found in the case of Florence LaSala, a woman who after having suffered two major stokes in 1980 told her family, friends and nurses that if she got worse, she did not want her life artificially prolonged. After another stroke some three years later Mrs. LaSala at age 78 fell into a persistent vegetative state. The petition of her family to remove her feeding tube was rejected because in the trial courts' words, "While LaSala may have expressed *generally* that she did not want artificially prolonged life, she didn't specifically say: 'No gastro-nasal feeding tube'" (Goldstein, 1993 at 8). That is, she did not meet the "subjective-specific intent" test established in *Eichner/Storar*. Since Florence LaSala's statements failed to meet the "seriousness of purpose necessary to satisfy the 'clear and convincing evidence' standard" demanded by New York court, she was forced to remain in an unresponsive vegetative condition for more than ten years of nursing home care at an annual cost of $85,000 till finally, in December, 1993, she died.

The final insult to patient's rights from this line of cases is found yet again in New York in the 1993 *Elbaum* case. There the Court of Appeals ruled that a family who had requested physicians at The Grace Plaza Nursing home to remove the feeding tube from Mrs. Elbaum when she lapsed into a well-diagnosed persistent vegetative condition had to pay for her care for that period of time during which the nursing home challenged the family's request until the Appellate Decision had ruled that, in fact, there was "clear and convincing evidence" of Mrs. Elbaum's wishes in the matter (*Elbaum*, 1993). The Appellate Division not only found that Jean Elbaum "while competent, repeatedly extracted a series of promises from her husband and family members, that reflected a resolve and purpose weighty enough to constitute 'solemn pronouncements' as to her desire that she did not wish to be sustained as a 'vegetable' and that no artificial feeding tubes be used to prolong her life if she reached that condition," it also learned that the nursing home had "stated that it would not act on those wishes even if it had irrefutable evidence of her wishes" because its goal as an institution "is to preserve life."

Despite these findings the Court of Appeals ruled that a provider could legitimately demand that a court make a determination of "clear and convincing evidence" before the provider is required to terminate life-sustaining treatment. The family would not only have to incur the legal expenses of that determination, it would also have to pay the institution for the "unwanted" treatment while the facility exhausted all legal challenges to its statement of the patient's wishes. All this, of course, "to protect the patient's rights."

New York is not alone in its imposition of a judicially-imposed "clear and convincing evidence" standard. The Missouri Supreme Court adopted a similar requirement in its *Cruzan* opinion. And the United States Supreme Court's in its *Cruzan v. Director, Missouri Department of Health* ruling upheld the right of a state to set such a standard -- by statute, or, as happened in these cases, by judicial fiat. In the Supreme Court's words: "Missouri requires that evidence of the incompetent's wishes as to the withdrawal of treatment be provided by clear and convincing evidence. The question, then, is whether the United States Constitution forbids the establishment of this procedural requirement by the State. We hold that is does not" (*Cruzan*, 1990 at 266).

On November 16, 1993 a three judge panel of the Superior Court of Pennsylvania established a different and even less workable standard in yet another case of a family requesting the withdrawal of medical treatment from a patient in a persistent vegetative condition. In its ruling in *Fiori* the Pennsylvania court stated: "[W]e find the quantum of proof necessary to discontinue the sanctity of life is to be measured by an equally high level of 'clear and convincing' evidence that the 'best interests' of the incapacitated person are being served." This determination, which the court describes as "emblematic of a society that cherishes life and the dignity of human life," is to be made in each and every instance by a court. The rationale for this standard is unambiguously announced by the Pennsylvania court: "First and foremost, our actions are motivated by the desire to preserve life."

Judge Phyllis Beck's dissent in this case spells out the problems of the standard adopted in *Fiori*: "[T]he clear and convincing evidence of best interests standards appears impossible to meet." That would certainly prove true of the patient in *Fiori* if, as the tribunal insists, trial courts must balance the burden of pain, discomfort of treatment or humiliation at the loss of dignity against the benefit of an extension of life. The PVS patient suffers no pain, no discomfort from his condition, is incapable of experiencing humiliation or loss of dignity, and could easily live seventeen more years in his present condition.

The practical effect of the *Fiori* standard, as Judge Beck notes, would be "continuing of life-sustaining treatment for all persistent vegetative state patients except those who had, while competent, expressed a specific desire not to receive such treatment." That seems to be a substantial deviation from the protection of "patients' rights."

This excursus into one line of cases demonstrates the dangers that await those who cast the difficult issues of bioethics onto the courts. I warned of that danger some fifteen years ago when first addressing the issue of patients whose terminal illnesses were made the subject matter of protracted legal battles (Paris, 1980). Yet courts persist in involving themselves in these cases to, as the Appellate Division of The New York Supreme Court stated in *Eichner*, "protect the rights of the incompetent and to mitigate a difficult ethical problem facing the medical profession."

A decade and a half of experience has shown how courts have fallen short of that goal. Rather it has established the correctness of the warning issued after the Court of Appeals ruling in *Eichner* and *Storar*: "If physicians continue to care for terminally ill incompetent patients in conformity with the highest traditions of the profession and make judgments on the propriety of actions in consultation with learned, prudent colleagues and the patient's family, the *Eichner-Storar* ruling will have little impact on the practice of medicine. If, on the other hand, physicians opt for legal approbation for their actions, they will place both the rights of their patients and the exercise of their professional responsibility in jeopardy" (Paris, 1981 at 1425).

That perspective was reiterated in Judge Beck's 1993 dissent in *Fiori* where he writes: "I conclude that the consent of a close family member along with the approval of two qualified physicians is sufficient to terminate life-sustaining treatment to a person in a long-term persistent vegetative state. I further conclude that except in certain unusual circumstances, courts should not be involved in the decision." To hold otherwise, to insist that only courts can provide the necessary safeguards to assure protection of life is in his view "a narrow and unhealthy view." It is, as he put it, "yet another expansion of the idea that courts are the repository of wisdom and the only institution available to protect human life and dignity." That such is not the case can be seen in Judge Warren Burger's warning in *Georgetown,* the first adjudicated case of a Jehovah's Witness refusing a life-saving blood transfusion: "There are myriads of problems judges are incapable of solving and this is one" (*Georgetown*, 1964).

In his 1980 Shattuck Lecture, Daniel Callahan warned of the dangers of elevating any one principle into an absolute (Callahan, 1980). He also cautioned against confusing law and ethics. Worse still would be to have law swallow up or replace ethics as the foundation for human behavior. That danger lurks in American bioethics today where as Professor Annas astutely observes, the first question rarely is: "Is this the right thing to do?" but "Is it legal?"

The apotheosis of law endangers any free society. Courts and judges, like all human institutions are fragile, fallible instruments not philosopher kings or deities. They operate in a democratic community with a limited mission and a limited mandate. To thrust greater claims on them is not only to distort their role but to endanger our "rights." The brief history of American bioethics demonstrates that danger.

Afterthought:

An opinion issued by the 4th circuit Court of Appeals in *In re Baby K* on February 10, 1994 [a week after The Bioethics Conference] illustrates the danger of physicians and hospitals petitioning the courts for resolution of bioethical disputes. In that case a pregnant woman insisted that "everything possible be done" for her anencephalic baby. At birth the infant was not breathing. The physician, following the mother's direction, resuscitated the infant and placed it on a respirator. The child was successfully weaned from the respirator and eventually placed in a pediatric nursing home. The pediatric intensivists at Fairfax Hospital told the mother that if the child again presented in respiratory distress they would not put her back on a ventilator. The mother's attorney warned that such a refusal would violate the federal "anti-dumping" statute, the Emergency Medical Treatment and Active Labor Act (EMTALA), that requires hospitals "to stabilize any patient presenting in the emergency room with a life threatening episode" regardless of the patient's inability to pay.

The hospital petitioned the federal court for injunctive relief. The trial judge ruled for the mother. The 4th Circuit upheld that judgment. Further it ruled that if no other hospital would accept the anencephalic child, under the federal statute Fairfax Hospital and its physician had to treat the child as the mother requested even if doing so was contrary to what they believed was "medically and ethically appropriate." Rejecting that reading of the statute, Judge James M. Sprouse wrote in his dissent that Congress "even in its weakest moments would not have attempted to impose federal control in the sensitive area, private area" of the patient-physician relationships.

The 4th circuit ruling surely fits within the rubric of "patient rights." The question that remains is does this judicial usurpation of medical judgment serve society well? Does it call out for the applause of a grateful nation?

* * *

In a commentary on *Davis v. Davis*, the Tennessee frozen embryo case in which the trial court had ruled that frozen embryos are "tiny human beings," George Annas wrote that in some of the best-known cases, including *Quinlan*, *Bouvia*, *Bartling*, and *Baby M,* lower court judges issued opinions that were "very wide from the mark" with regard to appropriate resolution of the bioethical issues involved (Annas, 1989 at 22). That phenomenon led Annas to conclude that "The opinions of these trial court judges suggest that lower courts are institutionally incompetent to deal with bioethical issues. Professional standards, blue ribbon commissions, and legislative bodies may be more appropriate."

Annas had it right.

Boston College

REFERENCES

Annas, G. (1979). Reconciling *Quinlan* and *Saikewicz*: Decision making for the terminally ill incompetent. *American Journal of Law & Medicine* 4:367-396.

Annas, G. (1981). Correspondence: Rights of the dying incompetent patient. *New England Journal of Medicine* 305:1222.

Annas, G. (1989). A French homunculus in a Tennessee court. *Hastings Center Report* 19(6):20-22.

Annas, G. (1993). Standard of care: The law of American bioethics. New York, N.Y.: Oxford University Press.

Callahan, D. (1980). Shattuck lecture -- contemporary biomedical ethics. *New England Journal of Medicine* 302:1228-1233.

de Tocquiville, A. (1990). Democracy in America. New York: Vintage Books.

Gilmore, G. (1977). The ages of American law. New Haven: Yale University Press.

Goldstein, M. (1993). A burial ten years too late. *Newsday* p.8.

Liacos, P. (1989). "Substituted judgement" a valid legal concept? *Issues in Law & Medicine* 5:2-9.

Marcel, G. (1965). Being and having. New York: Harper & Row.

Paris, J.J. (1981a). The Conclusion of the Brother Fox Case. *New England Journal of Medicine* p. 1425.

Paris, J.J. (1981b). Correspondence: Rights of the dying incompetent patient. *New England Journal of Medicine* 305:1222-1223.

Ramsey, P. (1970). The patient as person. New Haven: Yale University Press.

CASES

In the matter of Baby K, 832 F.Supp. 1022 (E.D. Va., 1993).

In the matter of Baby K, 16 S.3d 590 (4th Cir., 1994).

Brophy v. New England Sinai Hospital, 497 N.E. 2d 626 (Mass, 1986).
Buck v. Bell, 274 U.S. 200 (1927).
In re Conroy, 98 N.J. 321 (1985).
Cruzan v. Harmon, 760 S.W.2d 408 (Mo., 1988).
Cruzan v. Director, 497 U.S. 261 (1990).
Custody of a Minor, 385 Mass. 697, 434 N.E.2d 601 (1982).
In re Dinnerstein, 6 Mass. App. Ct. 466, 380 N.E.2d 134 (1978).
Matter of Eichner, 73 A.2d 431 (N.Y., 1980).
Elbaum v. Grace Plaza, 148 AD.2d 244 (N.Y.S., 1993).
In re Fiori, 1993 PA.Super.Lexis 3763.
In the matter of Nancy Ellen Jobes, 108 N.J. 394, 529 A.2d 434 (1987).
O'Connor v. Westchester County Medical Center, 72 N.Y.2d 517, 531 N.E.2d 607 534 N.W.S.ed 886 (Ct.App. 1988, amended 1989).
People v. Eulo, 63 N.Y.2d 34, 472 N.E.2d 286 (1984).
In re Quinlan, 70 N.J. 10, 355 A.2d 647 (1976).
Roe v. Wade, 410 U.S. 113 (1973).
Satz v. Perlmutter, 379 So.2d 359, 360 (Fla.1980).
In re Spring, 8 Mass. App. Ct. 831 (1979).
In re Spring, 380 Mass. 629 (1980).
Matter of Storar, 52 N.Y.2d 363, 73 A.2d 431 (1980).
Superintendent of Belchertown State School v. Saikewicz, 373 Mass 728 370 N.E. 2d 417 (1977).

MARTHA MONTELLO

MEDICAL STORIES: NARRATIVE AND PHENOMENOLOGICAL APPROACHES

USING LITERATURE TO TEACH MORAL REASONING IN MEDICAL EDUCATION

For the past few years, clinicians and medical educators have been discovering that old ways of conceptualizing and teaching bioethics are inadequate to new realities in medicine. In response, the profession has been attempting to clarify the competencies practitioners need to have in dealing with ethical issues and to find the best methods of teaching them. A growing number of medical educators who use literary and personal narratives to teach bioethics consistently observe that narrative explorations provide a highly effective method for teaching moral reasoning in medicine. Listening as students and colleagues read and interpret significant stories together, medical educators frequently witness an astounding process of moral development and ethics education. However successful the practice of using narratives to teach moral reasoning has often been, though, no existing theory has yet adequately explored the profound effects that reading literature has on ethics education during medical training. Although many educators already recognize a vital link between the experience of reading and the moral reasoning physicians use in encounters with patients, the profession as a whole needs a better understanding of what happens during reading that leads to moral development. Specifically, it needs to identify and explore the core processes set into motion in the act of reading that enhance competence in moral reasoning. Physicians and medical educators alike have much to gain from the investigations of an expanding collection of scholars and teachers in the humanities who argue for reading literature as a form of moral experience that offers unique contributions to the ethical practice of medicine.

Ethics, Narrative, and Medicine

Moral issues pervade clinical practice. Not confined to the intensive care unit or the transplant suite, ethics and moral action lie behind every medical encounter (Connelly & Dallemura, 1988). However commonplace a case may appear to the physician, illnesses often have profound moral dimensions that are of deep significance for the patient, the family, and ultimately for the physician, too (Neelon, 1994).

M. A. Grodin (ed.), Meta Medical Ethics, 109–123.

Since the time of Hippocrates, physicians have affirmed the profession's fundamental moral responsibility, the inextricable connection between clinical care and moral reasoning. New physicians still swear to the fifth-century B.C. in which they promise to do what is good for others and to avoid doing harm. During the past decade, however, increasingly rapid changes in the technology of medicine, combined with an aging society and the mounting pressures of cost containment, have generated a growing attention to medical ethics issues from both the profession and the culture-at-large and have heightened an awareness that all physicians need competence in ethical care. Faced with pervasive and complex dilemmas in such areas as resource allocation and end-of-life decisions, the medical profession is engaged in an urgent search for a theory and practice of medical ethics that can illuminate the issues and provide a real and present help. Medical educators, in particular, seek ways to train students not only in diagnosing and treating disease but also in recognizing and mediating ethical dilemmas.

Until recently, medical educators have relied heavily on bioethical theorists, who have been primarily concerned with adopting analytic frameworks of principles and rules to find solutions to bioethical problems. Contemporary ethical theory has attempted to secure for moral judgments the scientific ideals of objectivity, replicability, generalizability, and universality, though, against a rising frustration on the part of clinicians with the limits dealing with medical problems where ethics becomes a branch of decision theory (Hauerwas & Burrell, 1977). Real patients, physicians argue, are unique individuals who cannot be generalized. And real ethical issues in medicine, they insist, do not arise in the abstract, free from the subjective and contingent nature of the moral agents' beliefs, background, and character (Weicha, 1991). Instead, ethical issues arise from within the complex lives of specific individuals embedded in a particular context of family, community, and history.

In response, the focus of current discussion among medical educators has been moving away from attempts to connect problematic cases with formal philosophic theories, such as those of Kant, Rawls, or the utilitarians, and toward a more direct analysis of the particular cases themselves (Toulmin, 1972). Although judicious applications of general rules remain valuable guides to action and safeguards for personal rights, medical ethics has been evolving from an emphasis on formalist theories and "quandary" cases as paradigmatic concerns for moral analysis to a more person-centered, contextual understanding of the moral life and ethical decisions (Pincoffs, 1971).

Sometimes called narrative ethics, a contextual or interpretive approach to ethics focuses attention not on formalist principles but on the patient's life story. Narrative ethics responds to the insight that unless we can understand an illness as part of the story of a life-in-progress we cannot understand what has gone wrong or how to help (Hunter, 1990). Approaching the patient's experience as both a biomedical and personal part of an ongoing narrative allows the physician to listen for the way the patient makes sense of events and the meaning he or she attaches to the experience of illness (Brody, 1994). Within this framework, ethical analysis centers on what works best at this time in this one life. The unique situation of a particular patient shows the way to effective solutions to individual problems. Grounded in narrative knowledge of a particular patient's life, the meanings of singular human predicaments become the focus of ethical investigations that examine the moral issues people face in the context of lived lives.

Science, as Aristotle described it, seeks to establish general truths, universal laws of nature. Medicine, though, is not so much a science as a science-using enterprise, concerned with general rules that must at once be true and still apply to the individual and variant case, almost always as the case is in the process of changing (Hunter, 1991). Medical ethics, likewise, practices a clinical casuistry, like the casuistry of early modern theologians and that of our legal system, analyzing a specific case in order to relate that case reliably to a system of received principles. Such contemporary philosophers as Al Jonsen and Stephen Toulmin, who explore methods of reconciling the single, context-embedded case to the general principles of medical ethics, argue for the primacy of narrative in interpreting the individual case (Jonsen & Toulmin, 1988).

An adequate ethical theory recognizes the central role of narrative in the way we understand and make sense of our experience. We comprehend our lives as narratives and frame our moral choices through those narratives. We "live immersed in narrative," according to literary theorist Peter Brooks. All the stories we tell ourselves and each other, spoken and written, are part of our ongoing quest for a narrative structuring of our experience. Brooks observes that "our lives are ceaselessly intertwined with narrative, with the stories that we tell and hear told, those we dream or imagine or would like to tell, all of which are reworked in that story of our own lives that we narrate to ourselves in an episodic, sometimes semi-conscious, but virtually uninterrupted monologue" (Brooks, 1992 at 3). Fundamentally interpretive creatures, we seek out linear, time-bound patterns of experience to give us a sense of meaning and wholeness in living our own identity.

Contemporary scholars from various disciplines argue that narrative knowing is intrinsic to moral reasoning (Bruner, 1990; Sarbin, 1986; Spence, 1982). A disparate group, they nevertheless concur that ethical choices are based in a narrative understanding of virtue, within stories that distill a culture's values and a person's life history. Philosopher Alistair MacIntyre speaks for a growing company of cognitive psychologists, psychiatrists, theologians, historians, philosophers, literary theorists, and fellow philosophers when he describes the human being as essentially "a story-telling animal" for whom all moral decisions are made in the context of a life story:

> *[Man] is not essentially, but becomes through his history, a teller of stories that aspire to truth. But the key question is not about their authorship; I can only answer the question, 'What am I to do?' if I can answer the prior question, 'Of what story or stories do I find myself a part?' (MacIntyre 1981 at 216).*

In the same way, theologians Stanley Hauerwas and David Burrell have argued for the priority of narrative in moral reasoning, chastising traditional, formalist ethics for attempting to portray practical reasoning as separate from narrative context, for rejecting such crucial features as character, meaning, and contingency (Hauerwas & Burrell, 1977). Omitting the significance of narrative from ethical reflection, they aver, distorts any account of the moral experience. Scholars who find that human actions acquire their meaning only within narrative constructions concur with literary critic J. Hillis Miller's caveat for contemporary ethics: "There is no theory of ethics, no theory of the moral law and its irresistible stringent imperative, 'Thou shalt' and 'Thou shalt not,' without storytelling. Narratives, examples, stories...are indispensable to thinking about ethics" (Miller, 1987 at 3).

Explored by such twentieth-century moral philosophers as Hilary Putnam, Bernard Williams, Iris Murdoch, and Martha Nussbaum, the emerging field of ethical criticism is an outgrowth of the ancient interest in the relations between philosophy and literature documented in the writings of Plato and Aristotle and continued in modern times by writers as varied as Friedrich Schiller, Martin Heidegger, John Dewey, Samuel Taylor Coleridge, and Stanley Cavell. Contemporary ethical critics, such as Booth and Nussbaum, investigate the vital connection between the experience of reading and the moral reasoning readers use in living their lives. In *The Company We Keep: An Ethics of Fiction*, Booth explains that "even the life we think of as primary experience... is rarely experienced without some sort of mediation in narrative" (Booth, 1988 at 14). Drawing on specific examples from literature, such as readings from *Huckleberry Finn*, *Lady Chatterley's Lover*, and *Portrait of the Artist as a Young Man*, Booth analyzes the way our engagement with literature enhances, supplements, reorders, and interprets reality. In Booth's view, intelligent critical thinking about literature attends to the reader's experience during the hours of reading, to the quality of the life led while engaged with powerful stories.

Literature's Contribution to Moral Development

From Aristotle to Wayne Booth, philosophers and literary critics who argue for a narrative approach to moral reasoning locate ethics inquiry at the center of our engagement with literature. In studies that have far-reaching implications for literature in medical education, recent research in the cognitive sciences has begun to analyze the psychological processes at work in moral reasoning. Drawing on new discoveries in cognitive psychology, Mark Johnson's *Moral Imagination* explores the essential role of the imagination in ethical deliberation, offering a framework for describing patterns of moral reflection that support and complement the views of the ethical critics (Johnson, 1993). Concurring with other psychologists and psychiatrists who have ascertained the importance of the moral imagination for ethical thinking (Coles, 1989; Hillman, 1983; Bettleheim, 1975), Johnson goes further, investigating the cognitive structure of the moral imagination and the tools we use for moral reflection, such as metaphor, prototypes, frame semantics, basic lived experiences, and narrative. By deconstructing specific stories of how people make and justify moral choices, he explores how the imagination works in moral deliberation, what forms it uses as we create coherent narratives for our lives. Morality, as Johnson conceives it, is a matter of how well or poorly we create, or live out, a narrative that meets the on-going challenge of living a meaningful life. Moral reasoning, then, is "purposive," aimed at clarifying ambiguous situations, resolving dilemmas about how to act, and justifying our decisions to ourselves and others (Johnson, 1993 at 55). To these ends, we construct our lives as ongoing stories, within the constraints of our historical and social contexts and roles. Moral reasoning involves an imaginative narrative exploration of the possibilities for action within a present situation.

Since moral reflection is dependent upon narrative frames, upon creating and remembering stories, narrative is at the center of the moral imagination and forms its basic structure. Contrary to the Western philosophical tradition that moral reasoning involves identifying prearticulated laws and fitting them to specific situations, our actual practice involves recalling and constructing narratives to discern what is morally relevant in an indeterminate situation, to understand empathically how others experience things, and to envision a full range of possibilities open in a particular predicament. We recall stories, heard and read, to decide what parts of our experience to use and reject in making moral choices and in finding our way in new situations. Through narrative structures in our thinking, such as metaphor, plot, and context, we make sense of human action, evaluate character, and project possible resolutions to morally ambiguous or unfamiliar situations. Not simply an explanatory construct, narrative constitutes the way we explore our lives.

From our first attempts at moral thinking as children, we acquire a moral education through stories we hear. In the fairy tales read to us and the informal stories that surround us in family talk, we begin to "listen for stories," as author Eudora Welty puts it, as an early form of participation in the life around us (Welty, 1983). We learn to evaluate and justify our own actions and those of others through stories we tell to make sense of events, acquiring the way people think about their lives, make choices, and justify their decisions. Early on, stories emerge as the primary vehicle we use for moral deliberation. And we quickly become adept at using our imagination to project ourselves onto different sorts of situations, to explore various possibilities for continuing our own life story, and to discover how we feel about the likely results of particular actions. Stories allow us to follow the consequences of specific moral decisions over an extended time, tracing the various possibilities for action that are essential for moral reflection. Our primary task in moral development involves, in Johnson's words, "refining our perceptions of characters and situations and developing empathic imagination to take up the part of others" (Johnson, 1993 at 199). It is a well-cultivated, experientially-grounded moral imagination rather than a set of fixed moral laws that gives one the capacity to construct a meaningful life story.

Once we comprehend the power stories have to teach us about the contingencies and consequences of moral decisions, about the values that figure into the lives we choose to lead, and about what is required of us to lead the lives we most want, we begin to understand why literature so often plays such an effective role in our moral development. Philosopher Richard Rorty reminds us of the way we turn to novels, plays, and short stories, and not to moral philosophy texts, for our moral education (Rorty, 1982). In the fleshed-out, sustained narratives of literature, we come the closest to witnessing and vicariously experiencing another person's life. Imaginatively entering into the private worlds of the characters, we engage in acts of discernment, perception, and evaluation, discovering as we go what it is like to participate in the moral reality of others. At the same time we grow clearer about our own moral reality. As we read, we explore, learn, and change by entering into the imagined life.

Through literature, and not through traditional philosophy, we gain unique access to various views of the world and how one might live in it. Only literature offers a language and form that is as complex, contextual, allusive, and attentive to particulars as the experience of lived life. Philosopher and literary scholar Martha Nussbaum agrees with Rorty that a view of life is told and that some truths about human experience can be reliably and accurately rendered only by the narrative artist. In two highly acclaimed books that argue persuasively for the importance of literature in moral reasoning, Nussbaum draws on Aristotle's concept of the priority of the particular to describe a practical moral reasoning that recognizes the ethical significance of contingency, of conflicting obligations, of the unexpected, and of the emotions (Nussbaum, 1986, 1990). Along with other contemporary ethical critics such as John Gardner and Wayne Booth, she suggests that some literary texts, from Sophocles to Dickens to Proust to James are indispensable to philosophical inquiry in ethics, sources of insight and moral knowledge that can be gained in no other way. Through close readings of key passages from such works as James' *The Golden Bowl* and Dickens' *David Copperfield*, Nussbaum demonstrates the extent to which literary interpretation coincides with a practical moral reasoning that is finely tuned and nuanced, incapable of being rendered through any means less than art. Moral knowledge, as revealed through certain works of fiction, is more than an intellectual grasp of facts and rules; it is "perception," according to Nussbaum, and requires "seeing a complex, concrete reality in a highly lucid and richly responsive way,...taking what is there, with imagination and feeling" (Nussbaum, 1990 at 152). Literature is indispensable for its capacity to capture the morally salient particularities of our experience and to render the very processes by which we achieve moral vision.

Philosophers and critics such as Martha Nussbaum and Wayne Booth illustrate through close readings their claim that certain literary narratives are fundamentally works of moral philosophy and deserve our serious attention in the study of ethics. They concur, in this view, with J. Hillis Miller, who asserts that "ethics as a region of philosophical or conceptual investigation depends, perhaps surprisingly, on a kind of mastery usually thought to be the province of the literary critic" (Miller, 1987 at 3). John Gardner has observed that fiction is a moral "laboratory," a philosophical method through which the reader explores the way a singular person with a certain character, situated in specific circumstances, might live a life. The "art" of the fiction writer "controls the argument and gives it its rigor, forces the writer to intense yet dispassionate and unprejudiced watchfulness, drives him -- in ways abstract logic cannot match -- to unexpected discoveries and, frequently, a change of mind" (Gardner, 1978 at 108). Through literature, readers connect moral principles with concrete situations and gain a deeper understanding of life's various exigencies. By following characters, as novels do, over extended periods of time as they try to live by certain virtues, readers come to see what those virtues entail. Through the richly vicarious experience of reading, we make our own moral explorations.

Literary narratives offer readers not only a way to reflect on the consequences of choices and entanglements over time, but also a way to analyze the concrete particularities that form the subtle, intricate web of human commitments and relationships. Strengthening the ability and willingness to experience otherness and to recognize meaning as contextual, literature provides the best case studies in the world, with the texture and complexity of life itself (Hunter, 1990). D. H. Lawrence makes the point with characteristic bravado when he declares, "As a novelist, I consider myself superior to the scientist, the saint, and the philosopher, all of whom are masters of different bits of knowledge, but I get the whole hog" (Lawrence, 1923).

The Act of Reading

If the extended narratives of literature can be such effective vehicles for moral reasoning, what is it that happens to us when we read? What do we know about the act of reading that can explain its power and clarify its effects? Recent studies of the cognitive dimensions of the reading experience provide some of the first comprehensive accounts of the interpretive techniques readers use to find meaning in narratives, of how thought and emotion interact during the act of reading, and of the various ways knowledge gained from fictive worlds influences behaviors and judgments in the actual world. Notable among full-length research efforts to analyze the unique phenomenology of reading are cognitive psychologist Richard Gerrig's *Experiencing Narrative Worlds* (1993), poet Victor Nell's *Lost in a Book: The Psychology of Reading for Pleasure* (1988), and literary critic Matei Calinescu's *Rereading* (1993). Two decades of literary theory investigating the reader's response to literature now join contemporary cognitive psychology to suggest a coherent way of analyzing the experience of reading (Gerrig, 1993). In particular, the act of reading sets into motion three core processes within the reader: departure, performance, and change.

First, whenever we read literary narratives, we leave behind our own world in order to enter the narrative world. Like the cognitive process of dissociation, immersion in the world of a story renders the reader partially disconnected from the reality of the empirical world. The experience of being "lost in a book" mirrors the feeling of disorientation common to readers upon finishing a story and "re-entering" the actual world. Using Richard Gerrig's metaphor, the reader is a traveler "transported" some distance from his or her world of origin. But with a qualifier. By a "principle of minimum departure," articulated by M. L. Ryan, "we construe the world of fiction…as being the closest possible to the reality we know. This means that we will project upon the world of the [narrative] everything we know about the real world, and that we will make only those adjustments which we cannot avoid" (Ryan, 1980 at 406). The greater the departure from our own world, the more adjustments we must make in order to enter the fictive world. Conversely, the greater the skill on the part of the writer, the easier it is for the reader to travel great distances from his or her own world, and the less aware he or she will be of making the adjustments in order to enter. By convincingly rendering a common humanity in the most unlikely characters, writers have continued to draw generations of readers from every culture into the most distant of narrative worlds -- such as that of a Russian ax-murderer tormented by conscience (*Crime and Punishment*) or that of a barnyard pig pursued by fear of becoming sausage (*Charlotte's Web*) -- making the unfamiliar familiar at a fundamental, profoundly human level.

Second, in entering the narrative world, we willingly adopt the role which the text asks us to assume. Contemporary reader-response theory has given us a language and models for conceptualizing the reader's performance. Less a unified critical school than a loose collection of literary critics with a common point of departure, reader theorists focus on the reader as the decisive component of any meaningful narrative interpretation. From Walker Gibson's "mock reader" to Wolfgang Iser's "implied reader" and Umberto Eco's "model reader," their various terminology clarifies different aspects of the way making sense of literary narratives is dependent upon the reader's performance. Like a traveler expected to adopt local customs, the reader must acquiesce to the conditions which characterize the narrative world. Walker Gibson describes the reader's role by suggesting that "every time we open the pages of another piece of writing, we are embarked on a new adventure in which we become a new person. We assume, for the sake of the experience, that set of attitudes and qualities which the language asks us to assume, and, if we cannot assume them, we throw the book away" (Gibson, 1980 at 1). By adopting the role required by the story, the reader gains access to the lifeworld of the characters. "In reading," Iser says, "we are able to experience things that no longer exist and to understand things totally unfamiliar to us" (Iser, 1978 at 19). Seen this way, reading is an active process in which the reader participates in discovering meaning in a work. Umberto Eco goes so far as to say that the narrative text is "a lazy machine that expects a lot of collaboration from the reader" (Eco, 1993 at 128). Engaging the reader's memories, desires, psychological defenses, imagination, and insights, fiction functions the way games do, according to Eco, offering the reader limitless opportunities to engage his or her faculties for perceiving the world, for structuring and restructuring experience.

Third, and most significantly for our subject, we are changed by the journey. During the experience of reading, our very mental structures are altered. We put aside our actual life and enter another world, where we hear and see and feel the things the characters hear, see, and feel. And when we close the book and re-enter our own lives, that set of feelings and way of knowing is embedded in us, a part of us now. Wayne Booth suggests that we tend to "underestimate the extent to which we absorb the values of what we read...And even when we do not retain them, the fact remains that insofar as the fiction has *worked* for us, we have lived its values for the duration: we have been *that kind of person* for at least as long as we remained in the presence of the work" (Booth, 1988 at 41).

Until recently, assertions regarding the capacity of literature to bring about change in the reader have remained largely unsupported. Theorists from Aristotle to Freud have argued that the primary benefit of literature is pleasure, the catharsis achieved when the reader gratifies primal desires and fantasies surreptitiously. In this view, articulated by Norman Holland, reading literature has no formative effect; it simply offers materials that we adapt to our own "identity theme" in order to "symbolize and finally to replicate ourselves" (Holland, 1975 at 814). Each reader adapts portions of the text to fit his or her individual fantasies and defenses, rejecting the rest. But some psychoanalytic critics believe that reading literature yields more than emotional release and repetition of identity. Drawing on recent research in object-relations theory, these critics suggest that the act of reading offers the opportunity to re-form the self (Hymer, 1983; Roland, 1981). According to Alcorn and Bracher's research, what Holland calls "the infinite variations of identity" experienced by the reader may have long-term effects on the structure of the self (Alcorn & Bracher, 1975). Literature extends the reader's psychic map of the external world to take in unfamiliar territory, to include new environments, cultures, values, and behaviors. In addition, it reveals hidden primary values that have been repressed or ignored and brings them to the surface for conscious reflection. In this way, literary analysis parallels moments of what Meredith Skura calls "moments of integration and insight" in psychoanalysis, for the way frequently grants readers a shock of recognition, a tough self-scrutiny, with the concomitant possibility of changes in perspective and behavior (Skura, 1981 at 12).

Narrative Competence

Stories often possess the immediacy that connects so persuasively with human experience. However, we may be lured into making the easy assumption that reading literature makes better people or that studying the humanities naturally makes people more humane. When tempted by such facile correlations between intellect and character, we need only remember that a good number of Nazi SS officers loved their Goethe and Strauss and that university humanities departments are often anything but humane. What reading yields is competence, a set of skills that, interacting with cognitive processes set in motion through the act of reading, have profound implications for moral reasoning. Specifically, for the medical student or clinician who seeks competence in ethics and moral reasoning in encounters with patients and their families, it is worth exploring what constitutes narrative competence and how one best acquires it.

Clearly, physicians who read use the same skills all good readers intuitively exercise when reading stories (Charon, 1989). But two areas of narrative competence, in particular, prove essential to recognizing and responding to moral issues in medicine.

One is the ability to construct meaning when listening to or reading narratives. Physician and literary scholar Rita Charon reminds us that some of the most damaging mistakes doctors make in ethics decisions occur by replacing the patient's story with the doctor's agenda, a problem often caused or compounded by the doctor's lack of skill or interest in finding coherence in the patient's story (Charon, 1986). Doctors who become skilled, involved readers, however, are more likely to be competent at listening for a story to emerge from the patient's rendition of events. An attending physician who comprehends the way the reader contributes to the meaning made of a text will understand the necessity of self-awareness on the part of the doctor listening to patients. And a reading physician is more likely to be skilled in filtering, organizing, and interpreting disparate information, to be able and willing to puzzle out the meaning of seemingly disconnected events.

For instance, in the effort to construct meaning, the physician who reads and interprets such texts as William Faulkner's *The Sound and the Fury* has had practice in tolerating uncertainty, discontinuity, and ambiguity on the way to making sense of things. And a careful reading of Virginia Woolf's *To the Lighthouse* or James Joyce's *The Dubliners* yields a greater ability to identify and comprehend contradictory and multiple meanings. When clinicians and students read stories by women and minority writers with an ear to the silences and gaps in the texts, they learn to suspect power imbalance as a source of secrets in a story. They learn to listen as much for what is left unsaid as for what is said, to respect, as Henry James put it, "the power to guess the unseen from the seen." A reading doctor becomes a Jamesian witness, "one of those people upon whom nothing is lost" (James, 1909). A physician with narrative competence, then, is more likely to be able to hear the whole story from a patient, decipher its meanings, and recognize moral issues within the story, even where they may be less than obvious.

The other area of narrative competence which proves so essential to moral reasoning in medicine is the ability to adopt another person's point of view. This capacity, perhaps more significantly than any other, is strengthened through reading literary narratives. The essence of empathy is the ability to enter another person's world, to see from that perspective, to understand that experience from the inside out. Physicians are like readers, who, in F. Scott Fitzgerald's words, are granted "privileged glimpses of the human heart" (Fitzgerald, 1925). In order to recognize moral issues where they exist in the complex lives of particular individuals and to comprehend moral choices over the course of lived experiences of health and disease, physicians need the narrative capacity to imagine the richly textured moral life to which their glimpses grant them access.

Reading literary narratives calls forth and enhances empathy (Charon, 1993). It does not simply inform, but draws us into a life and leaves us changed. The poet Shelley understood that by exercising the imagination through reading we strengthen our capacity for empathy. In his "Defense of Poetry," Shelley uses metaphoric language that speaks to physicians today in describing the imagination as "the great instrument of moral good...that strengthens that faculty which is the organ of the moral nature of man, in the same manner as exercise strengthens a limb" (Shelley, 1965). Reading narratives by authors such as Mark Twain, Herman Melville, Shakespeare, and Toni Morrison draws us out of our own perspectives and into the context-rich experience of others. In such company as Huckleberry Finn, Billy Budd, Shylock, or Sula, we are morally educated, in the root sense of the word, "led out" of our own confined, necessarily limited world. Using the terms of Edmund Husserl, we have our "perceptual stance" altered every time we read a story (Husserl, 1975). The highly individual point of view or frame of reference from which each of us perceives and interprets the world of experience, Husserl insists, can with practice be shifted at will to provide our consciousness with access to unfamiliar reality.

Building narrative competence by reading and interpreting literary narratives with medical students and clinicians can strengthen the empathic skills and the willingness to exercise them so necessary to recognizing and responding to moral issues in medical encounters. Literary critic Roger Shattuck reminds us that, although it can never be a substitute for lived life, literature;

> *...acquaints us with a special and intensified repertory of feelings and events and possibilities. Later when we come upon an event, we may have a*

> *counterpart at hand... available. And the movement of our mind is to say, "This is it." For we have lived it once already.*
>
> *Literature can foreshorten the complex, two-part process of full-living; what we participate in through reading becomes the first half of that double process. Our own life, our personal experience, can then move directly into the second beat: recognition (Shattuck, 1963 at 133).*

Shattuck articulates precisely the benefit so many students and clinicians experience from reading literature while caring for patients. The sense of having "been here before" while paradoxically on unfamiliar ground in a clinical situation often arises from having experienced a similar situation while reading a story. The empathic connection with a fictive companion, whose values and moral concerns have become part of our experience, remains available as a counterpart to the current event. Reading affects readers by means of what Shattuck calls "the economy of life...by allowing them to achieve personal experience sooner, more directly, and with less groping" (Shattuck, 1963 at 134). Literature not only familiarizes readers with what may be encountered later in lived life but also provides a basis for the emotions and responses with which later events will be met.

Along with biomedical efforts to cure the body, physicians need the ability to care for the patient, to help someone who may be a stranger and very different in personality and background from the physician along on a journey that is "narratively right" for this individual life. To heal according to its fundamental meaning, "halle" -- the Anglo-Saxon root it shares with our words "health" and "whole," implies an ethics of medicine that requires narrative competence. To this end, we might wish that medical students and clinicians be not only well-educated in science, but also well-storied in ethics.

Every genuine work of literature intelligently read enlarges our capacity for the wisdom and experience necessary for mature moral reasoning. Reading and interpreting literature as part of medical education in bioethics offers both a content and a method; an accumulation of stories that continually build competence in moral reasoning by means of their limitless renditions of human experience. And a way of knowing that offers a means to see what otherwise remains obscure, to hear what otherwise remains silent -- and a limitless source of professional satisfaction and joy.

Harvard Medical School

REFERENCES

Alcorn, M. and Bracher, M. (1985). Literature, psychoanalysis, and the re-formation of the self: a new direction for reader-response theory. *Publications of the Modern* Language Association 100(3):342-354.

Bettleheim, B. (1975). *The Uses of Enchantment*. New York: Random House.

Booth, W. (1988). The Company We Keep: An Ethics of Fiction. Berkeley: University of California Press.

Brody, H. (1994). 'My Story is Broken; Can You Help Me Fix it?' Medical ethics and the joint construction of narrative. *Literature and Medicine* 13:79-92.

Brooks, P. (1992). Reading for the Plot: Design and Intention in Narrative. Cambridge: Harvard University Press.

Bruner, J. (1990). *Acts Of Meaning*. Cambridge: Harvard University Press.

Calinescu, M. (1993). *Rereading*. New Haven: Yale University Press.

Charon, R. (1986b). To render the lives of patients. *Literature and Medicine* 5:58-74.

Charon, R. (1989). Doctor-patient/reader-writer: Learning to find the text. *Soundings* 72:137-152.

Charon, R. (1993). The narrative road to empathy. In *Empathy and the Practice of Medicine*, ed. H. Spiro, M. G. M. Curnan, E. Peschel, and D. St. James. New Haven: Yale University Press.

Coles, R. (1989). *The Call of Stories*. Boston: Houghton Mifflin Company.

Connelly, J. and DalleMura, S. (1988). Ethical problems in the medical office. *Journal of the American Medical Association* 260(6):812-815.

Eco, Umberto (1993). *Six Walks in the Fictional Woods*. Cambridge: Harvard University Press.

Fitzgerald, F.S. (1925). *The Great Gatsby*. New York: Charles Scribner's Sons.

Gardner, J. (1978). *On Moral Fiction*. New York: Basic Books, Inc.

Gerrig, R. (1993). *Experiencing Narrative Worlds: On the Psychological Activities of Reading*. New Haven: Yale University Press.

Gibson, W. (1980). Authors, speakers, readers, and mock-readers. In *Reader-response criticism*, ed. J. Tompkins. Baltimore: Johns Hopkins University Press.

Hauerwas, S. and Burrell, D. (1977). From system to story: an alternative pattern for rationality in ethics. In *Knowledge, Value and Belief* 2:111-152. *The Foundations of Ethics and Its Relationship to Science*, ed. H. T. Engelhardt, Jr. and D. Callahan. Hastings-on-Hudson, N.Y.: The Hastings Center.

Hawkins, A. (1993). *Reconstructing illness*. West Lafayette, In.: Purdue University Press.

Hillman, J. (1983). *Healing fiction*. Barrytown, N.Y.: Station Hill Press.

Holland, N. (1975). Unity identity text self. *Publications of the Modern Language Association* 90:813-822.

Hunter, K. (1990). Overview. *Second Opinion* 15:54-69.

Hunter, K. (1991). *Doctors' Stories: The Narrative Structure Of Medical Knowledge*. Princeton: Princeton University Press.

Husserl, E. (1975). *Ideas*. New York: Collier Books.

Hymer, S. (1983). The therapeutic nature of art in self-reparation. *Psychoanalytic Review* (70):57-68.

Iser, W. (1978). *The Act of Reading*. Baltimore: Johns Hopkins University Press.

James, H. (1981). *Selected Literary Criticism*. ed. M. Shapira. Cambridge, England: Cambridge University Press.

James, H. (1909). *The Princess Casamassima*. (New York Edition) New York: Charles Scribner's Sons.

Johnson, M. (1993). *Moral Imagination: Implications of Cognitive Science for Ethics.* Chicago: University of Chicago Press.

Jonsen, A. and Toulmin, S. (1988). *The Abuse of Casuistry: A History of Moral Reasoning.* Berkeley: University of California Press.

Lawrence, D.H. (1923). *Studies in Classic American Literature*. New York: The Viking Press.

MacIntyre, A. (1981). *After Virtue*. Notre Dame, In.: Notre Dame University Press.

Miller, J. H. (1987). The ethics of reading: Kant, deMan, Eliot, Trollope, James, and Benjamin. New York: Columbia University Press.

Neelon, F. (1994). The Healer's Art. Boston College Magazine 52(4):38-45.

Nell, V. (1988). Lost In a Book. New Haven: Yale University Press.

Nussbaum, M. (1986). The Fragility Of Goodness: Luck and Ethics in Greek Tragedy and Philosophy. New York: Cambridge University Press.

Nussbaum, M. (1990). *Love's Knowledge*. New York: Oxford University Press.

Pincoffs, E. (1971). Quandary ethics. *Mind* 80:552-571.

Roland, A. (1981). Imagery and the self in artistic creativity and psychoanalytic literary criticism. *Psychoanalytic Review* (68):409-424.

Ryan, M. (1980). Fiction, non-factuals, and the principle of minimum departure. *Poetics* 9:403-422.

Rorty, R. (1982). *Contingency, Irony, and Solidarity*. New York: Cambridge University Press.

Sarbin, T. (1986). *Narrative psychology: the storied nature of human conduct.* New York: Praeger.

Shattuck, R. (1963). Proust's Binoculars: A Study of Memory, Time, and Recognition In 'a la Recherche du Temps Perdu'. New York: Random House.

Shelley, P. (1965). A defense of poetry. In *The Complete Works of Percy Bysshe Shelley*, ed. R. Ingpen and W. Peck. New York: Gordian. 7:109-140.

Skura, M. (1981). *The Literary Use of the Psychoanalytic Process.* New Haven: Yale University Press.

Spence, D. (1982). Narrative Truth and Historical Truth: Meaning And Interpretation In Psychoanalysis. New York: W. W. Norton & Co., Inc.

Toulmin, S. (1972). *Human understanding*. Princeton: Princeton University Press.

Welty, E. (1983). *One Writer's Beginnings*. Cambridge: Harvard University Press.

Wiecha, J. (1991). Ethics in medicine: are we blind? In support of teaching medical ethics at the bedside. *The Journal of Medical Humanities* 12(3):111-117.

LACHLAN FORROW

COMMENTARY ON 'NARRATIVE ETHICS'

THE CASE OF THE MISSING CASES

In building her case for the importance of what she and others call "narrative ethics," Martha Montello moves through several stages of argument. First, she criticizes what she views as the dominant "abstract" and "formalist" approach to ethical theory, especially as it is applied to medicine. Second, she describes advantages of a more "contextual approach" offered by "narrative ethics," concluding that "a mature, experientially-grounded moral imagination, not a set of fixed moral laws" (see Montello at 114) is critical to addressing moral issues in medicine effectively. She then describes connections between literature, the act of reading, and moral development, arguing that "reading changes readers" in ways that yield a "narrative competence" that has profound importance for moral reasoning. This "narrative competence," she suggests, involves three key components: the ability to construct meaning: the ability to negotiate aesthetic distance; and the ability to adopt another person's point of view. It is this last capacity, perhaps more than any other, that she believes is both strengthened by reading and crucial for moral reasoning in medicine.

Montello's first two claims are both important and controversial. A considerable literature has developed in the past decade about the limitations of "principle-based" ethics, and I will not undertake an extended discussion here.[1] A considerably more detailed characterization of the "abstract" and "formalist" approach to ethical theory that Montello criticizes would be necessary for such a discussion to proceed, at least to ensure that more than a straw man or caricature is being attacked. For example, Montello suggests that "real ethical issues in medicine...do not arise in the abstract. Instead, they arise in the complex lives of unique individuals within a particular context of family, community, and history." Few, if any, serious ethical theorists would deny this, and Montello herself goes on to agree that "judicious applications of principles and general rules remain valuable guides to action and safe-guards to personal rights." The point that a careful "contextual approach" to an individual situation should be included in any case analysis is important, but the subsequent application of principles -- even relatively abstract ones -- to that specific context is exactly what good principle-based moral reasoning involves.

M. A. Grodin (ed.), Meta Medical Ethics, 125–130.

Montello's third claim -- that what she calls "narrative competence" is central to moral development and that it is obtained through reading stories -- warrants careful assessment by anyone concerned with the ethical dimensions of medical education. Montello is surely correct in stressing the importance of developing skill in understanding the meaning of a patient's story, and in pointing out that damaging mistakes often occur when doctors replace a patient's story with the doctor's own agenda. She is also certainly right that in clinical care this problem is compounded by the limited skill or interest of physicians in actively searching for coherence in the stories of patients. Her report that "we are finding...that doctors who read are more likely to be competent at listening for a story to emerge from the patient's rendition of events" and that "a reading doctor is more likely to be skilled in filtering, organizing, and interpreting disparate information..." is provocative. These impressions of an experienced classroom teacher are important, even though one can reasonably ask for clearer empiric evidence before concluding that this is in fact true. Even if it is true, however, that does not by itself prove that we should devote more curricular time in medical training to reading fiction. An association between reading and competence in listening and interpreting may simply mean that qualities that lead physicians to be interested in reading also lead them to be interested and skilled in listening to patients.

Montello clearly believes more than this -- that if students can be encouraged to read more literary narratives then they will develop 'narrative competence' that will improve their moral reasoning in clinical situations. I suspect, however, that reading itself is not all that matters -- that *how* one reads is at least as important. Simply adding works of fiction to a medical school curriculum may not be as important as having highly-skilled teachers like Montello available to guide students in strengthening the attentiveness, critical questioning, and group discussion that good textual analysis involves. Even then, it is not clear that Montello's 'narrative competence' would be best developed through courses featuring the reading of fiction. Suppose a faculty member has responsibility for guiding students in how best to spend 10 or even 100 hours of a medical school year in developing their ability to understand patients' stories. Would that time really be best spent in reading and discussing works of fiction, rather than in listening to a dozen or more individual patients and then discussing understandings or misunderstandings of those patients' current life situations?

Montello is also clearly right that the "ability to negotiate aesthetic distance" has parallels with the ability to maintain appropriate "clinical distance" with patients, achieving a balance between detachment and overinvolvement. But again, in deciding how to allocate one's all-too-scarce hours of discretionary time, it is an open question whether time spent reading alone, or in discussion groups about books one has read, is a better way to strengthen this capacity than time spent with (and then later discussing) real patients. The same issue also obviously applies to Montello's third component of narrative competence -- the ability to adopt another person's point of view. Although I do believe that reading literary narratives can create and enhance empathy, I do not believe that it does so for all readers. For some of us, time spent reading fiction is an escape from the engagement with the real lives of other human beings, and this escape does not always leave us more interested or skillful in engaging deeply with the difficult work of struggling to help a real human being who is suffering.

For teaching purposes, there are at least two other features of literature that are helpful in the development of 'narrative competence'. First, one of the greatest challenges in medical education is finding ways of reliably exposing students to patients whose illnesses and lives present the sought-after learning opportunities. Literary cases (whether fiction or non-fiction) can be highly-efficient vehicles for ensuring that students are exposed to a wide range of issues, ideas, and varying perspectives. Second, in discussions about a real patient's story and how it can or should be interpreted, there is often considerable difficulty in pointing to any 'primary data' upon which conclusions or interpretations are based. Differences in interpretation become hard to resolve, and helping students to strengthen their ability to base interpretations in solid 'data' is difficult. Group interviews can be artificial, and after one-on-one interviews it can be nearly impossible without the use of videotape (which has its own logistical challenges) to ascertain exactly what was said, and how alternative interpretations of a patient's story might be developed and tested. In contrast, with works of literature, every reader has the same text. Whenever different student readers have different interpretations, there is an important opportunity to help students develop the discipline of looking at the actual text to support (or refute) an interpretation. As a colleague of Montello's, I have heard firsthand from her students about the ways in which they have been able to extrapolate from disciplined classroom discussions of literary texts to the development of greater discernment in listening to and interpreting the stories that real patients tell.

What is still needed, however, to justify enthusiasm for "narrative ethics" is a clearer articulation of the ways in which 'narrative competence' helps in addressing and resolving difficult ethical issues in clinical care. Competence in clinical ethics involves more than good listening and accurate, empathic interpretation -- most fundamentally it involves the capacity to make sound moral choices. In the next stage of discussions of the possible contributions that “narrative ethics” has, both to education and practice in clinical medicine, what we need most are specific, real-life case studies of “narrative ethics” in action. Just as real ethical issues in medicine do not arise in the abstract, assessments of the effectiveness of alternative analytic models -- such as the alleged differences between principle-based and narrative approaches cannot be done in the abstract. What is strikingly missing from most discussions about ‘narrative’ v. ‘principle-based’ approaches to cases, is exactly the presentation in full contextual detail of actual cases in which the two approaches are applied. As the field of narrative ethics evolves, we need to hear stories of difficult clinical -- ethical cases in which a narrative analytic approach appeared critical in reaching a satisfactory outcome. Let me conclude with one example from my own experience:

I and a colleague were called to join attending rounds at our hospital because the house staff were deeply troubled about a case which they summarized as follows:

> An 82 year old white male with moderately severe Alzheimer’s disease and no known family was transferred from a nursing home to the teaching hospital because of chest pain and worry that he was having a heart attack. This turned out not to be the case, but on further investigation he clearly had problems with swallowing, which included a pattern of chronic aspiration of food contents which had led to scarring on his chest x-ray of sections of his right lung. While in the hospital, he had both neurologic and gastrointestinal evaluations, and no clear cause for his swallowing difficulty was identified. He took in very few calories over his initial eight days in the hospital, and nutritional consultants advised that unless his caloric intake improved he was likely to become severely malnourished and die. The gastrointestinal specialists did not believe that he could eat safely and recommended that placement of a feeding tube be seriously considered. Psychiatric assessment was requested and the patient was found not to be depressed, but also not competent to participate effectively in decision-making. The house staff contacted the nursing home and found that there was no living will, no health care proxy, and no clear verbal advance directive. The medical team felt themselves in an agonizing situation where both alternatives before them -- placement of a feeding tube or possible progressive malnutrition -- were troubling. No one had a clear sense of how to proceed, and efforts to apply the “principle of autonomy” or the “principle of beneficence” did not seem at all helpful.

When we convened at attending rounds my colleague presented the following story which she had gained by contacting nurses at the nursing home and asking not about medical questions, but about the patient's personal life story:

> Mr. J. had worked for many years as a storekeeper with his wife as his close partner. He had retired fifteen years ago. They had been very devoted to each other and had no children or other close relatives. Mrs. J. had had a number of severe health problems and Mr. J. had had slowly progressive dementia of the Alzheimer's type. When Mrs. J. was first admitted to the nursing home about five years ago, he visited her twice a day, regularly going out on walks together. As his own condition slowly deteriorated, he moved into the same nursing home so they could spend as much time as possible together. In discussions about Mrs. J's care at a time when both were able to participate actively, a DNR status was entered for her and she died at the nursing home one and one half years ago. He was subsequently depressed and withdrawn for three months, but then, with active involvement of the nursing staff who had come to know him so well over several years, he fully rebounded. He became able to resume his daily walk and enjoy the company of the nurses, and seemed to be again thriving. Over the last six months, however, he had slowly become increasingly frail, with decreased appetite. With attentive and patient nursing assistance, however, they were able to get sufficient calories in during the routine nursing home meals so that his weight fell only very slowly. The staff of the nursing home, hearing about his experience as an inpatient, said that they would be very happy to take Mr. J. back and that they would also be very happy to continue to feed him in the way that they had before, by spoon. They said that it did not sound to them as if anything in his condition had really changed; and that now that it was clear that he had not had a heart attack they were eager to have him back with them again. If they were unable to give him sufficient calories to maintain his weight, they were confident that they could keep him comfortable and feeling loved.

By the end of this presentation, everyone participating in the attending rounds agreed on the proper course: immediate transfer back to the nursing home.

Although I believe that this case clearly demonstrates the importance and practical value of Montello's central thesis -- that ethical issues do not arise in the abstract, but rather in the complex lives of unique individuals within a particular context of family, community, and history -- it is not so clear to me that this case example demonstrates superiority of a "narrative" approach over a "principle-based" approach. A narrative understanding of the patient's situation, including especially several features of his life story, was absolutely crucial. But if any member of the medical team had been asked to explain why transfer back to the nursing home without a feeding tube was a better approach for this man than placement of a feeding tube, I suspect that themes of "autonomy" (what the patient would have wanted had he been able to participate in decision-making) and "beneficence" would have been central.

I believe that, as we look closely at cases for which 'narrative' approaches are claimed to be superior to 'principle-based' analyses, we will often find that advocates of 'narrative ethics' have presented a false choice. When attempting to choose, on moral grounds, among possible 'next chapters' in a patient's story, the kind of "narrative competence" that Montello emphasizes in her essay is clearly important. Nonetheless, when one arrives at the moment of moral choice -- of choosing one particular next chapter, the categories of traditional moral theory (whether or not they are strictly conceptualized as 'principles') will, I suspect, often remain crucial. Narrative competence is indeed a necessary component of overall competence in moral reasoning, but it is not sufficient.

Harvard Medical School

ENDNOTES

[1] See, for example: Hoffmaster B, Freedman B, and Fraser G (eds). Clinical Ethics: Theory and Practice. Humana Press. Clifton, NJ. 1989.

MARGARET A. FARLEY

NORTH AMERICAN BIOETHICS: A FEMINIST CRITIQUE

As the other essays in this volume indicate, there is more than one normative approach in North American bioethics. Sometimes these approaches are viewed as mutually exclusive, or at least in competition, as when we engage in debates about principles versus tradition, community, and narrative; or about ethics in distinction from law. Sometimes these same approaches are viewed as compatible, even complementary. The title assigned to my own essay suggests that all of these approaches (and their varying foundations) can be critiqued, perhaps from many directions but in particular from a feminist perspective. I will try to meet this assignment, but I can do so only in a very preliminary way. The reason for this is that the relationship between feminist theory and bioethics is very complex. Feminist theory, for example, is not in every way independent of other theories; nor is there one definitive form of feminist theory that represents all of the implications of feminism for bioethics. There are, for example, feminists who value ethical principles and feminists who privilege relationships over rules, feminists for whom legal traditions are important and feminists whose appeal to story and to history includes an appeal to religious traditions and communities of faith. Philosophically, feminists speak out of and back into a variety of schools -- classical, analytic, neo-Kantian, Marxist, pragmatist, deconstructionist.

Nonetheless, there are indeed what can be identified as feminist critiques of various approaches to bioethics as we know them today. The literature in this regard has grown remarkably in the last few years. Feminist journals have published special issues on medical ethics (*Hypatia*, 1989); new publications have appeared whose focus is on questions of women's health (*Women's Health Issues*); numerous volumes offer both collected essays and sustained feminist studies of problems in bioethics (Holmes & Purdy, 1992; Sherwin, 1992; Mahowald, 1993). I will not attempt to survey the efforts of feminists in this regard, but only to identify some elements in feminist theory that are or can be key to a feminist critique of bioethics.

Since even the term "feminism" can have more than one meaning (it is, in fact, a notoriously contested concept), let me begin by indicating what, in general, I will mean by it. Then, to provide at least a glimpse of the complexities within feminist analyses, I will appeal to a standard typology of feminist theories to suggest the sorts of concerns that can rise from each.

M. A. Grodin (ed.), Meta Medical Ethics, 131–147.

FEMINISM AND FEMINIST THEORY

The meaning I shall assume for the term "feminism" is this: Feminism is a position, a belief, a perspective, a movement, that is opposed to discrimination on the basis of gender. It is, therefore, opposed to sexism in all of its forms, whether in institutional practices and structures, attitudes and behavior, or beliefs, theories, and ideologies that establish or represent and reinforce such discrimination (as in, for example, gendered patterns of domination and subordination, gendered role differentiation, gender-biased unequal access to goods and services). More than this, feminism is opposed to other forms of unjust discrimination and patterns of domination and subordination; it takes seriously in its analysis the socially constructed connections between gender, race, class, age, sexual orientation, and other particular characterizations that can be the basis of discrimination and oppression.

Positively, feminism aims ultimately both toward equality of respect and toward the concrete well-being of all human persons regardless of gender. To achieve this aim, however, feminism is necessarily pro-women (but not thereby anti-men). Since discrimination on the basis of gender has been and remains pervasively discrimination against women, feminism aims to correct this bias. A bias for women includes a focal concern for the well-being of women and a taking account of women's experience in coming to understand what well-being means for women and men.

There are, however, quite varied strands of feminist thought, the most general of which are often identified as liberal, traditional Marxist, radical, and socialist (as in, for example, Jaggar, 1983).[1] Liberal feminism incorporates a view of human nature that emphasizes reason and individual autonomy. Its central moral principle is traditional philosophical liberalism's respect for persons. It bases this principle on the equal dignity of rational agents and on the requirements of rationality itself (that is, insofar as reason identifies unconditional moral obligations or provides the warrants for a social contract, it assumes self-legislation, self-governance, and self-responsibility).

The feminist version of liberalism exercises its critical function in challenging liberalism to consistency and to true impartiality in its recognition of and respect for every human person. It attempts to complete what it assumes to be a truly human moral point of view by (a) incorporating insights drawn from women's history and experience; (b) claiming for women a "sameness" with men as human persons and as citizens; (c) asserting the autonomy of individual women and the rights of self-determination for women as members of a group. Its goal is to have women included with men in the pool of human beings who are accorded similar respect and similar treatment. In regard to medical care, then, the liberal feminist emphasizes the need to treat women equally with men (for example, in medical research on women's as well as men's health care needs); the rights of women in regard to bodily integrity and informed consent; women's self-determination regarding sexuality and reproduction; the right of all persons to medical care, though not necessarily the need to reject a free market system in order to secure that right.

Discouragement with liberalism has grown among feminists (as among others), however. Its perceived failure to emancipate women (even after centuries of philosophical critique and political action) has convinced many feminists that an "additive" approach to ethical theory is not sufficient (that is, it is not enough simply to add women to the pool of beings who are acknowledged to be fully human). While few feminists want to lose civil liberties or a newfound sense of individual selfhood, many have come to demand of liberal norms and ideals more than a simple extension to include women (or other groups). Importantly, what this form of liberalism fails to do for feminists is to take serious account of the particular historical situations of women. It continues to separate areas of public life from private (so that while liberal ideals appear to alleviate some aspects of women's oppression, no significant change takes place in other aspects such as sexual relations, child rearing, and the support services of ordinary housework). Moreover, because the simple application of the principle of autonomy fails to reveal or address many of the life situations of particular women, liberal theory does little to change attitudes and policies that can get in the way of appropriate medical care for women. Without caricaturing liberalism or denying its value, its theoretical deficiencies mask its support of the subordination of some persons to others on the basis of gender, class, race, and other human particularities that liberalism claims to have transcended.

Not surprisingly, Marxist feminism has offered an important alternative for feminist critics of liberalism. Traditional Marxism presents an explanation for some of the failures of abstract rationality. It maintains that moral norms and ideals are not universal and ahistorical, grounded in an essential human nature; they are socially constructed. Biology, society, and physical environment, all limited and shaped by historical material needs, combine to construct humanity. Moralities are conventional; social goals are determined by those who are in power, though change can be influenced by the voices of the oppressed. Marxist theory thus targets the economic patterns whereby a dominant group protects the autonomy of some and limits the options of others. This theory is useful, therefore, for exposing the patterns of power in human enterprises, including, for example, the delivery of health care and the setting of the goals of science.

Yet, as attractive as Marxist analysis is for feminists, and as helpful as it has been in addressing the problems of liberal philosophy and political theory, it nonetheless falls short of what many feminists consider a necessary theoretical basis for social and political critique. In its preoccupation with production, it fails to take seriously the historical meanings of reproduction. It continues the liberal separation of the public world and the private. In short, traditional Marxism has insufficient room for addressing the social construction of gender. Within its framework, women as women cannot constitute a class, nor is race as such a determinant of class. As a result, Marxist theory is unable to provide adequate gender or racial analysis. The tools are therefore missing for some of the tasks of a feminist theory -- including a feminist critique of the foundations of bioethics.

Radical feminism, on the other hand, makes gender analysis the crucial task. Though "radical" feminism represents an unwieldy category, it clearly centers in the conviction that the most basic form of human oppression is patriarchy. From this perspective, patriarchy is neither a mere anomaly in an otherwise liberal system of justice nor a form of domination that is solely derivative from economic power. The radical feminist agenda contains commitments both to free women's bodies from the power of men and to free women's minds and hearts from the ideologies that mask their subordination. It is less concerned with issues of individual autonomy than with issues of community in which gendered power relations are exposed and transformed. The major clue to this transformation lies in retrieving an understanding of the differences between women and men, claiming a particular power in the dispositions and sensibilities of women.

Many feminists, however, find that radical feminism, too, is insufficient as a theory and as a political agenda. While radical feminism pays attention to gender, to women's experience, and to the integration of body and mind, it is finally not sufficiently historical for some feminists, not sufficiently political for others. Some fear that the new emphasis on differences between women and men is neither warranted nor wise; for it slips too easily into traditional stereotypes, and it often ignores the diverse histories of individual women and groups of women.

Nonetheless, radical feminist theory offers a particular vantage point for a feminist challenge to the system of medical care as a relational structure. While radical feminists may be less concerned than liberals about issues such as informed consent, they bring powerful tools of deconstruction to a prime example of patriarchy -- to a health care system in which the societal problems of gendered, racial, and class hierarchy are writ large. There is nothing abstract about the issues of power relations when they are situated not only between health care providers and recipients but within the community of health care providers themselves.

Socialist feminism is like Marxism in its assertions that understandings of individuals and society are socially constructed, and that prevailing world-views reflect the interests of the dominant class. It is like radical feminism in charging Marxism with failing to take particular account of gender in the analysis of oppression. Also like radical feminism, socialist feminists identify patriarchy as the central problem in both the public and the private spheres of human life. But socialists demand more critical analysis of women's experience than do at least some radical feminists, and they focus consistently on the interaction between gender and class (and race and age).

It might be argued that socialist feminism, precisely because it synthesizes many other strands of feminist theory, is better able to challenge bioethics as a field. It allows critical assessment of various moral epistemologies as well as normative approaches to systems that include science and technology, health care delivery and its financing. At the very least it can be said that socialist feminist theory intends to take on issues of universal morality, historical contextualism, theories of oppression, gender analysis, and distributive justice. My concern from here on, however, is not to identify the contributions of particular strands of feminist theory in the critique of bioethics but to turn to elements in the critique itself. Nonetheless, it will not do to forget entirely the variety of approaches that are all in some sense feminist.

SITUATED CRITIQUE

Feminist participation in bioethics is thus far primarily located in critiques of specific aspects of medical research, diagnosis, or care. Wherever in the spectrum of feminist theories one stands, the critique has tended to focus less on bioethical theories than on the actual structure and practice of medicine (McBride and McBride, 1981; Fisher, 1988; Macklin, 1993). Empirical data useful for this sort of critique is crucial, but it has only begun to be available. It is, therefore, part of a feminist agenda to foster studies that will provide more of it. Without such studies a feminist critique of medical ethics and of health care can be dismissed as rhetoric not connected with experience -- a charge that engages the central commitments of feminist methodology.

The data already available for gender analysis of the context and practice of medicine come from, by and large, two different locations. One might be described as the culture of physicians. It has to do with the genderization of physicians' training, career paths, clinical attitudes, and decisions. The other is the gendered experience of patients -- the differential treatment of male and female patients and subjects in research, diagnosis, and management of medical care. What studies we have of these locations constitute a bare beginning in regard to the issues of gender. Not only do they expose only the tip of an iceberg, but it is not yet clear how they are to be interpreted. They are, however, important as indicators of a problem and as stimulators for the development of theories appropriate to the problem.

Studies of the influence of their own gender on the experience of members of the medical profession include historical overviews (Bourdillon, 1988), studies of women and medical education (Bonner, 1992), sexual harassment among medical professionals (Baldwin, 1991; Komaromy, 1993; Lenhart, 1991), and gendered trends in models of physician-patient relationships (McDaniel & Naumburg, 1988). There are studies, for example, indicating that among physicians, women are more likely to be found in fields of primary care and not in surgery; women are in less lucrative specialties and are less likely to be self-employed (Cohen, et al., 1991; Martin, et al., 1988; Maheux, et al., 1989; Editorial, *Lancet*, 1991). Women and men physicians, according to some reports, approach physician-patient communication in different ways, relating differently to dying patients in particular (Dickinson & Tournier, 1993).[2] The general cultural socialization of women and men tends to persist through the socialization that takes place in the training of female and male doctors (Martin, et al., 1988).

When it comes to the gender of patients, differential treatment appears in access to medical care, in diagnosis and treatment, and in the focus of medical research. In 1991 the Council on Ethical and Judicial Affairs of the American Medical Association summarized many of the questions that have been raised in recent years about gender-differentiated medical care (JAMA, 1991). As evidence of gender disparity in health care, the Council pointed to studies showing that women make more physician visits in a year than their male counterparts, and women tend to receive more services per visit than do men (see, for example, Cleary, et al., 1982). Yet when it comes to some forms of diagnosis and treatment, men are more likely to receive them than women -- as, for example, is the case with kidney dialysis and transplantation (Held, 1988; Kjellstrand, 1988), diagnostic tests for lung cancer (Wells & Feinstein, 1988), coronary angiography and bypass surgery (Ayanian, et al., 1991).

How to interpret differences in medical interventions for women and men remains a matter of dispute. One explanation takes account of evidence that women are believed to be more emotional than men (Colameco, et al., 1983), so that women's medical complaints may be interpreted as grounded in anxiety rather than in physical causes. This explanation receives some support from other studies indicating a cultural tendency to take women's self-assessments and choices less seriously than men's. For example, court decisions in "right to die" cases show some patterns of acceding to male patients' wishes more readily than females' (Miles & August, 1990). In addition, it is almost legendary, if not yet statistically analyzed, that psychological problems are differently diagnosed in women and in men.

While gender differences, however stereotypically perceived, account for differential medical treatment of women and men, it is also the case, paradoxically, that women are treated differently from men on the basis of their assumed physiological similarities with men. Feminists have frequently observed that in medicine, as in other aspects of human life, men are considered the generic model of the human. This assumption has provided at least one reason for excluding women from a great deal of medical research (DeBruin, 1994). It has also led to the imposition of theories about male Type A personality onto the experience of women (Wallis, 1990). Other examples abound. Feminists now frequently argue, therefore, that women's health needs are indeed in important respects different from men's, and what similar and equal treatment requires is paying attention to those particular needs.

At the heart of much of the concern for women's medical care is women's reproductive potential. Here attention is certainly paid to differences between women and men. Ironically, however, valuation of women's reproductive capacities sometimes not only competes with but obscures other health values for women. Reasons for this go beyond sheer medical dilemmas of maternal-fetal conflict. Deep in Western philosophical and religious traditions is a tendency to equate women's identity with their reproductive and nurturing roles, and to value women not primarily for themselves but for their service to the species. It is difficult not to see this tendency reflected in, for example, the exclusion of women from major pharmaceutical research because of fear of potential as well as actual pregnancy and consequent fetal injury, or the inclusion of women in AIDS research only when it serves the goals of protecting their male sex partners or their fetuses (Levine, 1991; Faden, et al., 1994). This tendency is also visible in social policies such as "pregnancy clauses" that invalidate the living wills or medical proxies of women in at least thirty-four states. It is a tendency all too present in the development and use of reproductive technologies as well (see, for example, Lorber, 1987).

A few studies are available that begin to correlate gender with age, class, and race in order to evaluate differential treatment. It looks like, as in societal patterns as a whole, each of these factors compounds the problems of lack of access, discriminatory attitudes and decisions, and even policies (Perales &

Young, 1988; Davis, 1990; Cooper, et al., 1992). No one as yet knows, of course, what really explains all of the differences in the treatment that patients are likely to receive in their medical care. How significant are the correlations of gender with age, class, race, and disability is still debatable. The importance of further studies in regard to all of this, studies that will include an investigation of the social and cultural factors that characterize women's health needs and the response to these needs, is nonetheless no longer debatable.

Against the backdrop of various strands of feminist theory, as well as gendered experience in the structures and practices of medical care, it may be useful to consider key themes, or foci, for a feminist critique and reconstruction of bioethics. What I offer here is not in itself a critique, let alone a reconstruction, but a preliminary program for both.

CRITICAL THEMES

Among the many issues and themes that are presently relevant to the development of a feminist critique of bioethics, three of them seem to me to be particularly significant. These can be described in the following terms: (1) women's experience as a source for bioethics; (2) autonomy and relationality as features of persons and as principles in bioethics; and (3) embodiment and its meaning for science, technology, and the practice of medicine. These themes have been formative of feminist bioethics and also of the movement for women's health.

Women's Experience: Source for Bioethics

All forms of feminist theory, we have already noted, are committed to beginning with the experience of women. Underlying this commitment are a number of convictions, one of which is that experience rather than abstract reasoning is the first source of ethical insight and judgment. While this implies some confidence in the possibility of understanding experience, it by no means entails a simple epistemological access to objective reality. Feminists are as skeptical about objectivity and truth as are most late twentieth century theorists. Given past philosophical claims about the "nature" of women, feminists have strong reasons to question human certitude about the nature of anything. But on the other hand, feminists know the dangers of unmitigated relativism, of having no grounds for moral demands upon individuals and groups. On the contrary, out of our experience can come knowledge of ourselves and our world, sufficient to inform our desires and to clarify our responsibilities.

Many feminists acknowledge that experience is constituted and interpreted within the limits and possibilities of the languages we already have and the worldviews we already hold. Our experience of ourselves and our social world is shaped by the ways in which our society and traditions have given us eyes to see and ears to hear. "Society is in us before we are in society" (Harrison, 1985 at 153). This, however, does not mean that everyone's experience in a society is exactly the same, that one group's experience can be universalized to stand for the experience of all. Hence, aligned with a conviction about the importance of experience is a conviction that *women's* experience must be taken seriously by women and by the society as a whole in the discernment of ethical norms.

Recognizing the inadequacies of relying on the false universalization of men's experience as representative of all that is human, feminists' first methodological move was to claim the importance of women's experience. Under the challenge of women of color and women from diverse cultures, however, feminists have also come to acknowledge the inadequacy of universalizing the experience of one group of women (in this case, white, middle class, western women) to represent the experience of all women. Hence, the commitment to begin with women's experience includes a commitment to take serious account of the diversity in women's experience. It includes the obligation to hear the voices of all women, even privileging the voices of those who have previously been silenced most completely.

To take account of diversity is to pay attention to concrete particularity in the experience of individuals and of groups. This does not mean that no commonly accepted ethical norms can be found. Across race and class and gender, for example, feminists affirm a right to bodily integrity. Indeed, experience is diverse, but it is not completely unsharable. Experience yields different perspectives, but what is learned perspectively can be rendered at least partially intelligible to others whose perspective is different. Respect for diversity yields not insurmountable boundaries but the possibility of community.

When a commitment to take seriously the experience of women (in all of their diversity) is brought to a critique of bioethics it yields at least two things. First, it is impossible to dismiss the importance of experience in both the development and application of ethical principles. It is thus also impossible to dismiss the importance of the concrete particular always in favor of the abstract universal. Feminists, of course, are not the only ones to remind bioethicists of this. Indeed, ethics (and derivatively, bioethics) at its best has consistently acknowledged the importance of experience as the source and the test of general norms; and at its best, ethics has consistently recognized the impossibility of merely applying general rules as if there were an algorithm for moral discernment. Unfortunately, ethics, and the specialization of bioethics, is not always at its best. Hence, an ongoing enjoinder to attend to experience is not superfluous. Moreover, feminists bring a new force to the demand for deconstructing institutionalized categories, for critiquing theories of justice whose rules may either ignore or run roughshod over the spirits and bodies of concrete persons.

Secondly, it is not just experience that must be given its due; it is the experience of women. It is the experience of those who are in the majority of health care providers and recipients. It is, like all human experience, sometimes elusive, sometimes illusory, sometimes massively influenced by the meaning it has been given not primarily by women but by men. As such, it will not be easily retrieved, not easily interpreted, not easily brought to bear on the development of policy. But all of this makes the feminist methodological commitment more urgent and the data it yields more significant.

Autonomy and Relationality

Associated with the concepts of "autonomy" and "relationality" is a whole host of issues that have become crucial for feminist ethics generally and for feminist bioethics in particular. These include not only questions of the relative importance of freedom and relationship, but questions of an "ethics of justice" versus an "ethics of care," the nature of the human self and its meaning for professional commitments, the dynamics of power in interpersonal and social relations, and so on. Some of these issues overlap with a concern to begin ethical discernment with experience. Some of them lead to further concerns for human embodiment and for the generation of policies that protect and promote the well-being of all.

An early conviction of contemporary feminism was that at the heart of what is good for women is autonomy.[3] Autonomy, after all, is the feature of human persons that Western modernity identified as the basis for respect of persons. It is the core of the principle that requires treatment of persons as ends and not means only. It is what lies at the heart of the human self, the center of the modern subject. For women to claim autonomy was to claim a capacity to determine the meaning of their lives, a possibility of full identity as complete beings in themselves (not derivative from their relationships with men). Hence, as autonomous, women could claim respect as persons who are valuable in themselves and not only as instruments in the service of the community (of the human species, the family, or men). An important part of this claim was the right to bodily integrity, the right not to be touched or invaded or used as embodied beings without free choice or consent.

Autonomy is frequently the centerpiece of modern approaches to ethical theories of justice. Whether as the ground of a categorical imperative or the starting point of a social contract or a measure of all human interaction, it validates and informs ethical principles of justice. For women, who had been judged throughout Western history by philosophers and psychologists as not quite capable of the demands of justice, new self-identity as autonomous brought new assertions of the requirements and goals of justice.

But some women noted that the going theories of justice relied heavily on abstract principles and on ideals that had little to do with concrete individuals or with certain kinds of relationships. Carol Gilligan's work, in particular, challenged theories of moral development that enshrined principles of justice at the expense of principles of care (Gilligan, 1982). So was launched a new debate, not only among theorists generally but among feminist theorists in particular (Kittay & Meyers, 1987, and countless publications to follow).

While disagreement continues over the preferred approach to ethical discernment -- whether principles or relationships, equity or nonviolence, justice or care -- feminists tend now to agree on some things. Among all the strands of feminist thought, there is a general acknowledgment that autonomy as the central feature of the human personality is not without its theoretical and practical limitations. And whatever the variety of emphases, there is some common concern to include relationality (with varying conceptual content) in a feminist approach to ethical concerns. What is at stake here is a view of women, but also of men, in which the capacity for relationship is as significant for human persons as the capacity for self-determination. Not only can humans make choices, they can know and be known, love and be loved, participate in community in a way that is part of their very identity.

Like autonomy, however, relationality has its theoretical and practical limitations. Feminists tend to be aware, for example, of the destructiveness of an emphasis on relationship that fails to respect some degree of autonomy. They are more critical of situatedness in communities and traditions than are many recent communitarian philosophers. Women's experience of submersion in roles, the tyranny of traditions, and the potential for oppressiveness in closed communities, warn them of the need for moral limits to community as well as to individual autonomy. Similarly, an ethical emphasis on caring, when it is opposed to considerations of justice, holds dangers for women. Without justice, at least in a minimal sense, self-sacrificial caring can harm the one caring; without a just appropriateness in care, caring can harm the one cared for. Feminist theory, then, needs both autonomy and relationality.

Against exaggerated rationalism, it can show that autonomy is for the sake of relationship; against oppressive and repressive forms of communitarianism, it can maintain that relationships without respect for autonomy are destructive of both individuals and relationships.

The discernment of justice in caring and the expression of caring in justice are not, of course, easily achieved. The difficulties involved are not only the long recognized difficulties of clear-sighted ethical analysis or of the development of the virtues of wisdom and love. They are the difficulties (which post-modernism has placed in relief) of largely invisible patterns of power in every relationship. Nonetheless, feminist theorists have not despaired of unmasking gendered patterns of power, with the goal of enhancing both freedom and relation.

The meaning of all of this for bioethics is profound. An obvious case in point is the requirement of informed consent in the structures and practices of medicine. Failure to invite and obtain informed consent is a failure to respect an individual's autonomy and bodily integrity; it is a violation of the person. Yet a sole or even central emphasis on informed consent can result in a thinning of relationship; paternalism yields to an impersonal, distanced negotiation of rights and duties between strangers. The challenge is for freedoms to meet in a context of relationship -- a history of relationships, personal and social, familial and institutional, and a present relationship between health care provider and recipient. The goal is well-being, but a well-being that includes autonomy and an autonomy that serves well-being. We have not here a perfect world. Feminists know that too well. But they also know that critique advances an enterprise only when there is some clarity about the direction we wish it to take.

Embodiment

Embodiment, like autonomy and relationality, has been a central concern of contemporary feminist theory all along. The first stage of this concern was the feminist critique of Western dualisms that divide body and mind and that genderize the divide so that men are symbolically associated with mind and women with body. Feminists looked for the reasons for this sort of dualism, finding in philosophical and theological traditions the tendency to locate the essence of "woman" in childbearing functions. Women were thought to be "closer to nature" because of their biological roles, immersed in "matter" in a way that was physiologically fated (Farley, 1985). Since matter was traditionally devalued in relation to spirit, women's bodies and women themselves were devalued. They were interpreted as more "carnal" than men's bodies, more animal-like and less subject to rational control. The very exposure of these historical attitudes and beliefs made a feminist critique quite simple. Women turned to their own experience for new interpretations of their own bodies and of embodiment as such.

An early move of feminists was to reject the identification of women with their bodies. Anatomy is *not* destiny; women are no more reducible to their bodies than are men; women can transcend their bodies by knowledge and by choice. Paradoxically, this conclusion allowed women to take their bodies more seriously. They began to reclaim their bodies, refusing to reinforce the traditional dichotomy of body and mind. Thus, feminist theory also reclaimed the importance of women's bodies, understanding autonomy as embodied freedom and relationality as the capacity for embodied relationships. Women, it was argued, can live integrally as embodied spirits. Moreover, they can refuse to yield control of their bodies -- their embodied selves -- to men, to systems, to professionals, insofar as these threaten to instrumentalize them, to dominate or abuse them.

Influenced not only by their own experience but by developing philosophies, feminists have expanded their understanding of embodiment beyond individual bodies to contexts -- spatial (as in dwellings, geographical location, the whole universe) and social (as in family, lineage, city, institutions, civic society). Every dimension of embodiment, moreover, is socially constructed in its meaning. "Biological" reality (as women have learned) is not merely a biological given; it is interpreted in certain ways at certain times. The "carnality" of women's bodies, for example, is a social construct, relative to a certain time, history, culture, society. Since the way in which we interpret our bodyliness shapes our experience of it, it becomes part of embodiment, part of our embeddedness in concrete reality. Yet critical distance is possible. Feminism itself constitutes a form of critical distance from received meanings, a potential revolutionary force in the construction of meaning.

The significance of a focus on embodiment may appear obvious for bioethical theories. Yet it is important to draw out some of the implications of this focus. For example, the ways in which individuals experience medical care will depend importantly both on their own interpretation of their bodyliness and on the interpretations they receive from the providers of their care. In fact, these interpretations will almost inevitably be mutually influencing. And they will have everything to do with the form of the relationship between medical caregiver and recipient.

Or, in another example, the entire ethos of medicine is importantly shaped by interpretations of human bodyliness. It makes a difference whether bodies are objects to be fixed or embodied persons who present certain needs. It makes a difference to the meaning of disease and of disability what the reigning model is of the "perfect" body. And suffering, bodied suffering, though without its own language, nonetheless receives meaning that determines our response (Scarry, 1985 at 5-10). When a physician describes pain as "discomfort," this gives it at least part of its meaning; when a patient describes pain as "roaring," this not only expresses but influences its meaning; when diagnosticians ask for or use terms like "searing" or "burning" or "shooting" or "throbbing," a meaning is being clarified but it is also being shaped. When society approves policies regarding in vitro fertilization, it accepts a meaning for the suffering of infertility (Ryan, 1993).

It is not only feminists who point to the need to explore our interpretations and evaluations of embodiment, particularly in the context of medical care. But for feminists an urgent aspect of this exploration (this critical analysis, this deconstruction of hidden meanings, this social and political analysis) includes a consideration of gender (and race and age and class). Without gender analysis, we shall not understand some of the most important factors in the practice of medicine, the development of technology, the pursuit of science in a large ecosystem and a larger universe.

With the three themes -- women's experience, autonomy and relationality, and embodiment -- we have some sense of the concerns that feminists bring to bioethics as a discipline and to the structures and practices of medicine. To incorporate these concerns into a comprehensive critical theory, a number of things are still necessary. First, the concerns must be focused more sharply in relation to specific issues in bioethics. The methodological import of beginning not with hypothetical dilemmas but with concrete experience does not become clear until we explore the experience. Second, the pluralistic strands of feminist theory must be engaged so that, in particular, the issues of justice and care are not reconciled too quickly. The depth of a feminist critique will be missed if the tensions within it are not creatively probed. Third, the themes dealt with here must be expanded to include the critical work now being done by feminist theorists in the philosophy of science, ecological ethics, and political theory. And fourth, feminism's theoretical labors should not be abstracted from its perspective as a political movement.

Feminism is, after all, not only a theory but a movement. Its political concerns influence its theoretical parameters. This is not to say that feminist theory lacks intellectual integrity or that it is ideology merely at the service of political aims. Rather, it is simply to remember that insofar as feminism is a movement aimed at the well-being of women, it has an important interest in understanding what truly is for women's good. Insofar as feminism has an ultimate aim of enhancing the well-being of all human persons, its interests extend to understanding human good, individual and social.

As we have seen, feminist theory more often than not assumes or concludes to the social construction of many of women's needs and desires, the historical and cultural relativity of many of women's moral claims. Yet it rarely suggests total relativism and rarely accepts social construction without the sober possibility of critical distance. It presses for respect for diversity, but perceives difference as not so endless that we are without shared needs, common desires, and general duties. It is critical of absolute autonomy, yet it wants to preserve self-determination for women and for men. It embraces a relational perspective, but not to the extent that individuality is completely suppressed. It begins with experience, but experience is not all. Experience sometimes yields principles, sometimes tests them, sometimes shows them to be false; still, principles can carry us where we have not yet sufficient experience to go. Attention to the concrete reality of women is the order of the day, but it is an order that reaches beyond individual cases to wider contexts and to political action. The integrity of a feminist critique of bioethics, then, may not finally be separable from the integrity of a movement for all women's health.

Yale Divinity School

REFERENCES

American Medical Association, Council on Ethical and Judicial Affairs. (1991). Gender Disparities in Clinical Decision Making. *Journal of the American Medical Association* 266:559-562.

Ayanian, J.Z. and Epstein, A.M. (1991). Differences in the Use of Procedures Between Women and Men Hospitalized for Coronary Heart Disease. *The New England Journal of Medicine* 325:221-230.

Baldwin, D.C., et al. (1991). Student Perceptions of Mistreatment and Harassment During Medical School: A Survey of Ten United States Schools. *The Western Journal of Medicine* 155:140-145.

Bonner, T.N. (1992). To the Ends of the Earth: Women's Search for Education in Medicine. Cambridge: Harvard University Press.

Bourdillon, H. (1988). *Women as Healers: A History of Women and Medicine*. Cambridge: Cambridge University Press.

Cleary, P.D., et al. (1982). Sex Differences in Medical Care Utilization: An Empirical Investigation. *Journal of Health and Social Behavior* 23:106-119.

Cohen, M., et al. (1991). Gender Differences in Practice Patterns of Ontario Family Physicians (McMaster Medical Graduates). Journal of the American Medical Women's Association 46:49-54.

Colameco, S., et al. (1983). Sex Bias in the Assessment of Patient Complaints. *Journal of Family Practice* 16:1117-1121.

Cooper, L.Y., et al. (1992). Survival Rates with Coronary Artery Disease for Black Women Compared with Black Men. *Journal of the American Medical Association* 268:1867-1871.

Davis, A.Y. (1990). Sick and Tired of Being Sick and Tired: The Politics of Black Women's Health. In *Black Women's Health Book*, ed. E. C. White. Seattle: Seal Press.

DeBruin, D.A. (1994). Justice and the Inclusion of Women in Clinical Studies: An Argument for Further Reform. *Kennedy Institute of Ethics Journal* 4:117-146.

Dickinson, G.E., and Tournier, R.E. (1993). A Longitudinal Study of Sex Differences in How Physicians Relate to Dying Patients. *Journal of the American Medical Women's Association* 48:19-22.

Dornbush, R.L, et al. (1991). Medical School, Psychosocial Attitudes, and Gender. *Journal of the American Medical Women's Association* 46:150-152.

Faden, R., et al. (1994). Women as Vessels and Vectors: Lessons from the HIV Epidemic. In *Feminism and Bioethics: Beyond Reproduction*, ed. S. Wolf. New York: Oxford University Press.

Farley, M.A. (1985). Feminist Theology and Bioethics. In *Theology and Bioethics: Exploring the Foundations and Frontiers*, ed. E. Shelp. Boston: D. Reidel Publishing Co.

Farley, M.A. (1993a). Feminism and Universal Morality. In *Prospects for A Common Morality*, ed. G. Outka and J.P. Reeder. Princeton: Princeton University Press.

Farley, M.A. (1993b). A Feminist Version of Respect for Persons. *Journal of Feminist Studies in Religion* 9:183-198.

Fisher, S. (1986). *In the Patient's Best Interest: Women and the Politics of Medical Decisions*. New Brunswick: Rutgers University Press.

Gilligan, C. (1982). *In A Different Voice: Psychological Theory and Women's Moral Development*. Cambridge: Harvard University Press.

Harrison, B.W. (1985). *Making the Connections: Essays in Feminist Social Ethics*. Boston: Beacon Press.

Held, P.J., et al. (1988). Access to Kidney Transplantation. *Archives of Internal Medicine* 148:2594-2600.

Holmes, H.B., and Purdy, L.M., eds. (1992). *Feminist Perspectives in Medical Ethics*. Bloomington: Indiana University Press.

Hypatia. (1989). Feminist Ethics and Medicine. 4:2; Ethics and Reproduction. 4:3.

Jaggar, A.M. (1983). *Feminist Politics and Human Nature*. Totowa, N.J.: Rowman & Allanheld, Publishers.

Kittay, E.F., and Meyers, D.T., eds. (1987). *Women and Moral Theory*. Totowa, N.J.: Rowman & Littlefield.

Kjellstrand, C.M. (1988). Age, Sex, and Race Inequality in Renal Transplantation. *Archives of Internal Medicine* 148:1305-1309.

Komaromy, M., et al. (1993). Sexual Harassment in Medical Training. *The New England Journal of Medicine* 328:322-326.

Lancet. (1991). Editorial. 337:1007-1008.

Lenhart, S.A., and Evans, C.H. (1991). Sexual Harassment and Gender Discrimination: A Primer for Women Physicians. *Journal of the American Medical Women's Association* 46:77-82.

Levine, C. (1991). Women and HIV/AIDS Research: The Barriers to Equity. *IRB: A Review of Human Subjects Research* 13:18-22.

Lorber, J. (1987). *In Vitro* Fertilization and Gender Politics. *Women and Health* 13:117-134.
Macklin, R. (1993). Women's Health: An Ethical Perspective. *The Journal of Law, Medicine, & Ethics* 21:23-29.
Maheux, B., et al. (1989). The Professional Attitudes and Practice Characteristics of Male and Female Specialists. *Journal of the American Medical Women's Association* 44:154-158.
Mahowald, M.B. (1993). *Women and Children in Health Care: An Unequal Majority*. N.Y.: Oxford University Press.
Martin, S.C., et al. (1988). Gender and Medical Socialization. *Journal of Health and Social Behavior* 29:333-1343.
McBride, A.B., and McBride, W.L. (1982). Theoretical Underpinnings for Women's Health. *Women and Health* 6:37-55.
Miles, S.J., and August, A. (1990). Courts, Gender and 'The Right to Die.' *Law, Medicine, & Health Care* 18:85-95.
Perales, C.A., and Young, L.S., eds. (1988) *Too Little, Too Late: Dealing with the Health Needs of Women in Poverty*. N.Y.: Harrington Park Press.
Ryan, M.A. (1993). *Justice and Artificial Reproduction: A Catholic Feminist Analysis*. Yale University Dissertation. Ann Arbor: University Microfilms.
Scarry, E. (1985). *The Body In Pain: The Making and Unmaking of the World*. N.Y.: Oxford University Press.
Sherwin, S. (1992). *No Longer Patient: Feminist Ethics and Health Care*. Philadelphia: Temple University Press.
Wallis, L., and Klass, P. (1990). Toward Improving Women's Health Care. *Journal of the American Medical Women's Association* 45: 219-221.
Wells, C.K., and Feinstein, A.R. (1988). Detection Bias in the Diagnostic Pursuit of Lung Cancer. *American Journal of Epidemiology* 128:1016-1026.

ENDNOTES

1 There are many variations on this typology, but Jaggar's seems to me still the most useful for understanding feminist theory. My rendition of these types is adapted from an earlier essay (Farley, 1993a).

2 Some studies show conflicting findings on the issue of psychosocial attitudes among women and men physicians. See, for example, Dornbush, et al. (1991).

3 My discussion of this concept and the concept of relationality draws upon earlier essays in which I developed the relevant issues at greater length (Farley, 1993a; 1993b).

[illegible] (19[illegible]) [illegible] and [illegible]. *Women and Health* 13 [illegible].
[illegible], S. (1991) Women's Health: [illegible] Perspective. *The Journal of Family Medicine* [illegible]
[illegible] D., et al. (19[illegible]) The Professional Attitudes and Practice Characteristics of Male and Female Specialists. *Journal of the American Medical Women's Association* 46 [illegible].
[illegible], M.B. (19[illegible]) *[illegible] and Children [illegible]*. [illegible], N.Y.: [illegible] University Press.
[illegible] (19[illegible]) Gender and [illegible] Medical Health [illegible]. *Journal of Health and Social Behavior* [illegible].
McBride, A. [illegible] and McBride, W. [illegible] (19[illegible]) [illegible] for Women's Health. *[illegible] and Health* [illegible].
[illegible] (19[illegible]) [illegible] Gender [illegible] The [illegible]. [illegible].
[illegible], C.A. and Young, [illegible] (19[illegible]) *Too Little, Too Late: Dealing with the Health Needs of Women in Poverty*. [illegible]: [illegible] Park Press.
Rosen, [illegible] (199[illegible]) *[illegible]: A Feminist [illegible]*. Yale University Dissertation. Ann Arbor: University Microfilms.
[illegible], R. (198[illegible]) *The [illegible]*. [illegible] N.Y.: Oxford University Press.
[illegible] S. (19[illegible]) *The [illegible] Patient: [illegible] and Health [illegible]*. Philadelphia: Temple University Press.
Wallis, [illegible] and Klass, P. (199[illegible]) Toward Improving Women's Health Care. *Journal of the American Medical Women's Association* [illegible].
[illegible] and [illegible], R.A. (1988) [illegible] Diagnostic [illegible] of Lung [illegible]. *American Journal of Epidemiology* 128 [illegible].

[illegible]NOTES

[illegible] There are [illegible] from the [illegible] concerns [illegible] the most useful [illegible] of these types is adapted from an earlier essay (Sherwin, 199[illegible]).

[illegible] Some studies show conflicting findings [illegible] of psychosocial attitudes among women and men physicians, [illegible] for example, [illegible] et al. (199[illegible]).

[illegible] discussion of this [illegible] and the concept of [illegible] draws upon earlier [illegible] (Sherwin, 199[illegible]).

ADRIENNE ASCH

SOME THOUGHTS FOR PRACTICING BIOETHICS: EXTENDING THE FEMINIST CRITIQUE

In a wonderfully clear and succinct paper, Margaret Farley summarizes key feminist theories and then identifies three themes that warrant consideration from practitioners of bioethics and of medicine. I agree with her analysis of the different strands of feminist thinking and also concur that the themes of experience, autonomy and relationality, and embodiment all deserve more attention in the bioethics of the future than they have received to date. Thus, I will use this commentary to elaborate on her ideas and suggest some that are consonant with those she explicitly states that also need more attention from bioethics if it truly seeks to influence medical practice and public policy.

As this volume indicates, there is no one way to practice contemporary North American bioethics. Some bioethicists stress law and frame their thinking in a language of individual rights; some use utilitarian, Kantian, or communitarian theories to analyze particular cases in bioethics; others downplay existing moral theories and generalizations from cases or eschew them altogether, preferring to consider each case afresh, staying as close as possible to the nuances inherent in people's particular situations and relationships. I see these latter writers who are influenced by casuistry, and those urging bioethics to use stories to discern the ethical questions and solutions in a given situation, as relatively similar to one another (although they might disagree with this formulation) and as demonstrating a spirit and method that accords with Farley's call for heeding the life experiences and the specific relationships of the actors in each bioethics case (Arras, 1990). Some of Farley's proposals, then, should resonate with other approaches to bioethics found in this volume.

However, I am not contending that Farley's critique is captured by casuistic or narrative methods; nor is it either entirely inimical to or subsumed by rights-based or principle-driven approaches. Farley is one of a number of contributors to a growing feminist discussion of ethics generally and of bioethics in particular that developed in response to the psychological writing of Carol Gilligan and the philosophical writing of Nel Noddings. Feminists and others have debated the existence and implications of a "voice of care". Some philosophers have embraced the notion of an "ethics of care" in whole or in part, whereas others have questioned both its existence and its consequences (Scaltsas, 1992).[1] One of the virtues of Farley's approach is her acknowledgment that all human beings need "...value caring and

M. A. Grodin (ed.), Meta Medical Ethics, 149–155.

relationships" but that caring and relationships cannot flourish in an unjust society. Her appreciation of the importance of justice (about which I say more later) and her awareness that human beings must retain a sense of autonomy and separateness along with the possibilities for relationship leads me to claim that she values the protections afforded to all of us by rights-based theory and argument.

Farley points out that the authors who treat topics in medicine and bioethics from a self-consciously feminist standpoint have focused on aspects of medical research, diagnosis, or treatment and that their critique has concentrated less on bioethical theory than on the "structure and practice of medicine." As her text and bibliography reveal, there has been plenty to say about how medical training and practice enshrine sex-role stereotypes and about how women patients are neglected or short-changed. As part of the strategy to eliminate unjust distribution of resources and discrimination in medical training and practice, she urges that the field of bioethics should take seriously people's (especially women's) life experience. Although I agree with this assertion, I wish she had been more clear about the implications of women's experience for a re-fashioned and enriched bioethics. She reminds us that, as several essays in this volume indicate, feminists are not the only ones to argue for the value of basing bioethical discussion and theorizing upon the particulars of concrete experience. She is, perhaps, the one who most clearly suggests that such characteristics as sex, race, and class matter to that experience, and she urges that bioethics and medicine pay special attention to the views and experiences of those who have been most disadvantaged by existing social, sexual, and economic arrangements. She appears to be arguing that paying attention will somehow influence those in power to change the arrangements that have contributed to neglect, exclusion, and misery, but she does not explicate just what bioethics should call for or what medicine should do once they are compelled to listen to those they have ignored, or to recognize that not all people have similar experiences of illness, financial resources, social support, and the like.

Her critique is more pointed in commenting on implications of the other themes for bioethics. For example, she suggests that people's desire for both relationship and autonomy probably influences their views on the primacy of "informed consent" as a feature of their medical encounters. Yes, that women as well as men should be considered capable of making decisions about their own lives and about medical interventions is essential to respecting their personhood. But assuming that all they want out of a medical encounter is the opportunity to make a decision validates only one component of experience and omits people's desire to know that those who treat them also take an interest in them as whole human beings. The medical intervention is in the service of helping people get on with their life projects, and patients may be comforted and reassured when working with a professional who demonstrates an interest in their lives before, during, and after a medical procedure.

In considering embodiment and in urging that bioethics rethink its understanding of humans as embodied creatures, Farley makes one of her most significant contributions to a critique and a program for a bioethics of the future. Her essential argument is that how individual patients, families, and medical professionals view the body is powerfully influenced by cultural messages, and thus, adverse consequences that derive from such messages and views are remediable. She reminds us that historically, women were viewed as closer to their bodies than were men because of women's reproductive role. However, because the male body and male (read mental) activity constituted the admired and the good by the culture, women were perceived as "other", and their activities as well as their bodies were devalued. Feminist correction first announced that body, for neither males nor females, was synonymous with social destiny, and later radical feminist writings celebrated the cultural meanings of nature and of reproduction that had hitherto been used to relegate women to a second-class place in political and economic life. Farley avoids the pitfalls of essentialism noted by others (Scaltsas, 1992), and does not equate women's lives or virtues with their reproductive biology. She urges that bioethics acknowledge the importance of the body for women and for men and argues that how we think about medical practice depends upon how we think about bodies: as objects to be fixed, or as part of the total human being -- neither more nor less worthwhile than mind. I fear that the current ground-swell of enthusiasm among some feminist activists to create a specialty in "women's health" will only marginalize woman and permit all those in the medical profession who do not specialize in woman's health to again conclude that the "normal" body is male and that women are still other and someone else's department.

I extend Farley's arguments about the social construction of views about the body to bioethical views about health, disease, and disability generally. She suggests that how we think about health, disease, and disability may be influenced by our social and personal understandings of the body. We can extend Farley's critique of bioethical and medical thinking about women's bodies to attitudes toward the body generally, and to thinking about all people whose bodies to one degree or another need care, soothing, and healing. Since everyone requires some of these at some times, since only the kind or amount of that attention varies with the illness or impairment, if we viewed bodies and their variation as ordinary parts of the human experience, we might re-think our concept of the place of people with illnesses and disabilities in society. Do we view a person with a disease or disability as someone who has a "broken" body needing fixing, or as someone whose body differs from the statistical average, but as someone whose body is a variation on human experience? In other writing I have argued that bioethics was imbued with the belief that the problems ascribed to people who had chronic illness or disability (such as isolation, poverty, inability to participate in valued work and relationships) stemmed from their impaired, broken bodies alone and not from the attitudes toward impairment on the part of society or the medical profession (Asch, 1990; Asch, 1994). Farley points out that men's experience has been taken as the norm, and that what men have valued -- their mental life -- has been socially valued. Women have been perceived as "other" and that ascribed to them, the biological work of reproducing and feeding the young has been viewed as "other", not the norm, and thus devalued.

In this same vein, I submit that the norm has been the body that worked in a specified way, that did not interfere with performing valued tasks because it functioned perfectly and required no attention. People whose bodies do not fit the norm have been viewed as "other" and as different, even though the field of medicine exists because we understand that to one degree or another, all people's bodies need attention and healing. Yet the body, the focus of medical practice, and the people with physical problems, the focus of bioethics, have been viewed as "the other", as different. As a field invested in crisis medicine and crisis management that has had relatively little involvement with how patients and families manage daily life after an acute crisis, bioethics -- like most medicine itself -- has never gotten past the crisis of acute illness or traumatic disability to immerse itself in the reality of life with "broken" bodies. People with such bodies usually do not continue to view their bodies as "broken" or "other", but as part of their world and what they bring to their lives. However, because traumatic disability and people with such conditions as quadriplegia are conceived as "other", and outside possible human experience, most mainstream bioethics can continue to discuss the desires of Larry Macafee and Elizabeth Bouvia for physician-assisted suicide as "right-to-die" cases that are an understandable response to a "broken" body (Beauchamp & Childress, 1994), rather than a particular response of individuals to disability that is influenced by the cultural and social messages they have received about their bodies.

Although her critique concentrates on the themes of women's concrete experience, relationality and autonomy, and embodiment, Farley contends that feminism is a political movement as well as a theory for medicine and bioethics. She thus reminds us, but does not elaborate, her belief that the critique should serve to advance the goals of full equality and social participation of women and of others who have been historically disadvantaged and powerless. Susan Sherwin and Martha Minow are feminists whose theories explicitly challenge bioethics to reconsider medical practice and social policy in terms of how they exclude and perpetuate the powerlessness of disadvantaged groups. Both Sherwin and Minow argue that a central message of any critique of bioethics, medicine, and law is how these professions handle the problem of disadvantage and difference. Traditionally, women's bodies, or those of people with disabilities, have been viewed as "different", and the burdens and properties of difference have been ascribed exclusively to the "different" and powerless individual and group. Minow argues that difference is in the eye and mind of the person ascribing difference, and the person making the comparison. In fact, difference exists only when comparisons are being made, and comparisons need not include creating hierarchies that assign more value to one group and thus give one group greater access to resources and rewards than are given to another. "If the institutional arrangements we take for granted are part of the problem in assigning the burdens of difference to those who depart from the norm, then we should explore ways to adjust them -- ways in which the institutions themselves could change." (Minow, 1990 at 384).

The commitment to equality for those who have been powerless, and the commitment to re-shape institutions to enfranchise excluded and marginalized people can be illustrated in a feminist response to the bioethics treatment of such topics as age-based rationing of health care or of creating technology to facilitate post-menopausal pregnancies. Whereas many have argued against the notion that age should ever be a standard for denying medical care to individuals, it has been primarily feminists (Bell, 1992) who noted that the description of normal life span and of life biography, of when people should conclude that they have completed their expected life goals, all are based on a male construction of life goals; furthermore, age-based rationing that denied services to those over eighty years of age was virtually synonymous with further disadvantaging women, the group most likely to live into their eighties and to require medical and social services. The notions of life biography and of normal life goals, while appearing neutral, harm women who have often been disadvantaged in the medical, social, and economic arrangements in the rest of their lives. Similarly, although there may be many important concerns about using technology to create babies for post-menopausal women when poor women in developing countries and in North America fail to get adequate prenatal care, the objections to maternity for older women are disproportionate to objections to paternity for older men. Why is fatherhood at 60 acceptable but motherhood at 60 viewed askance? Feminist critiques would contend that what is at stake is not parenthood and the lives of children and parents, but actually unfortunate notions of who should and should not be mothers and what the institution of motherhood should mean.

In these examples I am sketching extensions of Farley's critique to encompass her concerns for equality and nondiscriminatory arrangements. I see it as both feminist and as consonant with critiques of bioethics coming from people with disabilities and from some sectors of the African-American community (Flack & Pellegrino, 1992); it is essentially a call to bioethics to adopt explicit thinking about power and social and economic arrangements as they influence the patient-family-professional relationships. It is a call to work for social justice and to focus on those questions of public policy that affect the medical services available to everyone in society. I believe that Farley's critique, along with the writings of other feminists she cites, should lead bioethics and medicine to focus their energies on matters of social justice and to consider how decisions about rationing of health care, development of new interventions and technologies, distribution of scarce resources, and treatment decisions contribute to a decrease in inequality or promote equality.

Wellesley College

REFERENCES

Arras, J. D. (1990). Getting Down to Cases: The Revival of Casuistry in Bioethics. In *Journal of Medicine and Philosophy,* Vol. 16, 331-350.

Asch, A. (1994). Disability: Attitudes and Sociological Perspectives. In *Encyclopedia of Bioethics,* 2nd edition, Warren T. Reich, (Ed.) New York: MacMillan.

Asch, A. (1990). The Meeting of Disability and Bioethics: A Beginning Rapprochement. In *Ethical Issues in Disability and Rehabilitation,* (B. S. Duncan and Diane Woods, (Eds.). New York: World Rehabilitation Fund, World Institute on Disability, and Rehabilitation International.

Beauchamp, T. L. and Childress, J. F. (1994). *Principles of Biomedical Ethics, 4th edition.* New York: Oxford University Press.

Bell, N. K. (1992). If Age Becomes Standard for Health Care Rationing. In *Feminist Perspectives in Medical Ethics,* H. B. Holmes and L. M. Purdy (Eds.) Bloomington and Indianapolis, IN: Indiana University Press.

Card, C. (Ed). (1991). *Feminist Ethics,* Lawrence, KS: University Press of Kansas.

Cole, E. B. and Coultrap-McQuinn, S. (Eds.) (1992). *Explorations in Feminist Ethics: Theory and Practice.* Bloomington and Indianapolis, IN: Indiana University Press.

Flack, H. and Pellegrino, E. D. (Eds.) (1992). *African-American Perspectives on Biomedical Ethics*. Washington, D.C.: Georgetown University Press.

Minow, M. (1990). *Making All the Difference: Inclusion, Exclusion, and American Law*. Ithaca, NY: Cornell University Press.

Scaltsas, P. W. (1992). Do Feminist Ethics Counter Feminist Aims? In *Explorations in Feminist Ethics: Theory and Practice*, E. Browning Cole and S. Coultrap-McQuinn, (Eds.) Bloomington and Indianapolis, IN: Indiana University Press.

Sherwin, S. (1992). Feminist and Medical Ethics: Two Different Approaches to Contextual Ethics. In *Feminist Perspectives in Medical Ethics*, H.B. Holmes and L.M. Purdy, (Eds.), Bloomington and Indianapolis: Indiana University Press.

ENDNOTES

[1] In addition to the works cited in Farley's essay, readers interested in the larger debate about feminist ethics should refer to the edited volumes of Card, 1991 and Cole and McQuinn, 1992.

ALFRED I. TAUBER

FROM THE SELF TO THE OTHER: BUILDING A PHILOSOPHY OF MEDICINE

I

How might we view the grounding of medical ethics in philosophy at large, or more specifically, how might we construct the foundations of a secular bioethics? This is easily perceived as an enormous undertaking, and even to suggest its outlines is a bit audacious. But audacity, or perhaps recklessness, should not inhibit philosophers, and so I embark cognizant of my peril. The literature on this topic is immense, and I have made no attempt to review it, nor even rigorously situate my argument with that of others. (See Engelhardt, 1986 and Grodin {this volume} for relevant reviews).[1] Most notably, there is no attempt here to deal with the typical concerns of most discussions construed as the domain of medical ethics, i.e. abortion, euthanasia, informed consent, etc. These may be regarded as particular aspects of the more encompassing issue of patient rights, or more formally, concerns with individual autonomy. Nor do I deal with the broad concerns of medical ethics such as distributive justice, public policy and health reform etc. My concern is an attempt to better define what I believe is the underlying basis of respecting patient autonomy and providing health care, namely the relation of the health care provider and the patient. What is the ethical basis of this relation? This essay explores what some might consider a restricted view of medical ethics, simply the doctor-patient relationship. I believe it is precisely at this encounter that we should devote our efforts in erecting a comprehensive philosophy of medicine that not only encompasses the aforementioned issues, but philosophically situates competing agendas of medical science and technology in their more appropriate places. My effort is then fundamentally concerned with defining the Self-Other relationship from which a comprehensive philosophy of medicine may be built.

Traditionally, "Otherness" emphasizes the responsibilities for Others, i.e. the community as governed by a given moral law. Obviously, adherence to a divine-inspired moral law characterizing this latter case long predates the Romantic reaction of the nineteenth century that asserted the primacy of the "expressive Self," the assertion of self-will and the ethical essentiality of the autonomous moral agent. This Enlightenment tradition relegates self-responsibility and freedom to a self-governing ethical agent. This is the ethical arena to which we assign the *Self*. Beginning with Kant, this Modern Man

M. A. Grodin (ed.), Meta Medical Ethics, 157–195.

was to undergo radical examination and reconstruction, and in its culmination with Nietzsche, an autonomous self-defining ethical being was heralded. My discussion begins with Nietzsche to highlight the cul-de-sac in which the principle of autonomy may situate ethics. I begin seeking the roots of a medical philosophy in what may fairly be regarded as the extreme modernist position of selfhood. The strategy I have chosen is to erect a scaffold between the "Self" and the "Other" on which to build an ethical edifice. The *Self* is the pole of autonomy, whereas the *Other* will serve as the contrasting position of what should be viewed as a dipole. In fact, Self and Other must, and can, only exist as linked. The question is how. I propose that the *Other* serves a constitutive role in defining the *Self*, a position that may fairly be regarded as a response to Nietzsche.

In a strong sense, many roads into twentieth century philosophy may be traced to Nietzsche. From Wittgenstein (Martin, 1989) to Heidegger (1979), Nietzsche's imprint is evident in the project to establish self-authenticity. He challenged the very legitimacy of the Self *qua* Self; the ontological basis of selfhood was in the process radically scrutinized. Some have carried it to a deconstructive finale, whereas a reactive denial was also aroused. And it is here, in the existential responses of Martin Buber, Franz Rosenzweig and their descendent, Emmanuel Levinas, that we find the contrast of what I starkly portray as the *Self-Other* dichotomy. This essay is thus crafted between the poles represented by Nietzsche, who affirmed the *Self* striving alone, and Levinas, whose *Self* is actualized in the encounter with the Other.

From these two disparate positions, distinct ethical philosophies emerge from which I will attempt to localize medicine's moral foundations. So after admitting that to ground medical ethics in a secularized philosophy has been a daunting task, and that the problem may be examined from many conceptual orientations and traced from any one of several points in modern intellectual history, in this essay, I have chosen to begin with Nietzsche as a central architect of what may be referred to as the "self-centered solution". My underlying thesis is that medical ethics must be based on the notion of the Self, both in the obvious terms of self-responsibility, but more fundamentally in the problem of Self as agent. It is in this regard that I first focus on Nietzsche's formulation of such an "entity" in the challenge of an ever-changing selfhood.

The Self in normal parlance implies permanency, a stable configuration. This common sensical notion has come under severe scrutiny ever since Hume challenged such an entity as a Self. The other destabilizing critiques of Rousseau, Hegel and later nineteenth century philosophers served as a major focus of philosophical inquiry of this period (Taylor, 1989; Tauber, 1994a), but by and large in the domain of biology and popular thought, the organism and personal identity were stable, that is, they were regarded as constant over time. This may have been sufficient in a pre-Darwinian world, but the epitome of evolution (which long preceded *The Origin of Species*) does not allow such stability. Change is of the essence - entities are evolving and thus elusive. The notions of change, progress, and becoming are imprinted on our Western consciousness. One might easily argue that the Self has been assaulted by deconstructionists as a contrivance or perhaps a convenience, hardly capable of serving as a regulative identity function from this fundamental instability bestowed by Darwinism. The philosophical consequences as to how Darwinism (more specifically the essential metaphysic of change) drove Nietzsche's construction of a Self based on evolution has been more fully argued elsewhere (Tauber, 1994c). Although a novel ethical position was espoused, Nietzsche's philosophy remained deeply connected to the overarching philosophical tradition from which it originated. Immediately this position assigns Nietzsche to the status of a modernist (i.e. Thiele, 1990; Pippin, 1991; Tauber, 1994a), who still attempts to construct a *Self* despite the assaults on positing such an entity at all. If we compare him to any of the post-modernists (e.g. Foucault {Tauber, 1994b}), Nietzsche is distinguished from them not by the problem of the "doubtful Self," but by his desparate efforts to affirm the Self's very legitimacy.[2]

This problem of identifying the Self, no longer tethered or stable is the basis of our philosophical unrest concerning its philosophical nature. And it is this basic issue of selfhood that confuses us in our attempts to formulate a philosophy of medicine, and more particularly firmly ground medical ethics in a more comprehensive philosophy. I suspect that in large measure the impediment to establishing a philosophy of medicine resides in the readily available "solution" to the issues concerning selfhood. As long as the Self remains in "doubt," we will be thwarted in finding a firm foundation for medical philosophy. It seems to me that a crucial first step in articulating such a philosophy is to firmly re-establish the foundations of a humane orientation in the affirmation of the Self as an ethical agent.

The argument developed here is that Nietzsche's ethic is based on an understanding of the organism that is a response to the Darwinian challenge of his time. From his understanding of organic being, Nietzsche placed the will to power as the foundation of organismic identity and from this base assigned health or sickness to the success of the organism in both integrating the competing inner drives and using them for self-aggrandizement. The ethic then develops from the demand to fulfill this *organic* identity. Nietzsche's "medical ethic" *arises* from the notion of health, or more pointedly to *how* health is to be achieved in a world where Zarathustra teaches to overcome. My initial motivation was stimulated by Nietzsche's exquisite delineation of what it means to be sick and which philosophical issues must be addressed in order to heal. After all, there are few modern philosophers who were so pre-occupied with their bodies. Obviously Nietzsche's medical illnesses and psychosomatic suffering dominated much of his everyday existence, and served as a dominant personal concern. Although this biographical fact is of interest in discerning the possible psycho-historical elements that might "explain" his philosophy, it is not particularly germane to my concerns of tracing how the *Self* becomes the focus of his inquiry. The true basis of my analysis resides in Nietzsche's metaphysical cognizance of the elusive, changing Self.

In his achievement of turning the problem of escaped essence into the very basis of the self's definition, we are the philosophical beneficiaries. But my conclusion is that Nietzsche's autonomous ideal is an insufficient basis for medicine's ethics, and I will therefore outline an alternative position, where the *relation* of Self and Other better serves as a foundation upon which to build medicine's moral philosophy. The weakness of Nietzsche's solution is its inability to satisfactorily account for an *Other*, namely the requirement of establishing the basis of *relation* - a Self with another. In this sense then the "self-centered" solution has a double meaning: first the *Self* is affirmed, but second, the Self is in a sense held captive to itself. Nietzsche's philosophy of the Self must fail as a basis of a comprehensive ethics, because he eschews the fundamental concern with intersubjectivity. After a Self is affirmed, it is the relation with others that constitutes the ethical encounter. Nietzsche only carries us part way. But to examine his thesis is useful for how he delineates the philosophical issues pertinent to defining selfhood in a post-modern world, where the challenge of ever-changing identity, contingent on cultural values and historical necessity leaves a subject, *qua* ethical agent, very much in doubt. Thus this essay approaches how one might ground medical ethics in its broader philosophical context by examining what I perceive as the fundamental question of how an ethical agent might be defined in the milieu of deconstructivist assault. We must turn to other philosophers to seek responses to how the Self, so elusive and "demoralized," might affirm an integral element of its core character, namely its ability to interact with an Other. All this is then preparatory to discussing how the essential philosophical tension is addressed, and why medicine must be grounded in an ethical formulation of the Self. These matters will be presented first from Nietzsche's perspective and then from that of Levinas' opposing view.

II.

Let us begin our discussion with Nietzsche's philosophy of the body.[3] Overall, Nietzsche clearly conceived of the body as a dynamic system emerging from favorable internal (and often unrecognized) struggle and competition. His conception of health, in view of such struggle, is not only the capacity of the body to overcome resistance, but its willingness to posit such resistance as well. All of these conceptions critically depend upon the centrality of the self's will to power. Nietzsche's clearest statements regarding the body are from *Thus Spoke Zarathustra*: "In the Despisers of the Body," Part I, Zarathustra declares:

> The awakened and knowing say: body am I entirely, and nothing else; and soul is only a word for something about the body. The body is a great reason, a plurality with one sense, a war and a peace, a herd and a shepherd. ...Behind your thoughts and feelings, my brother, there stands a mighty ruler, an unknown sage - whose name itself. In your body he dwells; he is your body (Nietzsche, 1885, 1959 at 146).

Nietzsche thus first establishes the fundamental status of the body (as opposed to consciousness, the soul, etc.) and its multiplicitous nature. Then, in *On the Genealogy of Morals* Nietzsche introduces the concepts of complexity, activity, and conflict, especially in essay 2, section 1. Therein he writes:

> To remain undisturbed by the noise and struggle of our underworld of utility organs working with and against one another; a little quietness, a little tabula rosa of the consciousness, to make room for new things, above all for the nobler functions and functionaries, for regulation, foresight, premeditation (for our organism is an oligarchy) - that is the purpose of active forgetfulness, which is like a doorkeeper, a preserver of psychic order, repose, and etiquette (Nietzsche, 1887; 1967b at 57-58).

Such a conception of the body is fully developed in *The Will to Power* (1904, 1907), which is fundamentally concerned with both reducing the exalted human to the animal, physiological level of the body and explicating the status of the body as such. Nietzsche reduces consciousness to the body in many places, for example:

> More and more decisively the question concerning the health of the body is put ahead of that of "the soul": the latter being understood as a state consequent upon the former, and the former at the very least as a precondition of the health of the soul (Nietzsche, 1904, 1967a at 72).[4]

Next, Nietzsche introduces the "drives," driven by individual wills to power. Every drive, in as much as it is active, sacrifices force and other drives: finally it is checked; otherwise it would destroy everything through its excessiveness (Nietzsche, 1904, 1967a at 372).

Nietzsche fully substantiates his account of the intra-organismically struggling, multiplicitous, hierarchical body, constructed of various antagonisms and alliances: What is common to all: the ruling drives want to be viewed also as the highest courts of value in general, indeed as creative and ruling powers. It is clear that these drives either oppose or subject each other (join together synthetically or alternate in dominating) (Nietzsche, 1904, 1967a at 359).

Thus, Nietzsche applies Darwinism to the body itself. Each drive is motivated by a need to discharge force, to vent its built-up will to power against actively sought resistances, which is the fundamental reduction of Nietzsche's conception of the body to multiple wills to power.[5] This formulation serves as Nietzsche's foundational conception of health.

With this short summary of Nietzsche's view of the body, we can now turn to his notions of health, which steadily evolved to eventually dominate his worldview, and ultimately would serve as a new morality. Although his views on health changed, i.e. different elements were added and elaborated over time, a consistent reading of "health" can be applied to all of Nietzsche's writings, even if certain of its elements at a given moment were more implicit than explicit. In general, the following six components characterize the Nietzschean conception of health: 1) Life is defined by struggle and disharmony at all levels, with the ability to harmonize and create order from chaos as a measure of individual power. This may represent Apollo taming Dionysus or the will to power, but the underlying conception is the same. 2) In the absence of truth, God, and absolute good and evil, one can only live well, looking for those values most useful to the good, powerful, self-creative life. Such resultant activities may range from aesthetic creation to warlike conquest in the name of such values. 3) Since self-creation involves constant redefinition in a changing environment, one must constantly pose resistances to oneself and overcome them. The inability to even pose such resistance represents sickliness (See Letteri, 1990 at 411; Nietzsche, *Will to Power*, 1904, 1967a, stanza #47, 29-30.). The inability to overcome such posed resistance reveals one's sickness. The ability to both pose and overcome such resistance represents health - great health. 4) Since each individual is the outcome of a unique, contingent history of struggle, and since greatness can be accomplished in many ways, no two types of individual greatness need be equal. Hence, there is no single static norm of health - the only constant of health is the degree of power which individuals expend successfully. 5) Health of the body and health of the mind are not only physiologically related, but operate according to parallel principles of resistance, struggle, and creative overcoming. Therefore, the great thinker is healthy when he can challenge his principles and incorporate anomalies into new and expanded world views. 6) Hence, the philosopher as physician of the soul and physician of culture functions by challenging prevailing principles and by forcing society and its individuals to acknowledge and incorporate anomalies in their own world views (Podolsky & Tauber, 1995).

To derive an ethic based on Nietzsche's conception of health requires a sensitive interpretation of several interwoven themes: first, the conception of the primacy of the body, second, truth is replaced with health, good and evil with good (health) and bad (sickness), and finally, a recognition of the centrality of the will to power, as Darwinian struggle. For Nietzsche, health is the manifestation of the will to power's actively searching for and overcoming resistances in a constant process of redefinition.[6] Health is defined as the will to seek resistance and overcome; it is a measure of the will to power, if any such measure exists. As Nietzsche noted of his task, well before Zarathustra, the issue becomes "how a new circle of duties may be derived from this ideal and how one can proceed towards so extravagant a goal" (Nietzsche, 1874, 1983 at 156). The ethic becomes a self-centered effort by which the thoughtless inertia of our lives is jolted into a constant critique of ourselves that directs its energies towards a self-defining ideal. In this sense, Nietzsche's thought is thoroughly permeated by an evolutionary metaphysic. Change is of the essence, but it must be harnessed in a self-fulfilling telos. The ethic is thus not only based on the underlying foundation of change recognized as an essential component of our being, but our being is transfigured into an ethical drive towards our self-perfection.

Nietzsche's philosophy assumes its most profound biological orientation in the Eternal Return, which is fundamentally organic in its implicit connotations of renewal, regeneration, recurrence. There are those who understand the Return as a cosmological principle; the reasons for rejecting this interpretation are amply argued elsewhere (Nehamas, 1985 at 142-167). Philosophically, Nietzsche uses the Return not as a theory of the world, but of the Self. The interpretation of eternal recurrence must reside in a consistent reading of Nietzsche's concepts of the will to power and its corollary, becoming as true being.

> Let us think this thought in its most terrible form: existence as it is, without meaning or aim, yet recurring inevitably without any finale of nothingness: "the eternal recurrence" (Nietzsche, 1904, 1967a at 35).

In a profound sense, Nietzsche envisions that the Return is the fulfillment of living each moment, each act, each choice without the demurrals of past remorse or future judgment. We are enjoined to live as if each moment is to be relived, unchanged, into eternity. Eternal recurrence is the final destination of a deeply rooted evolutionary process, a calling which should become an ethic of our biological being, independent of any transcendent principle. With that perspective, each moment is not only immutable, but precious, and forever accountable to ourselves. Nietzsche's recurrence does not refer "to a life precisely like this one, but to *this very life*" (Williams, 1952 at 100). "I come again, with this sun, with this earth, with this eagle, with this serpent - not to a new life or a better life or a similar life: I come back eternally to this same, selfsame life... to each again the eternal recurrence of all things...to proclaim the overman again to men" (Nietzsche, 1885, 1959 at 333). He thus would imbue the quality of eternity into every moment, and lead us to a supreme self-awareness of the ultimate and inescapable responsibility for our acts. The last element of the ethic then is to accept the irrevocability of every choice allowing us to assume the mandate of responsibility for our life, a life to be lived again and again, eternally.[7] If God is dead, then our morality must be based on our self-willed sovereignty. Responsibility then resides solely in the Self, whose identity is based on fully acknowledging the primacy of the will to power and living its mandate freed of false and encumbering moral restrictions. This is a commitment only the strong can assume, for the sick sigh, "If only I were someone else" (Nietzsche, 1887, 1967c at 122). If life is to be eternally recurrent, then we must accept living in the present in its full and self-sufficient complement. Time is framed not in the past or future, but accompanies us, moving steadily forward in the present. In this sense, Nietzsche accepts "becoming," but he does so with the particular proviso of apprehending the omnipotent present as full being, which in turn entails the rejection of becoming as an end or goal.

> The everything recurs is the closest approximation of a world of becoming to a world of being: high point of the meditation (Nietzsche, 1904, 1967a at 33).

Thus by removing extraneous moral contexts, life is lived as full and unencumbered will. The will, alone on its own axis, unselfconsciously knows no past or future.

> The will cannot will backwards; and that he cannot break time and time's covetousness, that is the will's loneliest melancholy (Nietzsche, 1885, 1959d at 251).

The Eternal Return, as an *ethical* mandate, becomes the ultimate assertion of that will. It is precisely the raising of man, the animal, from the one-dimensional will to a second ethical dimension: a moral exercise of will alters the Self, which thereby becomes freed and healed. The power of the eternal recurrence can be seen in its full expression in Nietzsche's radical reconstruction: the very past may be altered by the will in the present:

> The will is a creator. All "it was" is a fragment, a riddle, a dreadful accident - until the creative will says to it, "But this I willed." Until the creative will says to it, "But thus I will it; thus shall I will it" (ibid. at 253).

The present vision of the Self,thus defines the past and, if the present is accepted, then all that has led to that juncture has been enjoined. Most important, the past as forming the future is acknowledged. Thus to accept the present in Nietzsche's terms is to have willed all that led to this moment. Finally, "the significance of the past lies in its relationship to the future. And since the future is yet to come, neither the significance of the past nor its nature is yet settled" (Nehamas, 1985 at 160-61). Here then is an expansive ethic, in which a fully creative will is celebrated and redemption may be thus attained.

But by what guidelines would Nietzsche suggest that man alone, in the absence of another, can experience his full will and accomplish this mandate? Again he returns to biological criteria, where the organism is most fully alive - in a state that he called rapture. Rapture is attained in its highest context through the achievement of an aesthetic, which incorporates man's fully cognitive, emotional and spiritual strengths - each a manifestation of the will to power! The centrality of rapture in experiencing the aesthetic has been well-described as originating in Nietzsche's concept of the Dionysian, and this aspect will not be further discussed (see Heidegger, 1979). My purpose is simply to note this primal organic response of the Self to its experience, which captures man's biological sensibility and integrates the highest intelligent, cognitive functions with visceral emotion. Nietzsche is essentially curing nihilism, serving as "the teacher of the life-affirming Dionysian relationship to existence, of the morality of development and growth, and of the Übermensch (Overman) whose attainment lies in continual and creative self-overcoming and self-perfection" (Aloni at 5).[8] Moreover, since health is equated with the active search for obstacles to be overcome, at the cultural level the physician (and in fact each of us) should "educate ourselves '*against* our times'" (Nietzsche, 1874, 1983 at 146).[9] We might only allude to the contrast between Nietzsche and those who purportedly have followed him, specifically Michael Foucault. The contrast is offered only to highlight

Nietzsche's quest and ultimate affirmation of the Self with the post-modernist effort to deny that mandate (Tauber, 1994b).

Despite Nietzsche's disjointed writings, aphoristic style, and poetic hyperbole, there remains a consistency of purpose and direction of his thought. He endeavored to become physician to the soul, presenting a means towards achieving a transvaluation of values, an ethos of self-realization and growth. Not only is there an exuberance in his elucidation of will to power, it is firmly anchored in a characterization of the organic that is developed into a psychology guided by a normative ideal to "become." Foucault's ethics have no such orientation and arrive as an appendix to his major inquiry (Tauber, 1994b). The very idea of the Self is in question, which is the radical extension of Nietzsche's essential ethic, overcoming the Self. For Nietzsche the Self evolves, for Foucault its identity is always in doubt. Ethics is the casualty of Foucault's relentless dissection, for the Self is quite simply dissolved. Without the Self, an ethics is impossible, yet Foucault is exhilarated at the potential that a new awareness provides. In the examination of what constitutes selves in their cultural/historical context, Foucault does not seek "a new form of Self (that is, a new kind of ethic)... but makes modern ethics and morality optional as a form of human life" (Scott, 1990 at 55).[10] Instead of offering a structure of values, Foucault simply presents a "philosophical ethos consisting in a critique of what we are saying, thinking, and doing, through a historical ontology of ourselves" (Foucault, 1984 at 45). This is criticism, not ethics. In rejecting the metaphysics of subjectivity and arguing the contingency of the Self, Foucault has not elaborated any substantive alternative to humanism (Fraser, 1983 at 56). His "ethics" are left adrift in post-modern relativism. But he has (to his credit as an heir to Nietzschean skepticism) warned "against the erroneous variety of ways in which humanistic rhetoric has been and is liable to misuse and cooptation" (ibid. at 68). No small feat, but it can not be confused with his failed efforts to transcend humanism and replace it with something new.

The challenge bequeathed by Nietzsche is how the Self might *define itself* as it strives towards some undeclared and nebulous ideal. There is no "norm" that defines selfhood - that represents a pre-Darwinian notion of stable and definable boundaries. The Self evolves. Nietzsche's general formulation, so relevant to a philosophy of medicine, is often ignored. Consider, "The idea that a subject's health is identical with his ability to realize the goals *set by himself* is a promising approach suggested recently, and independently by two analytic philosophers, Caroline Whitbeck and Izymar Pörn" (Nordenfelt, 1987 at 65). Neither Brown (1985), Nordenfelt (1987), Pörn (1984), nor Whitbeck (1978, 1981) recognize the debt to Nietzsche for first articulating the underlying metaphysical argument for this position, and its application for our notions of health.[11] But each fails to articulate the primary source for their shared understanding of health in Nietzsche's writings, and thereby forfeit an important consideration of its full philosophical implications. Whitbeck's concerns with "ultimate goals" and Pörn's explicit introduction of "ideality" clearly resonate Nietzsche's own orientation.[12]

The very conceptual foundation of this understanding of organismal identity and integrity resides in a construction that echoes Nietzsche's essential principles governing the Self. The Self is not a given, established object, but lives as a dynamic and dialectical entity, evolving in time - developmentally and experientially. Its boundaries are ever-changing and thus the Self is constantly in the process of redefinition.[13] *Goalless* evolution, where only potentialities are recognized, allows for evolution to assume *sui generis*, a *value* in itself. No longer a "given," Man gropes toward the ideal. But this ideality is not a definable goal. In this sense, the ideal represents, alone and unqualified, evolutionary movement. Changes, adjustment, improvement are the responses of life to its challenges, both external and from within.[14] The ideal, the possible, the contingent potential has replaced our sense of finitude, a world with definable boundaries. Awash in this uncertain cosmos is the Self, whose own sense gathers tenuously within elusive categories and pliable structure.

We are still somewhat uncomfortable with the shifting foundations of this construct. We seek firmer definition, and we do so within a modernist tradition, as did Nietzsche. The striving for freedom as self-aggrandizement is clearly articulated by Nietzsche, the modernist, whose ideals still allow for autonomy and self-actualization. As elusive as such an identity might be, it still represents an attainable ideal.[15] Acknowledging that Nietzsche has offered us a challenging ethical mandate for the Self, it is still incomplete. The fundamental Nietzschean failure resides in the self-centered, even narcissistic pre-occupation with the self-contained Self. The positive ethic of self-responsibility and self-realization may easily be over-extended to "selfishness" or self-consuming narcissism. When so perverted, innervated energy is converted to power as domination. Nietzsche the cultural physician versus the proto-fascist is obviously a complex problem that continues to generate debate (e.g. Schultle, 1984; Aschheim, 1993), but few would argue that having enunciated his views of the Self, he satisfactorily dealt with the relation to the Other. To approach this issue we must turn to another venue altogether.

III

Emmanuel Levinas' philosophy has increasingly demanded attention.[16] He has argued in his major work, *Totality and Infinity* (Levinas, 1961, 1969) that philosophy must address the individual's unavoidable responsibility for others. His is a comprehensive ethic which would ground epistemology and metaphysics in this ethical encounter. The Self is not only epistemologically defined in relation to the Other, but the very nature of our being resides in that intersubjectivity. I outline his philosophy to present an alternative to the Nietzschean "self-centered" construction, and to highlight the inadequacy of the Übermensch ethic. The fundamental "grounding," of medical ethics must account for both "selfness" and "relation." I am aware that there is a split agenda in this essay. On the one hand, I have attempted to depict the autonomous position at the cusp where modernity precepts begin to converge with a post-modernist view of the contingent Self, doubtful of its elusive moral boundaries. The point of that exercise was to emphasize that for all its philosophical strength for arguing the autonomous case, there is no basis for establishing a relational component. The remainder of this essay poses the alternative formulation, where *relation* defines the Self. The concern in this latter case is not so much to situate particular ethical problems as to ground medical practice *in toto* within an ethical orientation. I believe it is on the foundation of a relational philosophy that a comprehensive medical philosophy should be built. Levinas' argument represents an interesting and potentially fecund path for such a philosophy to pursue.

Levinas is fundamentally an existential phenomenologist, and it is in the framework of an ontological inquiry that his argument is structured.[17] His thought is heavily indebted to Husserl's phenomenological analyses, where the attempt to examine how phenomena appears in our consciousness, to grasp our lived experience, regulates Levinas' own approach. I have summarized Husserl's philosophy of the Self elsewhere (Tauber, 1994a), and suffice it to simply state here that "the I, even in its purity as a 'pure ego' — sheer 'I-hood' — is individual as act" (Kohák, 1978 at 203). It is at this point of action that Levinas initiates his own phenomenological project. For Levinas, the Self must detach itself from being and thereby discover its alterity and thus itself. He distinguishes a consciousness that does not "think" but "lives" non-reflectively. Thought begins with a reflection on this primordial consciousness, and in thought the outside world then exists as non-self. Thought represents to itself what is extrinsic to it and thus perception and appropriation is defined by this self-consciousness. Alterity is established only in the non-reciprocity of relation, where the Self moves beyond the ease of living without reflection to recognizing that "Being is exteriority, and exteriority is produced in its truth in a subjective field, for the separated being" (Levinas, 1961, 1969 at 299). In the radical separation *and* relationship with the *Other* (produced simultaneously), the subject becomes a "host," or in the vocabulary of this essay, a true *Self.* "Separation is the very act of individuation ... The fact of starting from oneself is equivalent to separation" (ibid.). This is a crucial step in erecting the ethical framework, which is in direct opposition to the Nietzschean view, namely the self-aggrandizing aspirations of natural (non-reflective) man are negated, if not destroyed, through the encounter with the Other.

I would simply note here, as an aside, that Levinas is not posing the Self in a totally novel fashion. There are antecedents of the Self fashioned in relation to Others in Hegel and Marx. Note that Sartre too would adopt a Self in a contextual perspective. We are in fact together-in-the-world; it is through the Other's responses that I get a sense of the quality of my own being. Moreover, in carrying out my own projects, I inevitably infringe on the world of others. This is a basic phenomenological construct: As intentional activity, consciousness makes itself *be* by its choice of action in the world. The Self is essentially engaged in the world and responsible for what both itself and the world become. Ethical responsibility with regard to others rests on the recognition that in acting on the world one inevitably changes it for others, as well as for oneself. This is the same starting point for Heidegger, Sartre and Levinas. A dramatic separation then occurs.

Like Heidegger, the question of authenticity is the focus of Levinas' inquiry. But Levinas is no Heideggarian, and he robustly rejects him at several points. First, note Nietzsche's relevance for Heidegger (1979), in particular how power constitutes being, which according to Levinas prohibits power from even becoming the source of values. Perhaps more fundamentally, Levinas argued that our genuine ipseity resides in our recognition of the infinite, which cannot be understood through reason. Since Heidegger places the *power* of reason as the modus of understanding being, he cannot, according to Levinas, establish an understanding of the infinite, which is fundamental to understanding the Other.[18] The ability to recognize the Other, to establish ourselves in relation to the Other and thereby define ourselves is the central theme of Levinas' thought.[19]

This realignment of how the Self is grounded rests most fundamentally in recognizing the infinite Other (and the need for transcendence - the very basis of ethical existence), and in the social domain of human existence where man must live with (similarly self-fulfilling) others. *Relation* then defines the Self. This construction extends to the body, which in Levinas' view forms only the "adverb" from which self-reflective consciousness emerges: "The body appear[s] not as an object among other objects, but as the very regime in which separation holds sway, as the 'how' of this separation and so to speak as an adverb rather than as a substantive" (Levinas, 1961, 1969 at 163). Note the body is accorded a special locus in the universe of objects, but in the Levinasian world, it is relegated to a subordinate adverbial status, unlike the primacy afforded the body in Nietzsche's philosophy. The consequences from an ethical point of view are crucial; the selfness of the Self does not reside as body qua body (the primacy of the biological), but in self-reflectiveness (which posits an internal disjunction) and encounter with subsequent definition of Self by the Other.

In a sense, the vital Self -- the unconscious, non-reflective Self, the Nietzschean will -- is only the prelude to the Self that recognizes itself through the Other. According to Levinas, the Self is only fully realized in relation. The will of Schopenhauer and Nietzsche is no longer sufficient towards defining the Self, and the body has lost its dominance, albeit not its orienting role.[20] Levinas acknowledges that experience begins with the body, that we engage the world and establish ourselves in that world through the body, which thus provides our point of view and serves as the "cross-roads of physical forces [and by standing] on the earth, to be in the Other" (Levinas, 1961, 1969 at 164). But at the same time, the Nietzschean pre-occupation with self-definition of selfhood is eclipsed by reaching *out* of the body into the world. More importantly, to be human for Levinas is the ability to separate, to self-reflect on our very consciousness. In this very act of contemplating our "Self," what distinguishes ourselves as perceiving and feeling beings, is to discover the very basis of our humanity. Thus to separate, first to recognize that we are in fact a Self, then to separate ourselves from the world and thus define ourselves within that context, is but preliminary to the final separation of the finite from the infinite. The separated being is no longer one with the totality of being. Here, in the knowledge that the world and ourselves are situated in an infinity of space/time is to acknowledge that we must encounter, engage and recognize the infinite Other.

Levinas seeks man's true nature in his confrontation with the infinite. And how is the infinite perceived? The isolated Self -- in Levinas' terms, the Self in its ironic totality -- is extroverted to face "infinity." The encounter with the *face*, as a metaphor of the infinite, eclipses circumscribed totality. The structure of the encounter in its simplest format is that we are defined by our encounter with the infinite, with the Divine Other, and by extrapolation such encounters with the (mundane) *Other* -- the metaphorical face -- serves the same existential function. In short, Levinas seeks in the face a transcendence of totality to infinity, which is the encounter that fully actualizes the Self. Levinas then is diametrically opposed to Nietzsche, who would regard the Other as a resistance, a *face* to be contended and overcome. It is the transfiguration of power that is at stake here. Force and countervalent force are measures of totality, and as already explained, Levinas seeks in the face a transcendence of totality. Thus the *face* serves as the means to reaffirm (perhaps in different guises) our ethical encounter with the infinite. Man cannot be regarded in his complete potential without the inclusion of his fundamental relation to the infinite, and it is the *face* that expresses infinity.

> The face is present in its refusal to be contained. In this sense it cannot be comprehended, that is encompassed... The Other remains infinitely transcendent, infinitely foreign; his face...breaks with the world that can be common to us, whose virtualities are inscribed in our nature and developed by our existence (Levinas, 1961, 1969 at 194).

In dialogue, the need to respond to the Other finalizes the Self's own reality. This attention to the Other is not an actualization of a potential because it is not even conceivable without the Other. This is the point where Levinas makes his most interesting conjecture: the Other, specifically the encounter with another person, ultimately defines the Self:

> It is only in approaching the Other that I attend to myself. This does not mean that my existence is constituted in the thought of others. An existence called objective... does not express me, but precisely dissimulates me (Levinas, 1961,1969 at 178).

The encounter with the world is always "personal" or self-centered. In Nietzsche's view everything is oriented to the perceiving subject. "I am stuck with myself and my own intentionality, stuck like an insomniac who cannot find any way to escape the assimilating power of consciousness. The Self as ipseity is isolated and secluded" (Gibbs, 1992 at 182). But in the encounter with an Other there is both the presentation of vulnerability of that face and the astonishment of its incomprehensibility. More than framing the response, the encounter actualizes the Self. To be self-contained, or self-sufficient, to exist in Levinas' terms in a totality is to deny the infinite. The presence of the face challenges this complacency, permitting man to acknowledge "the difference between being and phenomenon, [to] recognize his phenomenality, the penury of his plenitude, a penury inconvertible into needs which, being beyond plenitude and void, cannot be gratified" (Levinas, 1961, 1969 at 179-180). In short, as long as the existence of man remains confined to inferiority, it is limited to the phenomenal. To exist for or with another offers the unique possibility to live in more than interior existence (ibid. at 182). "This means concretely: the face speaks to me and thereby invites me to a relation incommensurate with a power exercised, be it enjoyment or knowledge" (ibid. at 198). For Levinas, "the epiphany of infinity is expression and discourse," where a being presents itself and to which the I must respond (ibid. at 200). The presence of the face is not to be ranked among other meaningful manifestations, nor a modality of coexistence, nor even of knowledge, but is "the primordial production of being" (ibid. at 305).

From this position, Levinas constructs his ethics, for beyond defining the Self, he would make the encounter with the Other explicitly moral. In final analysis, the Self can fully actualize itself only in engagement, and engagement for Levinas denotes response. Herein, the ethical dimension is revealed, for to respond is to exhibit the Self's *responsibility* to (for!) the Other. The face, more specifically the encounter with that face, becomes a moral space, the locus of the possibility of all those expressions that are the basis of a moral life. Perhaps it is useful to think of this space as one of ethical possibilities, filling "the content" of a person's view of the world. But more, Levinas would build into our ordinary experience the demand for a moral response: "the epiphany of the face is ethical" (ibid. at 199). Encounter and confrontation, the resistances of Nietzsche's will, have become in Levinas' moral universe, self -definitional.

A fascinating antecedent position is expressed by Descartes in the third *Meditation,* and I wish to discuss it as a means of situating Levinas in the modernist - post-modernist debate. Descartes wrote, "In some manner I had within me the notion of the infinite before I had the notion of the finite, that is, that of God before that of myself" (Descartes, 1968 at 124). Descartes sensed the infinite as constitutive of his very selfhood; Levinas encounters the infinite and thereby fully actualizes the Self. There are obviously powerful repercussions in these opposing positions. Most critics characterize Levinas as a post-modernist, and this contrast with Descartes might exemplify the modernist divide. For Levinas must seek the infinite Other by casting for the divine upon a sea of doubt. To define Self through the Other is an uncertain, if not potentially haphazard endeavor. Contrast this quest with the Cartesian affirmation. Although framed in his own deep skepticism, Descartes is still able to proclaim the I with a certitude we no longer possess. Note, both the Self and the Other are affirmed, essentially together. But our age is characterized by no such security. As Wittgenstein wrote in his early notebooks (1914-1916), it seems almost with a sigh echoing through the rest of the century, "The I, the I is what is deeply mysterious" (Wittgenstein, 1979 at 80e). But Levinas defies this post-modern placement, because he essentially ends in the same position as Descartes. First, he recognizes in a deep sense the possibility of the infinite as constitutive. After all, there must be some motive force to drive the Self out of its circumscribed totality. In Levinas' attempt to contrast, and still link himself to this Cartesian passage, he wrote in "God and Philosophy" (originally published in 1975) that we begin with "the idea of the *Infinite, Infinity in me* [as] ...a passivity of consciousness" (Levinas, 1987a at 160). Here, he recognizes a pre-conscious potential, which can only be actualized in self-conscious engagement. Then the Self is ultimately realized as it actively encounters the infinite. The sequence is a primordial, unreflective consciousness, separating to contemplate the world, and itself, which finally leads to encounter with the Other. The seeking out of the Other, the perception of the face as infinite, is motivated by sensing the incompleteness of totality, which represents a vague Cartesian intuition of the divine Other. But for Levinas this pre-conscious, passive sense of the divine is both unformed and ontologically vague, in sharp contrast to Cartesian indisputable belief. Nevertheless, there is a finalization: Through encounter the Self will be realized. There is an end point -- elusive, uncertain, and problematic -- but at least there is potential closure. On this basis I resist assigning Levinas to the post-modernists.

So to recapitulate, the structure of Levinas' argument might be summarized as follows: the Self is held together by the understanding of what it is not. The triviality of our everyday lives obscures the alterity of the Other. In the rigorous, contemplative pursuit of the Other, in the sphere of the intersubjective, we must truly encounter the Other, ethically, i.e. in *response*. The Self cannot contain the infinite, which by its very definition must be separated from the Self, residing in a radically different domain, beyond our comprehension. We might only "approach" or "intend" the infinite, but in so doing, we become truly realized. It is then in the face as an expression of the infinite we recognize the limits of our experience as "totality." Totality is used ironically: we are not true selves until we face the infinite. The contrast with Nietzsche is again striking, for in this formulation Levinas asserts the absolute negation of our powers. "We abandon the will to power; we will not will. What resists us is non-resistance, an 'ethical resistance'. The face is that which appears before us as unmediated; it is an epiphany, a direct and true presentation of the non-self" (Wyschogrod, 1974 at 93). This existential encounter might be viewed as profoundly emptying the Self of itself, and placing the Self in question. But Levinas regards ethics as an "optics," the "royal road" by which relation to truth is to be established (Levinas, 1961, 1969 at 29). In this reading, Levinas defies a post-modern label. And regarding our dominant concern, man's ethical relation to the Other is ultimately prior to his ontological relation to himself or to the totality of things that we call the world. To truly encounter an Other as a stranger, an unknown and an unreducible to our sameness, forces us to place everything that we are into question. This encounter is the essential challenge of selfhood:

> To be I is, over and beyond any individuation that can be derived from a system of reference, to have identity as one's content. The I is not a being that always remains the same, but is the being whose existing consists in identifying itself, in recovering its identity throughout all that happens to it. It is the primal identity, the primordial work of identification (ibid. at 36).

And it is the intersubjective encounter that affords this self-definition. As we recognize the Other, the infinite, the non-self, we discover ourselves.

I am defined as a subjectivity, as a singular person; as an "I," precisely because I am exposed to the Other. It is my inescapable and incontrovertible answerability to the Other that makes me an individual "I." So that I become a responsible or ethical "I" to the extent that I agree to depose or dethrone myself - to abdicate my position of centrality - in favor of the vulnerable Other (Levinas, 1986 at 27).

Nietzsche would no doubt scoff at such a proposal. Fully resounding a Biblical ethos, Levinas clearly has the deity on his agenda.[21] He unabashedly follows the existentialism of Kierkegaard and Buber,[22] reconfirming *homo religiosus* from a phenomenological critique of ontology. Metaphysics thus precedes ontology (Levinas 1961, 1969 at 42ff), and it is an ethical metaphysics that grounds his entire philosophy.[23]

Before I proceed in my attempt to apply this position to medicine, let me address the most obvious objection to Levinas' argument. Perhaps the most succinct counter-proposal is Sartre's "Hell is Others," the summary statement in his play *No Exit*. As Hazel Barnes has written (1989), if Hell is Others, it is because of the tyranny of the look by which one person turns the Other into an object. This language is not entirely metaphorical. I *am* an object, though not exclusively so. In extreme cases my body may be literally manipulated or treated as a thing, as for example, the Jew in the Holocaust. According to Sartre, in normal circumstances, human relations are a fluctuating battle of subjects and objects which nobody finally wins. Psychologically the goal is to secure one's own being. The one who cherishes the illusion of being only a subject precludes the possibility of inter-relation or growth from contact with others, for in such encounter, we must recognize that we become objects too. It is this incessant dialectical engagement of *Self* and *Other*, where each is defined by the Other that the phenomenological project is focused. We are all both subjects and objects. To escape from the dehumanized final objectification is what Sartre calls "the look," and Levinas, "the face." The exchange must become the mutual pledge and invitation to acknowledge and accept the respect for each other's subjectivity, our respective selfness. I believe Levinas has pointed at how such a project is approached -- we recognize the divine infinite in the Other, assume *response-ibility* for it, and thereby, define ourselves. Alterity begets ipseity through responsibility. This is the crucial twist to simple encounter: we are defined by responsibility for the Other.

IV

Nietzsche to Levinas! How might one begin to sketch in a philosophy of medicine on such a tensioned manifold? I believe it is precisely upon this tension that such a philosophy must be erected. The conflict in fact begins at a common point - the Self. Each seeks to identify the basis by which the unity of the Self may be understood, and dispel those attempts that would disallow such a being (And each does so as a post-rationalist!) This is actually a crucial commonality at a time when the very legitimacy of selfhood beyond mere convenience and contingency is more than the faint howlings of a small cadre of critics. The implications are profound for *any* ethics. To participate in any ethical dialogue a responsible agent must be a *Self*, an integrity of being. The tension between Nietzsche and Levinas rather resides in how to establish the ethical foundation of the responsible agent. For Nietzsche, the competitive nature of man is determinant, and from a metaphysic of change and eternal recurrence, we must become committed to an ethos of overcoming, to perpetually struggle and re-define ourselves. Levinas would confront eternity in exactly the opposite fashion: we become selves *in* the encounter with the Other, not by means of self-generated actualization as Nietzsche believed. For Levinas, autonomy is a mark of irresponsibility.[24] Whereas Nietzsche proclaimed the death of God as the liberation that demanded self-responsibility, for Levinas, death is death of the Other. We can not assert, nor define ourselves without the Other.[25] It is this divine-inspired "Otherness" to which Levinas alludes and would not escape. He has, however, performed a marvelous sleight of hand. The infinite Other has been presented in the neutral terms of existentialist phenomenology.[26] The question remains as to how influential such a formulation might become.

To complete the theme introduced at the beginning of this discussion, the ethical enterprise must encompass two distinct, albeit overlapping positions. The first resides in positing and respecting the autonomous agent. This is the fundamental problem of selfhood and given the challenges of his time and the direction assumed by his post-modernist followers, Nietzsche clearly represents a crucial formulation of the modernist "Self" role. The threads of that concern appear in a highly woven matrix dealing with questions of individual autonomy and self-reliance (see endnote #15), which have served as the foundation of many bioethical philosophies (e.g., Engelhardt, 1986).[27] The contrasting element to the basic concern with autonomy resides in the relational aspect, the "Otherness" of responsibility. The most obvious point to be made, and also the most important, is that in medicine the "problem" of the Other vanishes. If "Hell is the Others" reflects the practical limits of Levinas' metaphysical ethics, medicine begins with that question already resolved. By dictate, by fiat, by assumption the Other is "given" by the ethical responsibility accepted by the healer. Physicians and nurses are in principle committed to the care of the patient, and in this fundamental sense, the health care provider is in fact defined by this responsibility. In a trivial sense, the physician-patient relation is already presented *a priori* as one of responsibility. In this setting, medicine offers us a particularly interesting application of Levinasian ethics. The religious origins of medicine are readily exposed and serve in his cause...and our own. At heart I see modern medicine, even in its highly technical and scientific garb, as only a more sophisticated application of the healing arts to the ministries of care, to the sufferer. The archetypal role of the physician still draws upon the patient's implicit trust in the healer, and this role is fundamentally based on an ethical commitment of caring. The medical encounter is thus by definition ethical as Levinas poses the Self-Other encounter.

Thus in medicine, it is irrelevant whether Levinas has attempted a sleight of hand regarding the secularization of his ethical formulation. He is defended by sympathetic critics such as Robert Gibbs (1992) and Susan Handelman (1991) as placing Jewish philosophy in the post-Hegelian tradition of reorienting (if not replacing) philosophy. They regard the thought of Hermann Cohen, Walter Benjamin, Franz Rosenzweig, Martin Buber, Gershom Scholem and Levinas as having stimulated important responses in twentieth century literary criticism, sociology, and philosophy itself. But others are less enthused. Consider John Caputo who recently wrote that Levinas' ethics were a fable that borders on ineffability (almost) and bears repeated telling. "I never tire of hearing it retold...What Levinas says is impossible, but that is why I love it. Thinking the impossible, trying to think the impossible, is among the most important tasks of philosophy, which leaves what is possible to the other disciplines. The impossible is what pulls us out of our most sedimented thoughts and opens new possibilities" (Caputo, 1993 at 82).

Caputo views the "absolutely Other" as poetic and hyperbolic. Although he respects Levinas as a poet, or prophet, ultimately the verdict is harsh - Levinas is too pious, his poetics are too grave. "I tire easily of always wearing black" writes Caputo (ibid. at 83). One might agree, but recall physicians and nurses wear white, which in this case is an interesting contrast - opposite and yet the same. Healing priests, dressed in white, have *chosen* to assume this calling, this responsibility. It must form the existential basis of themselves as healers. They in fact *are* defined by their Other - the patient. Fundamentally, for the healer there is no choice - his or her calling is this ethical self-definition.

And it is here that I believe the Levinasian argument has its most profound impact. In his scheme, the Other defines the Self in their relation. We have already seen that the character of the relation is given by the unique mission of medicine as caring. The full phenomenological address of the patient sufferer, with respect to his autonomy, will frame the healer's response, not by virtue of the physician's power, her medical science and technology that work to cure disease, but because of her commitment to heal. The patient no longer is a scientific object, an Other, but becomes part of a dialectical relation that defines both healer and sufferer as a singular unit. The ethics demands priority because it is the relation that defines the medical encounter. Science must serve ethics. The relation of doctor and patient is ethical and dominant over all other concerns.

So finally, how might we situate medical ethics, or more specifically, how might we ground the particular requirements of a medical ethics in its broader philosophy? The first question, by the parameters drawn here, is how would medical philosophy appear if it was *based*, à la Levinas, in ethics, rather than, let us say, Truth? Concerning the relation of ethics to epistemology and for that matter, metaphysics, one might recall the game played as children -- "rock, paper, scissors." Simultaneously, two players throw out a fist, a flat hand or two fingers. The fist symbolizing a rock, breaks the scissors, represented by two fingers, but paper, the flat hand, covers the rock; note however the scissors cut the paper. Neither rock, paper, nor scissors is inherently superior to the others, each has its relation to its counterparts. The case to be more fully explored is the position of ethics relative to the other domains of what constitutes philosophy of medicine. An ambitious, and worthwhile project is to examine a philosophy of medicine based not on epistemology or metaphysics, but instead on ethics. Simply, one might consider the case of ethics prior to truth and its consequences for a philosophy of medicine. Obviously medicine is committed to science, to establishing a rational praxis, but the problem is to place our science in its proper humanistic role. While invoking science and technology, the physician should place these resources in their appropriate context, guided by the underlying ethos of his endeavor -- to heal. The medical scientist would objectify disease -- the patient as object; the ethical physician would care for the patient, which obviously includes the use of her scientific tools, but regard these as auxiliary to her primary *relation*, her responsibility as an ethical agent.

This is potentially a radical and far-reaching proposal. I cannot consider here how this position impacts on such classic medical ethics problems as human experimentation, death and dying, reproduction or abortion. The validity of this approach must be tested in such particular issues, but here I am content with presenting the relational philosophy alone as a basis of all medical practice. It may well be that the true impact of my argument is to be felt in how we situate medical ethics in general. Is medical ethics to remain an attachment to medical education and practice, or can it be moved to center stage? After all, medical ethics is hardly a pillar of contemporary medical education. The erosion of *any* concern with ethics may be traced to the end of the nineteenth century, when physiology and its close cousin, medicine, rode upon the broad shoulders of newly-defined positivist principles (Canguilhem, 1989). This new standard of knowledge was to apply an "objective" natural science to physiology and health. The observer would distance himself as far as possible from the object of scrutiny. The challenge of a laboratory-based medicine, as opposed to a bedside-oriented clinical practice was clearly discerned as a dangerous development by such leading physicians as William Osler, Richard Cabot, and Francis Peabody at the beginning of the century (Tauber, 1992; Dodds, 1993). They argued the position presented here, not in explicit philosophical terms, but in defense of the patient as sufferer and ward of the physician. Their warnings however were quickly drowned, for from the laws of physics and chemistry, a new medicine would arise; powerfully and inexorably, we are its beneficiaries. But a profound irony emerged as medicine assumed its new legitimacy in laboratory-based sciences: medicine lost its own boundaries and focus. No longer possessing its own theory, medicine sought its explanatory roots in other scientific disciplines (Tauber, 1992). A medicine constructed on its own principles was subsumed to a medicine based on other sciences. These would define the basis of medical theory, offer it their criteria, and regulate disease as designations defined by sciences that had in fact no normative. Physics has no *value* in its descriptive practice, but physiology does in the context of suffering. But in the objectification of the patient, medicine's fundamental ethos was stolen and with it medical ethics as a crucial constituent of medicine's theory or practice. An ethos based on intersubjectivity -- the *interaction* of physician and patient -- is the commonality of the healing art in all cultures. With our positivist approach, the legitimacy of the interpersonal relation is not necessarily denied, but it is too often subordinated to laboratory-derived facts. Science and technology are pre-occupied with different concerns, and these may indeed come into play, but must be understood in the context of medicine's unique agenda.

When the patient became a scientific object, the ethical relation of the healer to her client was fundamentally altered. We have been so preoccupied with establishing those parameters by which patient autonomy will be respected, through what may broadly be referred to as judicial constraints or guidelines, that a thorough examination of the philosophical basis of the physician's ethical relation to the patient pleads for attention. "Strangers at the bedside" to borrow David Rothman's phrase (1991), have appeared to protect the patient from the physician. These are not only the bioethicists, lawyers, administrators, and economists, but the physicians themselves. Physicians are estranged from their patients and self-consciously seek guidance, directives, orders and shared responsibilities to practice ethically. Medical ethics has become a tag or an appendage to the health care industry. Like any industry in our society, it too requires careful governance to protect its consumers. Patients do not trust their physicians as they did a generation ago, and physicians have largely lost their sense of professional autonomy (Rothman, 1991). Beyond the social and economic repercussions of this change, we are witness to a markedly altered ethical relationship between patient and healer. In many respects, the physician-as-god is happily fading rapidly in our collective memory, but with what model has the demigod been replaced? Please note, physician power, for all of its dangerous applications still demanded physician responsibility. If the physician is to share responsibility with other members of the health provider complex, what remains the basis of his moral commitment and how is it to be defined? The self-protective adversarial model is obviously evidence of failure. This is a highly complex issue, which has convoluted social and economic aspects, but I believe it remains fundamentally a philosophical problem. To posit an ethical metaphysics for medicine is no less than to claim that the very foundation of medicine is to find and assert its own philosophy.

For those hungry for particular applications of such a philosophical orientation, I will only note that when basing medical philosophy in an ethics, certain epistemological issues are immediately realized. Specifically, if the doctor-patient relationship is constructed as an ethical phenomenological model, then the erotetic logic employed by the physician is markedly altered. If the patient does not reside in this "protected" enclave, he is but another object of biological inquiry, and thus the very nature of medical epistemology is affected (Toulmin, 1993). As Sartre noted, the objectification of illness as "disease," i.e. as a "being-for-others," alienates the Self from the body. In illness, the body is experienced in a fundamentally different manner, and the patient not only becomes aware of pain or dysfunction, but attempts to find "meaning" by objectifying the soma. The physician is of course party to this objectification process as she attempts to scientifically define the disease by what Husserl would refer to as the "naturalistic attitude." This is the alienation intrinsic to the experience of illness (Leder, 1992; Toombs, 1992).

A phenomenological analysis seeks to suspend this "natural standpoint" which essentially views the world as given, and takes for granted the experiencing subject. In medicine, such an orientation assumes a deeply ethical position as others have argued before me (Pellegrino, 1979; Kestenbaum, 1982). From this vantage, the medical encounter is based on viewing the patient not as a "case," a diseased entity, but as an experiencing, in fact suffering, individual. Being ill alters our very selfhood, changing our fundamental relationship to our bodies. The ill lose freedom of action through impairment. The patient's dependence upon others for recovery, and hence his loss of freedom from the power of others, exposes him to increased vulnerability and consequent weakening of his self-image. The phenomenological approach squarely addresses this problem, by building a medical ethics that recognizes as a first principle the humanity of the ill. Medical ethics written from the phenomenological perspective regards the patient experiencing illness as more than simply an object of study. Illness is dehumanizing. The Self is damaged, and the task then is to restore the patient's full sense of identity. The medical scientist might be satisfied with "patient-as-disease," but the caring physician is guided by her recognition of the suffering person, *in toto.*

From this orientation, important distinctions are made between apprehending the body in "lived experience" (normal, everyday) as opposed to the disruption initiated by illness and its care (Toombs, 1992 at 49ff). Focusing upon the clinical narrative, Toulmin (1993) and others (reviewed by Toombs, 1992 at 103-119) recognize that the patient's rendition of the disease experience offers crucial insight to the physician, both as scientist and empathetic, that is, ethical, healer. The doctor-patient relationship as a communicative problem has a voluminous literature. I might cite only two recent studies that on the one hand emphasize the silence of misinformation that passes for clinical dialogue, and on the other hand offers the means by which such communication might be improved. In a study by Jay Katz, written only a decade ago (1984), the abuse of patients by insensitive physicians who were unable to freely discuss patient distress and illness experience already seems alien. Katz carefully documented dialogue that no doubt still occurs, but there is a general demand that physicians exercise their authority with non-paternalistic compassion and with proper respect of patient "rights," i.e. autonomy. This change in the doctor-patient relationship (albeit incomplete and hardly universal) probably reflects a significant cultural shift in regards to various power relations that may be traced to feminist critiques, empowerment movements of various kinds, and a responsive judiciary. These changes have filtered into medicine so that when Roter and Hall (1992) deal with doctor-patient communication, this study can already assume a new standard. They attend to analyzing the various causes of physician insensitivity and address how to improve verbal interactions between doctor and patient, with a stronger mandate to support their agenda.

These orientations towards a more personal, if not compassionate medicine, I believe reflects the underlying phenomenological attitude. Beyond obtaining information that may be important in tending to the patient's medical needs, a patient's phenomenological description of the illness experience presents the physician with the problem of suffering, with the profound disruption, uncertainty and pain that disease imposes. This is the domain implicit to any discussion that attempts to improve the doctor-patient encounter as humane. Suffering cannot be reduced to an objectified medical science alone, and thus from this perspective, the physician must confront the full panorama of illness as personal experience to heal. In Levinas' scheme, this phenomenological encounter is explicitly articulated as ethical.

Note however, this is not what Pellegrino and Thomasma (1981) propose of the physician and patient as meeting like friends dedicated to the good of health. This is what is discussed as beneficence -- mutual sympathy and the interest in the common pursuit of the good life. Such a relationship assumes that the doctor and patient share the same medical ideals, have no economic or social conflicts of interests, and embrace the same moral values. These are of course broad, and too often unwarranted assumptions. But beyond the problems of establishing a common social ground, this approach does not establish an *a priori* ethical relationship. The physician-patient encounter in the philosophy I have advocated is fundamentally ethical. No contingencies and no caveats. The relationship alone is the *sine qua non* of medicine. So in this respect, the discussion concerning the relative positions of autonomy and beneficence, in the Levinas scheme I have advocated, takes on a new twist. Beneficence is a guiding element in the physician-patient encounter, but it is only a product of the primary relational commitment. Beneficence moves from ethical dominance, to a result of a more fundamental ethical mandate. In short, although obviously important, beneficence cannot serve as the defining parameter.[28]

Finally, when alterity *defines* ipseity, the autonomous Self is problematic. Heretofore, I have paid uncritical homage to patient autonomy, but we must note just as the Self is defined by the Other in the Levinas equation, the Other is also a Self, and is defined reciprocally. But in medicine, the equation between Self and Other is complicated because the symmetrical relationship has been lost. There is now the requirement of patient trust in the physician's care, which is hardly reciprocal. In this dependence, grades of freedom have necessarily been forfeited. The relation between equals in the original Levinasian scheme has lost its parity. The equation has assumed a new complexity, and the casualty is autonomy, so much the subject of recent bioethics. Complete patient autonomy must honestly be labeled a fiction. Patients must be informed, they must be free to make choices, and they are ultimately responsible for accepting medical risks, but these are degrees of autonomy. The patient ultimately relies to a varying extent on the health professional for guidance. I do not advocate a paternalistic stance, but autonomy under this critical gaze has lost some of its sacrosanct character. Starkly stated, autonomy had already vanished from my original description of Levinas' ethical universe. Now as I attempt to situate medical ethics as an application of such a relational philosophy, I must acknowledge that the engagement of Self and Other no longer possesses the equality of free encounter.

Important implications for the ethical construction outlined here arise from this acknowledgment. For instance, one might consider that there are in fact layers of physician responsibility that might range from a fiduciary role of the pathologist or radiologist, who has no personal contact with the patient, to a comprehensive responsibility of the primary care provider who assumes total care of her patient. These different ethical roles would then translate into alternative relationships with the various auxiliary functions of medicine, each assuming its role relative to the primacy (or essentialist position) of the primary physician. It may well be that the current popular appeal of primary care is precisely in recognizing that the return to a full ethical encounter with the patient is the true basis of medicine, not in the technocratic application of the scientific armamentarium. Thus the level of physician involvement, or personal commitment to the patient as Person, largely defines the ethical boundary. With that delineation, differing epistemologies may then be imposed. For instance, if the doctor-patient encounter is characterized as "active-passive," the patient *qua* person has little role to play in the diagnostic or therapeutic events. Such is the case with the comatose patient in an intensive care unit or on an operating table. In what Szasz and Hollender (1987) refer to as the cooperation mode, the physician still commands virtually total autonomy and instructs ("commands") the patient how to deal with his illness. But in the mutual participation setting, the patient-doctor relationship markedly shifts. In this last case, treatment is mutually defined, the notions of health and disease, i.e. the therapeutic aims and success, are reoriented to allow the patient to take an active role in establishing goals and helping himself. A "partnership" ensues and the role of physician as empathetic facilitator is emphasized. In this last scenario, the characteristics of patient and disease take on radically different meanings than those operating passively in the first example.

When we regard the patient, we discern that the power of the Levinasian construct is most aptly applied from the physician/nurse towards the patient. The relationship's reverse vector is encumbered by dependence. As described, disease compromises the patient's freedom, and thus autonomy has necessarily been relinquished in this existential state of illness. The issue of restoring the patient's full sense of selfhood might be construed as uncomfortably passive in this scheme. My rejoinder simply resides in the essential ethical commitment of the healer to help re-establish the sufferer's complete identity. To fulfill the trust given her, the health professional is committed to re-confirming the Other's selfhood. The relationship may not be symmetrical as the patient suffers, but the goal of healing is in fact to affirm an equal exchange between full selves. The healer's success is in the patient again becoming his true Self. Recall, autonomy, in the mode of self-sufficiency, is not even possible in the Levinasian equation, and thus the loss of autonomy from Levinas' philosophical lexicon only emphasizes the markedly divided position from that of Engelhardt (1986), for instance. A specific study of their respective positions would be of interest, but as I have already indicated, the structure of their arguments could hardly be more diametrically polarized. I believe that in a full examination of these contrasting philosophies, the impact of Levinas' metaphysical ethics may be most profoundly appreciated.

These remarks are made only as a first attempt to discern how we might sketch in the most relevant consequences of Levinas' philosophy for medicine. He has clearly offered us an alternate ethical portrait from this perspective. I recognize the focus of concern has shifted from the patient, i.e. the autonomous subject, to the relational issue, and therefore, in the overall context of this essay the comparison between Nietzsche and Levinas has not allowed an equal opposition. But this shift alone is highly significant in that the focus of medical ethics as proposed here would deliberately attempt to bring a realignment in the manner we might construct a philosophy of medicine from a primary concern with autonomy to one focused on a morality based upon a relational ethic. When we seek to define the philosophical relation of patient and healer, the entire enterprise of healing is exposed to scrutiny. From this perspective we can now ask how might the notion of an ethical medicine situate itself within the ethos of a reductionist science? How will a scientifically dominated medicine comprehensively and effectively incorporate the ethical position as fundamental to practice? Although I suspect that the repercussions may be quite startling, I am the first to admit that a systematic attempt to apply Levinas' general thesis to medicine is a most ambitious venture. In this scheme, the physician must define herself in relation to her patient, as a face -- as a person. The doctor of course must diagnose disease and administer care, but these latter functions in the view espoused here are subordinate to the primacy of the doctor-patient relation. This is fundamentally an ethical encounter, which then, as a secondary matter leads to a specific epistemological question: what is the disease? The issue of the patient, i.e. the suffering person in her "infinity" is established first. The ethics underlies the epistemology. Without this prioritization, we are doomed to a myopic technocratic medicine.

Medical ethics must face this challenge of establishing the physician's identification with the patient, for in truly seeing the patient, she most fully defines herself. Thus the task of medical ethics is very much centered on the physician-patient encounter, where each is scrutinized as a *relational* Self. By posing the issues in this fashion I have attempted to explicitly present what I perceive to be the essential problem in philosophy of medicine, or more to the point, *The* problem of medicine, which so poignantly and dramatically exhibits the very issue of post-modern selves in a post-modern world. We seek to ground a moral view in respect to different beliefs and cultural demands. Such an ethics must situate itself in mutual respect. The strategy of placing the relational component as paramount represents a fecund attempt to protect the Other from becoming an object. Ultimately, if that Other becomes definitional to ourselves, care and responsibility become operational. And this at base is the rich possibility of translating our world view into an ethical space, wherein we become true selves. Medicine is a unique crucible in which to test these precepts. Ultimately I believe to be Human is to be moral, and if philosophy is to help us understand who we are and how we order and engage the world, I see the ethical component not as an attachment, but the foundation of such a philosophy. At this locus, medicine is naturally situated, or as Aristotle so aptly affirmed, "The philosopher should begin with medicine, the physician should end with philosophy."[29]

Boston University

REFERENCES

Aloni, N. (1991). *Beyond Nihilism. Nietzsche's Healing and Edifying Philosophy*. Lanham: University Press of America.

Aristotle. (1931). *The Works of Aristotle, Volume III*. Translated and edited by W. D. Ross. Oxford: Clarendon Press.

Aristotle. (1973). *De Sensu and de Memoria*. Translated by G. R. T. Ross. NY: Arno Press.

Aschheim, S. E. (1993). *The Nietzsche Legacy in Germany, 1890-1990*. Berkeley: University of California Press.

Barnes, H. E. (1989). Sartre. In *Ethics in the History of Western Philosophy*, ed: R.J. Cavalier, J. Gouinlock and J. P. Sterba. New York: St. Martin's Press. pp. 335-365.

Bernasconi, R. (1988). Failure of communication as a surplus: Dialogue and lack of dialogue between Buber and Levinas. In *The Provocation of Levinas*, ed. R. Bernasconi and D. Wood. London: Routledge. pp. 100-135.

Birch, C. (1988). The post modern challenge to biology. In *The Reenchantment of Science. Post Modern Proposals*, ed. D. R. Griffin Albany: State University of New York Press. pp. 69-78.

Blondel, E. (1991). *Nietzsche. The Body and Culture*. Translated by S. Hand. Stanford: Stanford University Press.

Boorse, C. (1977). Health as a theoretical concept. *Philosophy of Science* 44: 542-573.

Brown, W. M. (1985). On defining disease. *The Journal of Medicine and Philosophy* 10: 311-328.

Canguilhem, G. (1989). *The Normal and the Pathological* [1966]. Translated by Carolyn R. Fawcett. New York: ZONE Books.

Caputo, J. D. (1993). *Against Ethics*. Bloomingdale: Indiana University Press.

Ciaramelli, F. (1991). Levinas' ethical discourse between individuation and universality. In *Re-reading Levinas*, ed. R. Bernasconi and S. Critchley. Bloomington: Indiana University Press. pp. 83-105.

Descartes, R. (1968). *Discourse on Method* and *The Meditations*. Translated by F. E. Sutcliffe. London and New York: Penguin Books.

Dodds, T. A. (1993). Richard Cabot: Medical reform during the Progressive Era (1890-1920). *Annals of Internal Medicine* 119: 417-422.

Engelhardt, H. T., Jr. (1986). *The Foundations of Bioethics*. NY: Oxford University Press.

Foucault, M. (1984). Politics and ethics: An interview. In *The Foucault Reader*, ed. P. Rabinow. New York: Pantheon Books. pp. 373-380.

Fraser, N. (1983). Foucault's body-language: A post-humanist political rhetoric? *Salmagundi* 61:55-70.

Gibbs, R. (1992). *Correlations in Rosenzweig and Levinas*. Princeton: Princeton University Press.

Hand, S. (1989). *The Levinas Reader*. Oxford: Blackwell.

Handelman, S. A. (1991). *Fragments of Redemption. Jewish Thought and Literary Theory in Benjamin, Scholem, and Levinas*. Bloomingdale: Indiana University Press.

Heidegger, M. (1979). *Nietzsche*. San Francisco: Harper and Row.

Katz, J. (1984). *The Silent World of Doctor and Patient*. New York: The Free Press.

Kestenbaum, V. (1982). Introduction: The experience of illness. In *The Humanity of the Ill Phenomenological Perspectives*, ed. V. Kestenbaum. Knoxville: The University of Tennessee Press. pp. 3-38.

Kaufmann, W. (1974). *Nietzsche. Philosopher, Psychologist, Antichrist*. 4th Edition. Princeton: Princeton University Press.

Kohák, E. (1978). *Ideas and Experience. Edmund Husserl's Project of Phenomenology in Ideas I*. Chicago: University of Chicago Press.

Kolb, C. (1990). *Nietzsche as Postmodernist. Essays Pro and Con*. Albany: The State University of New York Press.

Leder, P. (ed.). (1992). *The Body in Medical Thought and Practice*. Dordrecht: Kluwer Academic Publishers.

Letteri, M. (1990). The theme of health in Nietzsche's thought. *Man and World* 23: 405-417.

Levinas, E. (1969). *Totality and Infinity* [1961]. Translated by A. Linguis. Pittsburgh: Duquesne University Press.

Levinas, E. (1973). *The Theory of Intuition in Husserl's Phenomenology*. Translated by A. Orianne. Evanston: Northwestern University Press.

Levinas, E. (1978). *Existence and Existents*. Translated by A. Linguis. Dordrecht: Kluwer Academic Publishers.

Levinas, E. (1986). Dialogue with Emmanuel Levinas. In *Face to Face with Levinas*, ed. R.A. Cohen. Albany: State University of New York Press. pp. 13-33.

Levinas, E. (1987a) *Collected Philosophical Papers*. Translated by A. Linguis. Dordrecht: Martinus Nijhoff Publishers.

Levinas, E. (1987b) *Time and the Other*. Translated by R. A. Cohen. Pittsburgh: Duquesne University Press.

Levinas, E. (1989). Martin Buber and the theory of knowledge, in *The Levinas Reader*, ed. S. Hand. Oxford: Blackwell. pp. 59-74.

Levinas, E. (1990a) *Difficult Freedom. Essays on Judaism*. Translated by S. Hand. Baltimore: The Johns Hopkins University Press.

Levinas, E. (1990b) *Nine Talmudic Readings*. Translated by A. Aronowicz. Bloomington: Indiana University Press.

Levinas, E. (1991). *Otherwise than Being or Beyond Essence* [1974]. Translated by A. Linguis. Dordrecht: Kluwer Academic Publishers.

Martin, G. T. (1989). *From Nietzsche to Wittgenstein. The Problem of Truth and Nihilism in the Modern World*. New York: Peter Lang.

Moles, A. (1990). *Nietzsche's Philosophy of Nature and Cosmology*. New York: Peter Lang Publishing.

Nehamas, A. (1985). *Nietzsche. Life as Literature*. Cambridge: Harvard University Press.

Nietzsche, F. (1956) *The Birth of Tragedy*, [1872]. Translated by F. Golffing. Garden City, New York: Doubleday Anchor.

Nietzsche, F. (1959). *Thus Spoke Zarathustra*, [1885] in The Portable Nietzsche. Edited and translated by W. Kaufmann. New York: Penguin Books. pp. 112-439.

Nietzsche, F. (1962). *Philosophy in the Tragic Age of the Greeks*. Translated by M. Cowan. Washington DC: Regnery Gateway.

Nietzsche, F. (1967a). *The Will to Power*, [1904]. Translated by W. Kaufmann and R. J. Hollingdale. New York: Vintage Books.

Nietzsche, F. (1967b). *On the Genealogy of Morals*, [1887]. Translated by W. Kaufmann and R. J. Hollingdale. New York: Vintage Books.

Nietzsche, F. (1974). *The Gay Science* [1882]. Translated by W. Kaufmann. New York: Vintage Books.

Nietzsche, F. (1983). *Schopenhauer as Educator* [1874]. *In Untimely Meditations*, translated by R.J. Hollingdale. Cambridge: Cambridge University Press.

Nietzsche, F. (1986). *Human All Too Human*, [1878]. Translated by R. J. Hollingdale. Cambridge: Cambridge University Press.

Nietzsche, F. (1990). The Philosopher as Cultural Physician. In *Philosophy and Truth, Selections from Nietzsche's Notebook of the Early 1870's*. Edited and translated by D. Breazeale. Atlantic Highlands: Humanities Press, International. pp. 69-76.

Nordenfelt, L. (1987). *On the Nature of Health. An Action - Theoretic Approach*. Dordrecht: Kluwer Academic Publishers.

Pasley, M. (1978). Nietzsche's use of medical terms, In *Nietzsche: Imagery and Thought: A Collection of Essays*, ed. M. Pasley. Berkeley: University of California Press. pp. 123-158.

Pellegrino, E. D. (1979). *Humanism and the Physician*. Knoxville: University of Tennessee Press.

Pellegrino, E. D. and Thomasama, D. C. (1981). *A Philosophical Basis of Medical Practice*. New York: Oxford University Press.

Peperzak, A. (1993). *To the Other. An Introduction to the Philosophy of Emmanuel Levinas*. West Lafayette, IN: Purdue University Press.

Pippin, R. A. (1991). *Modernism as a Philosophical Problem*. Oxford and Cambridge: Basil Blackwell.

Podolsky, S. H. and Tauber, A. I. (1995). *Nietzsche's conception of health - the idealization of struggle*. Submitted.

Pörn, I. (1984). An equilibrium model of health. In *Health, Disease, and Causal Explanation in Medicine*, ed. L. Nordenfelt and B.I.B. Lindahl. Dordrecht: D. Reidel Publishing Co. pp. 3-9.

Romanell, P. (1984). *John Locke and Medicine*. New York: Prometheus Books.

Roter, D. L. and Hall, J. L. (1992). *Doctors Talking with Patients/Patients Talking with Doctors: Improving Communication in Medical Visits*. Westport, Conn: Auburn Home.

Rothman, D. J. (1991). *Strangers at the Bedside. A History of how Law and Bioethics Transformed Medical Decision Making*. New York: Basic Books.

Schutle, O. (1984). *Beyond Nihilism. Nietzsche Without Masks*. Chicago: The University of Chicago Press.

Scott, C. E. (1990). *The Question of Ethics. Nietzsche, Foucault, Heidegger*. Bloomington: Indiana University Press.

Szasz, T. and Hollender, M. H. (1987). A contribution to the philosophy of medicine: The basic model of the doctor-patient relationship. In *Encounters Between Patients and Doctors. An Anthology*, ed. J. D. Stoeckle. Cambridge: The MIT Press.

Tauber, A. I. (1992). *The Two Faces of Medical Education/Flexner and Osler Revisited*. J. Roy. Soc. Med. 85:598-602.

Tauber, A. I. (1994a). *The Immune Self: Theory or Metaphor?* New York and Cambridge: Cambridge University Press.

Tauber, A. I. (1994b). Nietzsche and Foucault: On the transvaluation of values, In *Papers in Honor of Robert S. Cohen*, ed. M. Wartofsky. Dordrecht: Kluwer Academic Publishers.

Tauber, A. I. (1994c). A Typology of Nietzsche's Biology. *Biology & Philosophy*. 9: 24-44.

Tauber, A. I. and Chernyak, L. (1991). *Metchnikoff and the Origins of Immunology. From Metaphor to Theory*. New York and Oxford: Oxford University Press.

Thiele, L. P. (1990). *Friedrich Nietzsche and the Politics of the Soul.* Princeton: Princeton University Press.

Toombs, S. K. (1992). *The Meaning of Illness. A Phenomenological Account of the Different Perspectives of Physician and Patient.* Dordrecht: Kluwer Academic Publishers.

Toulmin, S. (1993). Knowledge and art in the practice of medicine: Clinical judgement and historical reconstruction. In *Science, Technology, and the Art of Medicine*. eds. C. Delkeskamp-Hayes and M. A. Gardell-Cutter. Dordrecht: Kluwer Academic Publishers. pp. 231-250.

Whitbeck, C. (1978). Four Basic Concepts of Medical Science. *PSA* 1: 210-222.

Whitbeck, C. (1981). A Theory of Health. In *Concepts of Health and Disease: Interdisciplinary Perspectives*, ed. A. L. Caplan, H. T. Engelhardt, Jr. and J. J. McCartney. Reading, Massachusetts: Addison-Wesley Publishing Co. pp. 611-626.

Williams, W. D. (1952). *Nietzsche and the French.* Oxford: Basil Blackwell.

Wittgenstein, L. (1979). *Notebooks.* 1914-1916. 2nd edition. ed. G. H. Von Wright and G. E. M. Anscombe. Chicago: University of Chicago Press.

Wyschogrod, E. (1974). *Emmanuel Levinas. The Problem of Ethical Metaphysics.* The Hague: Martinus Nijhoff.

ACKNOWLEDGEMENTS

This essay was given in a condensed version as my Inaugural Lecture in the Department of Philosophy at Boston University, February 7, 1994. I am indebted to the critical comments made by Bob Cohen, Anne Dubitzky, Charles Griswold, Michael Grodin, Victor Kestenbaum, and Allen Speight. Although they cannot be held accountable for what is argued here, they are heavily invested in their encouragement of this project, and I am most grateful to each for their support.

ENDNOTES

1 A typical argument that begins with the Lockean-Kantian autonomous agent is the underlying focus of this anthology. This position is perhaps best defended by Engelhardt, whose primary concern is to preserve the province of autonomy, and thus he argues that ethics can only be based on society's commitment to resolve

moral controversy by agreement; he rejects any hierarchy of values as canonical. Beyond the political desire of establishing a peaceable community, this position espouses "a transcendental condition, a necessary condition for the possibility of a general domain of human life" (1986 at 42), i.e. mutual respect. He explicitly places beneficence subordinate to individual autonomy, and by mixing positions advocated by Locke, Kant, Rousseau, Mill and Rawls, Engelhardt essentially offers a political philosophy for ethics. I am presenting an approach that might be regarded as underlying the basis for "mutual respect" and other similar positions not founded on autonomy per se. I am not so much attacking the notion of autonomy as attempting to demonstrate its metaphysical boundaries. It is in this sense that "building a philosophy of medicine" was chosen for my title.

2 This claim has been contested by those who place Nietzsche as the first post-modernist (e.g. Kolb, 1990). In any case, Nietzsche's radical critique of the self initiated the modernist-post-modernist debate (Tauber, 1994a, 1994b).

3 The following discussion of Nietzsche's concepts of the body and health, although based on my previous work (1994a; 1994c), is expanded in Podolsky and Tauber (1995). The exposition presented here is largely based on this latter essay.

4 This should be read in the context of *The Gay Science*, stanza #120 - as well as *Will to Power*, stanza #674 which is also very appropriate for this reading.

5 *The Will to Power* is especially rich for the argument advanced here. Beyond stanzas #490, #492, #660, note in #641, "A multiplicity of forces, connected by a common mode of nutrition, we call 'life'" (at 341); #673, "Theory of chance. The soul a selective and self-nourishing entity, perpetually extremely shrewd and creative...To recognize the active force, the creative force in the chance event: - chance itself is only the clash of creative impulses" (ibid. at 355). Thus an interesting account of intra-organismic contingency resulting from innumerable drives and too many individual causes to be able to be reduced to determinism is a recurrent Nietzschean theme. In stanza #674 Nietzsche bolsters such a claim by writing: "In the tremendous multiplicity of events within an organism, the part which becomes conscious to us is a mere means" (ibid.).

6 "This means that for Nietzsche health is essentially overcoming (Letteri, 1990 at 410) ... Health is ... the free admission of weakness into the arena of struggle with the aim of conquering it and thereby becoming stronger.... The sickly will does not dare to search for resistance. ... It is inspissated, exhausted, incapable of the task - the self-appointed task, in the case of the healthy will - of grappling successfully with hindrances to its drives (ibid. at 411). ... In short, it appears that for Nietzsche 'healthy' equals 'good' and 'sick' equals 'bad' ... With him we move beyond good and evil into the demoralized - yet still, of course, value-laden

- realm of health and sickness." Note that this replacement is also noted by Aloni, 1991 at 30.

7 "Morality is a morality of the base which does not grow to the summit, as do the doctrines of Plato, Spinoza, Kant and Schopenhauer, which infuse transcendent being into human volition....Nietzsche's passionate desire to liberate morality from transcendence is consistent with this biological tendency of his morality" (Simmel, 1907, 1991 at 178-179).

8 Thus, for Aloni sickness = nihilism = passivity, whereas health = eudaimonism = active overcoming of resistance. Health is an individual measure of self-creation, with no two individuals possessing the same type of "health," as he writes: "*The* way does not exist and ... the condition necessary for the development of noble and healthy cultures is constant interacting and contesting between many types of authentic, noble, and creative individuals" (Aloni, 1991 at 9). Such an overall conception reduces to the elimination of the conceptions of truth and the ability of humanity to know Truth, and the call for man as "interpreter, form-giver, and creator, who is driven by a 'desire for edification,' vitality, or power and whose distinguishing mark lies in his capacity to give meaning and value to things through a continual generation of descriptions of man and world" (ibid. at 22). This, for Aloni, represents edifying, "healing" philosophy.

9 For an example of such philosopher-physicians in action, Aloni turns, as do all Nietzsche scholars, to the Greeks. Chapter VIII details such an elaboration, centering upon the spirit of agony, the noble (aristocratic) morality, the life-affirming tragic view of life, and the use of creation via art. As such, Aloni both defines the healthy man as the active, self-creator, and the philosophical physician as he who challenges society's beliefs by offering resistance to it which must either be overcome or which will destroy it. Of course, this book does not deal with the physiological notion of health, however, it effectively explores the concept of health as a modus to the understanding of Nietzsche. Parenthetically note, the quote, "educate ourselves against our age," was Nietzsche's referral to how we might emulate men of genius, which in this case was Schopenhauer.

10 Because he does not endeavor to "replace one kind of subjectivation with another" (Scott, 1990 at 55), Foucault maintains distance and detachment in the process of his analysis. "His [Foucault's] language and movement of thought...are not ethical... The question of ethics of liberation is characteristic of his discourse" (ibid. at 53).

11 The approach towards defining health taken by these authors is, in my opinion an appropriate response to the objective one adopted by Boorse, who argues that

health is simply the absence of sickness or illness (Boorse, 1977). Brown (1985) critiques each strategy.

12 For discussion of Nietzsche's conception of health as an "idealization of struggle" see Podolsky and Tauber (1995).

13 The broader historical context of this claim is made elsewhere (Tauber & Chernyak, 1991; Tauber, 1994a).

14 There is no stable norm, no given, no static entity. The very character of evolution disallows permanence in any sense, and in each instant, the organism must encounter its environment and itself to evolve - that is respond. Life is dialogical - an ongoing and ceaseless dialogue between organism and its world. In a world of flux, relativity and indeterminism, evolution replaces rigid hierarchy and ordered cosmic forces. Probability has replaced a mechanistic determinism, and our new understanding of cause arises from disparate and indefinite sources of likelihood. If we truly are heirs of Darwin, then we remain unhinged in a world of chance, bereft of the predictability of an ordered world of deterministic causality, as Darwin himself lamented: "I cannot think that the world is the result of chance; yet I cannot look at each separate thing as the result of Design...I am, and shall ever remain, in a hopeless muddle" (Letter from Charles Darwin to Asa Gray, quoted by Birch, 1988 at 75). Darwin is expressing an ancient vexation, for despite constant change, an entity *has* an identity. How do we discern that character and what is it? Depending on the philosophy considered the problem becomes to establish the criteria of *identity*, or to perceive the governing Form (Aristotle) or to discern the hidden Idea (Plato).

15 In this reading of Nietzsche, modernity's essential failing was that "it had not been modern enough, that the restless, perpetually self-transforming, anomic, transient spirit of modernism had to be affirmed much more honestly and consistently" (Pippin, 1991 at 7). The argument for such a radicalized modern venture, to truly free the self, assumed its most exuberant expression in Nietzsche, but can be traced as well from Baudelaire through the anti-bourgeois sentiment that fueled much of fin-de-siècle's emotive energy. The self as independent and self-determining self-consciousness, always in action both as moral agent and ultimately in its knowledge of the world, constitutes in a strong sense the end result of the modernist quest that began with Kant (Tauber, 1994a).

16 Levinas was born in 1906 in Kovno, Lithuania. In 1923 he went to Strasbourg and studied with Husserl and Heidegger in Freiberg. In 1929 Levinas published the first French translation of Husserl and an important introduction to his thought. After settling in Paris, Levinas taught at the Normal School, a training institution for teachers of the Alliance Universelle Isráelite, a modern school network for

Jewish communities through the Mediterranean. Only in 1961, did Levinas obtain a university position after publishing his major work, *Totality and Infinity*. His other major work, *Otherwise than Being or Beyond Essence* was published 1974. He eventually became Professor of Philosophy at the Sorbonne, and has recently become an important voice of European philosophy. Levinas' philosophical roots are easily traced to Husserl, and to a lesser extent Heidegger, however, Levinas is perhaps better linked to Martin Buber, and most particularly Franz Rosenzweig (Gibbs, 1992; Handelman, 1991; Wyschogrod, 1974).

17 The phenomenological concerns of Levinas pervade his work, but his explicit relation to the movement is not discussed here. Several of his shorter phenomenological essays are collected (Levinas, 1989, 1987a) and his most important monographs translated (1978; 1973; 1987b). His major statements are *Totality and Infinity* (1961, 1969) and *Otherwise than Being or Beyond Essence* (1961, 1991), of which the former has been distilled in this discussion. Probably the best introduction to *Totality and Infinity* is Levinas' 1957 article "Philosophy and the Ideal of the Infinite" translated by Linguis (1987 at 47-60) and Peperzak (1993 at 88-119), who also offers an extensive commentary on this essay and the larger work that it summarizes.

18 In addition, Levinas views Heidegger as a pagan; "to heed the voice of being is to leave natural existence unquestioned and unjustified" (Wyschogrod, 1974 at 15). Levinas as a Jewish philosopher thus views Heideggerian atheism as paganistic, rooted in pre-Socratic texts and thus fundamentally anti-Biblical. This is the most obvious root of Levinas' antipathy, but the deeper issues may reside with Heidegger's sympathy to Nietzsche's entire philosophical project of the self, which may be easily viewed as a powerful precursor to Heidegger's own version of the Übermensch, *Dasein*. See Peperzak (1993) for further comparison of Heidegger and Levinas.

19 What Levinas finds is that both Heidegger's authenticity and Husserl's transcendental ego reduce the existential world by giving undue primacy to the self and its relationship to itself. The alterity of the other person is more fundamental than "the being of the being who asks about being" (Gibbs, 1992 at 8).

20 Note "consciousness does not fall into a body" (Levinas, 1981, 1969 at 155), i.e. it is not "trapped by matter but rather represents a suspension of the body corporeality" (Wyschogrod, 1974 at 59).

21 "[T]he 'I' becomes itself through its substitution for the other...The 'I', as substitution, is a task of responding for the other -- and as such becomes an infinite task through this inversion. Levinas calls this task ethics, but this is a translation of the "Hebrew" term *sanctification*" (Gibbs, 1992 at 187).

22 The contrasts with Buber are explored by Bernasconi (1988) and Levinas himself (1989). Those debts to Kierkegaard are mentioned only briefly by Ciaramelli (1991); the most complete comments to date are those given by Gibbs (1992), who notes "Buber's relationship [I-Thou] is reciprocal. The result, according to Levinas, is that Buber provides for a relationship that does not recognize the height of the other and the fundamental inability to imagine the polarity reversed" (1992 at 189).

23 "Responsibility for the other preexists any self-consciousness, so that from the beginning of any face, the question of being involves the right to be. This is what Levinas means when he mentions the face of the other: I do not grasp the other in order to dominate; I respond, instead to the face's epiphany. As such, what is produced in a concrete form is the idea of infinity rather than totality. The relations is metaphysical, and precedes any ontological programme" (Hand, 1989 at 75). Ciaramelli (1991) notes that to pass from ontology to ethics requires an inversion: We must first postulate freedom of will, since it is absent from the ontological realm, and then submit free will to the rule of rationality in the attempt to find criteria for human action that are universally intelligible and valid. To speak in the name of *logos* places philosophers under obligation in two ways: 1) affirm an intelligibility that manifests the structure of reality, and 2) allow everyone to recognize himself in this rationality. To obey the logos, we must be autonomous, and in turn moral obligation is justified by referring to the inherent rationality of the ethos. "This submission to the authority of the logos goes hand-in-hand with the primacy of ontology.... The understanding of ethical discourse that we find in the work of Levinas is quite divorced from this view. Levinas does not treat 'ethics' as one branch of philosophy amongst others....'ethics' means an anarchical assignation of the particular subject to morality by the appeal of the other. 'First philosophy' is no longer ontology or ontological metaphysics, but ethics. Ethical obligation arises not from logical and ontological universality of reason which discloses to knowledge criteria for freely determined action, but rather immediately from the uniqueness of the moral situation itself....[M]oral obligation binds us because it takes hold immediately, before understanding or decision on the part of the subject" (p.85). *Totality and Infinity,* the work upon which my summary is based, still attempts to present its account within the constraints of ontological language; *Otherwise than Being* (1991) disengages altogether and in this respect is a more challenging work.

24 "That my freedom depends on the other, and that even my refusal (my free choice) originates in the other's freedom, is one of the most contentious and most important insights of Levinas....The rejection of the self-centered self is not identical to the dissolution of the self....The self is de-centered by an other who then appears as the center of my agency, producing an other-centered self. This

option is a valuable one for post-modernism. But autonomy… appears… as unethical" (Gibbs, 1992 at 222). The theological origins of this position are pursued by Gibbs (1992 at 223ff).

25 The stark differences between Levinas and Nietzsche are legion but note that a crucial argument represents a different view of our biological natures. Levinas emphasizes the cooperative aspects of biology, the struggle is subordinated to the seeking of pleasure, fulfillment of desire, the satiety of living. The encounter of the face *trusts* that there is to be no murder, that to meet is to exchange, and relation allows each party to *exist*. Levinas describes a non-Darwinian ethos, where Nietzschean struggle is replaced with a celebration of interaction in the intersubjective encounter.

26 It is hardly a secret that Levinas' philosophy is closely linked to his religious writings on Biblical and Talmudic texts. The roots of Levinas' philosophy in his understanding of man's relation to God may be gleaned from translated essays (1990a). More formal accounts may be found in "God and Philosophy" (1987 at 153-173), as well as alluded to in his major texts. Thus far, the most extensive analyses in English regarding the Jewish foundation of Levinas' philosophy are to be found in Gibbs (1992), Handelman (1991) and Wyschogrod (1974). There is of course an interesting irony: "Levinas' discussion of Judaism requires Judaism to seek out philosophy, to seek out a 'Greek' translation of its thought. And what is almost more scandalous is that Levinas does not claim to borrow or translate from the philosophical tradition into Jewish thought" (Gibbs, 1992 at 157).

27 This essential Lockean position, as modified by Kant, has been the subject of various post-modernist critiques. I have reviewed these issues elsewhere (Tauber, 1994a) and would not attempt to further delineate them here.

28 Engelhardt argues that beneficence is subordinated to the principle of autonomy and serves as a source of tension: "Concerns with mutual respect and concerns with common welfare appear sufficiently distinct so as not to allow a means for a mediation of their tensions. At best one will be able in particular communities commonly to agree to particular ways for understanding claims of beneficence. Yet even under the best of circumstances, such agreements will not be sufficiently complete or detailed to avoid tensions between the rights and obligations of individuals within the morality of mutual respect versus what appears right or wrong to do within the morality of common welfare" (Engelhardt, 1986 at 87). This is of course reminiscent of Kant's rejection of the beneficent philosophy of Shaftesbury and Hutcheson, and the alternate tack of asserting virtue as utilitarianism advocated by Christian Wolff.

[29] This Aristotelian aphorism is cited by Romanell (1984) as an epigraph, but he gives no reference, and I surmise that it in fact is a construction from two separate passages from *Parva Naturalia*, a group of short treatises on subjects of physiological psychology. Near the beginning of the chapter on sense perception, Aristotle wrote, "It falls within the province of the natural scientist[s] to survey the first principles involved in the subject of health and disease… [they] do not stop until they have run on into medicine, and those of our medicine men who employ their art in a more scientific fashion, use as the first principles of medicine truths belonging to the natural sciences" (Aristotle, 1973 at 44-45). Later, near the end of the chapter on respiration, he wrote, "For physicians of culture and refinement make some mention of natural science [philosophy], and claim to derive their principles from it, while the most accomplished investigators into nature [philosophers] generally push their studies so far as to conclude with an account of medical principles" (Aristotle, 1931 at 480b). I am much indebted to Professor Wolfgang Haase of Boston University for finding these passages and clarifying the origin of the quoted epigraph.

ALLEN SPEIGHT

SELF AND OTHER IN ETHICS: A RESPONSE TO ALFRED I. TAUBER

In sketching the outlines for a medical ethics that would direct practitioners' concerns from the technocratic aspirations of much contemporary medicine to a reconceived notion of medicine as the art essentially concerned with healing, Alfred I. Tauber has suggested the basis not only for a more comprehensive philosophical grounding for medical ethics but also for a new philosophy of medicine. His claim that medicine is fundamentally ethical has roots in the tradition of American medical ethics (in the writings of Osler, Cabot and Peabody), but what is bold about Tauber's project is his choice of philosophical allies.

By seeking in the philosophy of Emmanuel Levinas a source for a philosophy of medicine centered on the physician-patient relationship, Tauber offers a provocative way of shifting the terms of debate in medical ethics away from an over-concern with such issues as patients' rights and physician paternalism. Levinas' notion of "ethics as first philosophy" is, in the first instance, a potentially quite suggestive starting-point for medicine's own self-definition with respect to other scientific pursuits: because medicine in contrast with other scientific fields of inquiry has as its fundamental purpose the task of healing, ethics may, following Levinas, be taken to be a sort of "first medicine" -- that which defines, rather than as ancillary to, practitioners' understanding of what they do. What is more difficult to see -- and what will be the focus of my response here -- is concretely what sort of medical ethics would follow from a Levinasian model. This general question is tied to a further issue of a historical sort concerning the origins of Levinas' project in a rejection of a tradition of philosophical ethics grounded in autonomy.

Tauber argues for his thesis by framing the issue in the stark terms of a dialogue between the rival philosophical claims of Nietzsche and Levinas: if Nietzsche's concern for a radical sort of self-determination opposes the equally radical claim of Levinas concerning the demands of the Other, the two nevertheless share a certain set of assumptions concerning the claims of the earlier rationalist tradition in ethics; most especially, the assumptions embedded in the Kantian notion of moral autonomy.

What I should like to suggest here is that, by framing the relation between Self and Other as represented by a dialogue between Nietzschean and Levinasian positions, Tauber has perhaps left out of account some strategies associated with the rationalist tradition of autonomy which might

M. A. Grodin (ed.), Meta Medical Ethics, 197–201.

contribute to his project of redefining medical ethics around the patient-physician relationship. These strategies may in the end prove necessary as well to remedy some deficiencies in a Levinasian approach to medical ethics.

The comparison with these earlier strategies prompts, then, a re-framing of Tauber's question at its most general level: if construing a Self-Other relation is the task of an ethics, what are the minimal conditions for that construal? What issues, in other words, must any ethical theory -- whether general or applied -- determine, if it wishes to give a full account of the relation between Self and Other? I would suggest, at least provisionally, the following three concerns: (1) self-consciousness: how is Self, and Other, respectively grounded? (2) responsibility: is the relationship of responsibility between Self and Other one which is symmetrical or asymmetrical? (3) determination of content: does the relation as defined yield a set of concrete duties that can be practiced?

A look at these three issues can help explore in general what is involved in a task such as the one proposed and compare as well the extent to which Levinasian and Kantian models are helpful for providing concrete answers.

1. Self-Consciousness

The first of our issues concerns the need in any ethical relation for the Self to have a sufficient consciousness of itself as agent in order to act: Tauber takes it as his "underlying thesis" that "medical ethics must be based on the notion of the Self, both in the obvious terms of self-responsibility, but more fundamentally in the problem of Self as agent." The question that Levinas pointedly raises is whether that sense of Self-as-agent is not fundamentally dependent on an Other which offers "resistance" to the merely egoistic projects of the acting subject. Levinas thus criticizes the earlier philosophical tradition for the primacy it places on a self-consciousness that stems from the self's sense of its autonomy. What is offered in its place is a notion of Self which is dependent on the Other: "To realize my responsibility for the Other, I myself must be free and independent; but the sense of my selfhood is my being-for-the-Other" (Peperzak, 1993 at 25).

It is only worth saying here that what Levinas sees in the "resistance" of the Other as necessary for genuine self-consciousness is something that is not only preserved in his Other-centered ethics, but also may be said to be a constitutive part of the tradition of autonomy itself. Levinas himself did suggest that he felt "particularly close" to the practical philosophy of Kant, particularly the distinction between persons and things implicit in the famous second formulation of Kant's categorical imperative (Levinas, 1989 at 128).[1] This formulation of the moral law from the tradition of autonomy involves at its root some sense of the necessary "resistance" of others to projects of my own inasmuch as those others are, as I am, rational agents, capable of acting on the categorical imperative: I cannot merely act on my desires with respect to other human beings, but must accord them a respect which stems from the basic respect deriving from the moral law itself.

Admittedly, the respect for Other inherent in the tradition of autonomy does not allow what Levinas seeks to capture in the uniqueness of the demands the Other places on me ("to utter 'I'... means to possess a privileged place with regard to responsibilities for which no one can replace me and from which no one can release me" [Levinas, 1969 at 245]). Yet, if the concern is for a medical ethics grounded in a Self-Other relationship that fully respects the place of the Other, an ethics which takes autonomy as its first principle at least has sufficient means for establishing such respect.

2. Responsibility and Symmetry

The second issue concerns what sort of obligation Self and Other reciprocally owe: is the relationship of responsibility between Self and Other symmetrical, or -- as Levinas' project seems to suggest -- inherently asymmetrical at its origin? Tauber's use of Levinas here for a medical ethics seems particularly appropriate, since the asymmetry that exists at the root of the Levinasian Self-Other relationship (I am infinitely responsible for the Other, but I cannot claim the same obligation from him) correlates in some sense in the medical case with an inherent asymmetry in the physician-patient relationship. As opposed to the obvious need for some symmetry of responsibility in a general ethics, it is the doctor whose responsibility is chiefly at issue in the practice of medicine, whereas the patient's own relation is one inevitably of dependence.

Tauber acknowledges this asymmetry in saying that "the power of the Levinasian construct is most aptly applied from the physician/nurse toward the patient" and suggests a possible Levinasian answer for filling in the relation from the patient's perspective: that, while the doctor-patient relationship may not be symmetrical as the patient suffers, the healer's ultimate goal is to return the patient again to his "true Self." Yet a further problem remains in the asymmetry inherent in physician responsibility: if the physician's responsibility for the patient is rooted in an "infinite" responsibility for the Other, what guidelines are there for denying appeals of the patient that the physician himself finds clearly harmful and unethical? Whether such an issue is to be resolved, as Kant thought, as a consequence of the universality and respect for humanity implicit in the notion of autonomy, or requires a further integration of the principles of autonomy and beneficence

(Engelhardt, 1986 at 69, 77), it is clear that the tradition of ethical thought which takes autonomy as its primary principle again offers concrete guidance. It is still unclear to me how a Levinasian approach gives us the tools for resolving this issue, which has in effect pointed to our third concern, which I find presents the most substantial and general objection to Tauber's proposal.

3. Determination of Content

The final question which must be asked of any ethical theory concerned with the relation between Self and Other is whether that theory can specify a set of concrete duties sufficient for action. Tauber points to the necessity for such a concrete determination of ethical content in his suggestion that a medical ethics must incorporate a number of "layers of physician responsibility," ranging from the merely "fiduciary" role of pathologists and radiologists who have no patient contact to the "primary care provider who assumes total care of her patient."

The problem of discriminating a concrete set of ethical responsibilities is a problem, of course, which faces both the tradition of autonomy and Levinas' project. Yet there has been, starting with Hegel, a series of attempts within that tradition itself to specify ethical content without losing a fundamental attachment to the claims of free and rational agency.

Strikingly, given the seriousness with which it takes the distinctiveness of the concrete Other, Levinas' account of the Other loses the sort of concreteness of Tauber's picture of varied medical responsibilities or Hegel's articulated set of ethical commitments, returning us to something closer to the Kantian view of ethical non-particularity. If the Other is, as Levinas puts it, "the first individual to come along," someone to whom I have a "responsibility that goes beyond what I may or may not have done to the Other" (Levinas, 1989, at 83), it may reasonably be asked whether such a description can encompass the range of relations that a physician actually has to concrete Others. Such relations are constituted by unique Others, with whom I have a specific history defined by the deeds we have reciprocally shared. What I owe them has in some measure to do with how I have already come to be related to them (In this connection, Tauber rightly distances himself from the suggestion of Pellegrino and Thomasma that physician and patient might relate to one another as friends, since -- even with the included qualifiers that they "share the same medical ideals, have no economic or social conflicts of interests and embrace the same moral values" -- such a beneficence-based medical ethic seems not to respect the inherent concreteness and variety of one's relationships to others that cannot be expressed in the exclusivity of a friendship).

It is, then, the difficulty of determining a set of concrete ethical duties which, as Tauber himself suggests, poses the greatest test of the validity of his approach. In examining the questions involved for any ethical determination of the Self-Other relation, I hope to have shown not only what generally would be needed to test the possible "fecundity" of a Levinasian medical ethics but also that the tradition of autonomy which Levinas rejects has within itself already elements which are useful for the project which Tauber has defined as most crucial -- that of reconstruing medicine as an essentially ethical endeavor.

Boston University

REFERENCES:

All the works cited here are already in Tauber's bibliography, with the exception of the following:

Levinas, Emmanuel. "Is Ontology Fundamental?" Translated by Peter Atterton. In *Philosophy Today* 33, 1 (Summer 1989): 121-29.

ENDNOTES

1 This affinity between Kantian moral philosophy and Levinas' project with respect to the demands of the other is discussed further in Jan de Greef, "Ethique, reflexion et histoire chez Levinas," *Revue philosophique de Louvain* (1969), 431-460 and in Bettina Bergo, "The God of Abraham and the God of the Philosophers: A Reading of Emmanuel Levinas' 'Dieu et la Philosophie,'" *Graduate Faculty Philosophy Journal* 16 (November 1992): 113-164. I am especially grateful to Ms. Bergo for her criticism of an earlier draft of this response.

INDEX

Adams, J. L., 81
Alcorn, 118
Alexander, L., 85
Alexander, Shana, 92, 97
Andrews, Lori, 63
Annas, G., 83, 97
Aquinas, St. T., 2, 35
Ariston, 31
Aristotle, 2, 18, 29–31, 41, 42, 45, 57, 111, 112, 113, 115, 118, 185
Asch, A., 149
Augustine, 42

Barnes, H., 174
Beauchamp, 35, 36, 38, 50, 56, 58
Beecher, 5
Bellah, 70
Benjamin, W., 176
Bentham, 29, 38, 68
Bleich, 11
Booth, W., 112, 115, 118
Bouvia, E., 152
Boyajian, Jane, 62
Bracher, 118
Brock, 35
Brody, 35
Brophy v. New England Hospital, 99
Brown, W. M., 166
Buber, M., 158, 176
Buck v. Bell, 98
Burrell, D., 112
Bush, G., 16, 98

Cabot, R., 178
Calinescu, M., 116
Campbell, J, 87
Caplan, 61, 85
Caputo, J., 176, 177
Casey, 84
Cavell, S., 112
Charon, R., 119
Childress, 35, 36, 38, 50, 56, 58
Cicero, 32, 33, 34, 35
Clark, B., 90
Clinton, Bill, 16, 70, 84, 92, 98
Cohen, H., 176
Coleridge, S. T., 112
Cruzan v. Director, Missouri Dept. of Health, 85, 104
Cruzan, Nancy, 85

Davis v. Davis, 106
Descartes, R., 29, 172–73
Devettere, R., 27, 49, 53, 54–59
Dewey, J., 112
Dickens, 115

Eco, U., 117
Eliot, T. S., 93
Engelhardt, 35, 183

Farley, M., 131
Faulkner, W, 119
Fay, Baby, 90
Feldman, 11
Fitzgerald, F. S., 120
Fletcher, 4, 11, 55
Forrow, L., 125
Foucault, M., 165, 166
Frankena, 39
Freud, 78, 118

Gardner, J., 115
Gerrig, R., 116
Gibbs, R., 176
Gibson, W., 117
Gilligan, C., 141, 149
Griswald v. Connecticut, 63
Grodin, M., 1

Handelman, S., 176
Hauerwas, S., 112
Healey, 3
Hegel, 158, 169
Heidegger, M., 112, 158, 169
Himes, Kenneth, 71, 74, 75, 76
Himes, Michael, 71, 74, 75, 76
Hippocrates, 2, 18, 110
Holland, N., 118
Homer, 43
Hume, 38
Husserl, E., 120, 168

Isaiah, 43
Iser, W., 117
Ivy, A, 85
Izymar, 166

Jacobovitz, 11
James, H., 115, 119
John XXIII, 72
Johnson, Mark, 113
Jonsen, 33, 39, 53, 111
Jordon, E., 92
Joyce, J., 119

Kant, 28, 29, 35, 38, 41, 42, 55, 110, 157, 198, 199
Katz, J., 181
Kearn, 11
Kevorkian, J., 92

LaRochefoucald, 77
Lawrence, D. H., 116
Leo XIII, 71
Levi, E, 43
Levinas, E., 158, 168–75, 176, 181, 182, 183, 197, 199

Macafee, L., 152
MacIntyre, A., 112
Maimonides, M., 2
Mannheim, 78
Mappes, 38
Marx, 78, 169
McCann, D., 75
McCormick, 11
McFadden, 3
Melville, 120
Mill, J. S., 28, 29, 35, 38, 41, 55
Miller, J. H., 112, 115
Minow, M., 153
Montello, M., 109
Moore, G. E., 80
Morrison, T., 120
Moses, 43, 45
Munson, 37
Murdoch, I., 112
Myrdal, G., 83

Nell, V., 116
Neoptolemus, 45
Newton, 29
Nietzsche, 158–67, 169, 170, 175, 183, 197
Noddings, N., 149
Nordenfelt, L., 166
Nussbaum, M., 112, 114, 115

O'Connor v. Westchester County Med. Ctr, 102
Odysseus, 45

Osler, W., 178

Paris, J, 97
Peabody, F., 178
Pellegrino, 13, 35, 181, 200
Percival, 3
Philo, 34, 35
Pieper, J., 70
Pius IX, 71
Pius XI, 73
Plato, 2, 18, 29, 112
Pörn, I., 166
Potter, R., 77
Proust, 115
Putnam, H., 112

Quinlan, 85
Quinlan, Karen, 87, 89

Ramsey, P., 6, 11, 99
Rawls, J., 54, 110
Reagan, R., 16, 70
Relman, A., 91
Rockwell, 71
Roe v. Wade, 63, 84, 98
Rorty, R., 114
Rosenzweig, F., 158, 176
Rosner, 11
Rothman, D., 179
Rousseau, 158
Ryan, M. L., 116

Sartre, 169, 180
Schiller, F., 112
Schlesinger, A. Jr., 83, 93
Scholem, G., 176
Schopenhauer, 170
Scotus, 69
Seneca, 31
Shakespeare, 120
Shannon, T., 61, 77, 78
Shattuck, R., 120, 121
Shelley, P., 120
Sherwin, S., 153
Shklar, Judith, 36
Skura, M., 118
Socrates, 29
Solomon, 45
Sophocles, 43, 45, 115
Speight, A., 197
St. Paul, 45
Starr, Paul, 92

Tauber, A., 157
Thomasma, D., 181, 200
Toulmin, 33, 53, 111, 180
Troeltsch, 78
Truog, R., 49
Twain, 120

Veatch, R., 35, 36

Walters, 38
Weber, 78
Webster, 84, 98
Welty, E., 114
Whitbeck, C., 166
Williams, B., 112
Wilson, J., 66
Wittgenstein, 158
Wolfe, Naomi, 91
Woolf, V., 119

Zarathustra, 160, 161, 163
Zembaty, 38
Zeno, 31

Boston Studies in the Philosophy of Science

105. F. Burwick (ed.): *Approaches to Organic Form.* Permutations in Science and Culture. 1987 ISBN 90-277-2541-1
106. M. Almási: *The Philosophy of Appearances.* Translated from Hungarian. 1989 ISBN 90-277-2150-5
107. S. Hook, W.L. O'Neill and R. O'Toole (eds.): *Philosophy, History and Social Action.* Essays in Honor of Lewis Feuer. With an Autobiographical Essay by L. Feuer. 1988 ISBN 90-277-2644-2
108. I. Hronszky, M. Fehér and B. Dajka: *Scientific Knowledge Socialized.* Selected Proceedings of the 5th Joint International Conference on the History and Philosophy of Science organized by the IUHPS (Veszprém, Hungary, 1984). 1988 ISBN 90-277-2284-6
109. P. Tillers and E.D. Green (eds.): *Probability and Inference in the Law of Evidence.* The Uses and Limits of Bayesianism. 1988 ISBN 90-277-2689-2
110. E. Ullmann-Margalit (ed.): *Science in Reflection.* The Israel Colloquium: Studies in History, Philosophy, and Sociology of Science, Vol. 3. 1988 ISBN 90-277-2712-0; Pb 90-277-2713-9
111. K. Gavroglu, Y. Goudaroulis and P. Nicolacopoulos (eds.): *Imre Lakatos and Theories of Scientific Change.* 1989 ISBN 90-277-2766-X
112. B. Glassner and J.D. Moreno (eds.): *The Qualitative-Quantitative Distinction in the Social Sciences.* 1989 ISBN 90-277-2829-1
113. K. Arens: *Structures of Knowing.* Psychologies of the 19th Century. 1989 ISBN 0-7923-0009-2
114. A. Janik: *Style, Politics and the Future of Philosophy.* 1989 ISBN 0-7923-0056-4
115. F. Amrine (ed.): *Literature and Science as Modes of Expression.* With an Introduction by S. Weininger. 1989 ISBN 0-7923-0133-1
116. J.R. Brown and J. Mittelstrass (eds.): *An Intimate Relation.* Studies in the History and Philosophy of Science. Presented to Robert E. Butts on His 60th Birthday. 1989 ISBN 0-7923-0169-2
117. F. D'Agostino and I.C. Jarvie (eds.): *Freedom and Rationality.* Essays in Honor of John Watkins. 1989 ISBN 0-7923-0264-8
118. D. Zolo: *Reflexive Epistemology.* The Philosophical Legacy of Otto Neurath. 1989 ISBN 0-7923-0320-2
119. M. Kearn, B.S. Philips and R.S. Cohen (eds.): *Georg Simmel and Contemporary Sociology.* 1989 ISBN 0-7923-0407-1
120. T.H. Levere and W.R. Shea (eds.): *Nature, Experiment and the Science.* Essays on Galileo and the Nature of Science. In Honour of Stillman Drake. 1989 ISBN 0-7923-0420-9
121. P. Nicolacopoulos (ed.): *Greek Studies in the Philosophy and History of Science.* 1990 ISBN 0-7923-0717-8
122. R. Cooke and D. Costantini (eds.): *Statistics in Science.* The Foundations of Statistical Methods in Biology, Physics and Economics. 1990 ISBN 0-7923-0797-6

Boston Studies in the Philosophy of Science

123. P. Duhem: *The Origins of Statics.* Translated from French by G.F. Leneaux, V.N. Vagliente and G.H. Wagner. With an Introduction by S.L. Jaki. 1991 ISBN 0-7923-0898-0
124. H. Kamerlingh Onnes: *Through Measurement to Knowledge.* The Selected Papers, 1853-1926. Edited and with an Introduction by K. Gavroglu and Y. Goudaroulis. 1991 ISBN 0-7923-0825-5
125. M. Čapek: *The New Aspects of Time: Its Continuity and Novelties.* Selected Papers in the Philosophy of Science. 1991 ISBN 0-7923-0911-1
126. S. Unguru (ed.): *Physics, Cosmology and Astronomy, 1300-1700.* Tension and Accommodation. 1991 ISBN 0-7923-1022-5
127. Z. Bechler: *Newton's Physics on the Conceptual Structure of the Scientific Revolution.* 1991 ISBN 0-7923-1054-3
128. É. Meyerson: *Explanation in the Sciences.* Translated from French by M-A. Siple and D.A. Siple. 1991 ISBN 0-7923-1129-9
129. A.I. Tauber (ed.): *Organism and the Origins of Self.* 1991 ISBN 0-7923-1185-X
130. F.J. Varela and J-P. Dupuy (eds.): *Understanding Origins.* Contemporary Views on the Origin of Life, Mind and Society. 1992 ISBN 0-7923-1251-1
131. G.L. Pandit: *Methodological Variance.* Essays in Epistemological Ontology and the Methodology of Science. 1991 ISBN 0-7923-1263-5
132. G. Munévar (ed.): *Beyond Reason.* Essays on the Philosophy of Paul Feyerabend. 1991 ISBN 0-7923-1272-4
133. T.E. Uebel (ed.): *Rediscovering the Forgotten Vienna Circle.* Austrian Studies on Otto Neurath and the Vienna Circle. Partly translated from German. 1991 ISBN 0-7923-1276-7
134. W.R. Woodward and R.S. Cohen (eds.): *World Views and Scientific Discipline Formation.* Science Studies in the [former] German Democratic Republic. Partly translated from German by W.R. Woodward. 1991 ISBN 0-7923-1286-4
135. P. Zambelli: *The Speculum Astronomiae and Its Enigma.* Astrology, Theology and Science in Albertus Magnus and His Contemporaries. 1992 ISBN 0-7923-1380-1
136. P. Petitjean, C. Jami and A.M. Moulin (eds.): *Science and Empires.* Historical Studies about Scientific Development and European Expansion. ISBN 0-7923-1518-9
137. W.A. Wallace: *Galileo's Logic of Discovery and Proof.* The Background, Content, and Use of His Appropriated Treatises on Aristotle's *Posterior Analytics.* 1992 ISBN 0-7923-1577-4
138. W.A. Wallace: *Galileo's Logical Treatises.* A Translation, with Notes and Commentary, of His Appropriated Latin Questions on Aristotle's *Posterior Analytics.* 1992 ISBN 0-7923-1578-2
Set (137 + 138) ISBN 0-7923-1579-0

Boston Studies in the Philosophy of Science

139. M.J. Nye, J.L. Richards and R.H. Stuewer (eds.): *The Invention of Physical Science.* Intersections of Mathematics, Theology and Natural Philosophy since the Seventeenth Century. Essays in Honor of Erwin N. Hiebert. 1992 ISBN 0-7923-1753-X
140. G. Corsi, M.L. dalla Chiara and G.C. Ghirardi (eds.): *Bridging the Gap: Philosophy, Mathematics and Physics.* Lectures on the Foundations of Science. 1992 ISBN 0-7923-1761-0
141. C.-H. Lin and D. Fu (eds.): *Philosophy and Conceptual History of Science in Taiwan.* 1992 ISBN 0-7923-1766-1
142. S. Sarkar (ed.): *The Founders of Evolutionary Genetics.* A Centenary Reappraisal. 1992 ISBN 0-7923-1777-7
143. J. Blackmore (ed.): *Ernst Mach – A Deeper Look.* Documents and New Perspectives. 1992 ISBN 0-7923-1853-6
144. P. Kroes and M. Bakker (eds.): *Technological Development and Science in the Industrial Age.* New Perspectives on the Science–Technology Relationship. 1992 ISBN 0-7923-1898-6
145. S. Amsterdamski: *Between History and Method.* Disputes about the Rationality of Science. 1992 ISBN 0-7923-1941-9
146. E. Ullmann-Margalit (ed.): *The Scientific Enterprise.* The Bar-Hillel Colloquium: Studies in History, Philosophy, and Sociology of Science, Volume 4. 1992 ISBN 0-7923-1992-3
147. L. Embree (ed.): *Metaarchaeology.* Reflections by Archaeologists and Philosophers. 1992 ISBN 0-7923-2023-9
148. S. French and H. Kamminga (eds.): *Correspondence, Invariance and Heuristics.* Essays in Honour of Heinz Post. 1993 ISBN 0-7923-2085-9
149. M. Bunzl: *The Context of Explanation.* 1993 ISBN 0-7923-2153-7
150. I.B. Cohen (ed.): *The Natural Sciences and the Social Sciences.* Some Critical and Historical Perspectives. 1994 ISBN 0-7923-2223-1
151. K. Gavroglu, Y. Christianidis and E. Nicolaidis (eds.): *Trends in the Historiography of Science.* 1994 ISBN 0-7923-2255-X
152. S. Poggi and M. Bossi (eds.): *Romanticism in Science.* Science in Europe, 1790–1840. 1994 ISBN 0-7923-2336-X
153. J. Faye and H.J. Folse (eds.): *Niels Bohr and Contemporary Philosophy.* 1994 ISBN 0-7923-2378-5
154. C.C. Gould and R.S. Cohen (eds.): *Artifacts, Representations, and Social Practice.* Essays for Marx W. Wartofsky. 1994 ISBN 0-7923-2481-1
155. R.E. Butts: *Historical Pragmatics.* Philosophical Essays. 1993 ISBN 0-7923-2498-6
156. R. Rashed: *The Development of Arabic Mathematics: Between Arithmetic and Algebra.* Translated from French by A.F.W. Armstrong. 1994 ISBN 0-7923-2565-6

Boston Studies in the Philosophy of Science

157. I. Szumilewicz-Lachman (ed.): *Zygmunt Zawirski: His Life and Work.* With Selected Writings on Time, Logic and the Methodology of Science. Translations by Feliks Lachman. Ed. by R.S. Cohen, with the assistance of B. Bergo. 1994 ISBN 0-7923-2566-4
158. S.N. Haq: *Names, Natures and Things.* The Alchemist Jābir ibn Ḥayyān and His *Kitāb al-Aḥjār* (Book of Stones). 1994 ISBN 0-7923-2587-7
159. P. Plaass: *Kant's Theory of Natural Science.* Translation, Analytic Introduction and Commentary by Alfred E. and Maria G. Miller. 1994 ISBN 0-7923-2750-0
160. J. Misiek (ed.): *The Problem of Rationality in Science and its Philosophy.* On Popper vs. Polanyi. The Polish Conferences 1988–89. 1995 ISBN 0-7923-2925-2
161. I.C. Jarvie and N. Laor (eds.): *Critical Rationalism, Metaphysics and Science.* Essays for Joseph Agassi, Volume I. 1995 ISBN 0-7923-2960-0
162. I.C. Jarvie and N. Laor (eds.): *Critical Rationalism, the Social Sciences and the Humanities.* Essays for Joseph Agassi, Volume II. 1995 ISBN 0-7923-2961-9
Set (161–162) ISBN 0-7923-2962-7
163. K. Gavroglu, J. Stachel and M.W. Wartofsky (eds.): *Physics, Philosophy, and the Scientific Community.* Essays in the Philosophy and History of the Natural Sciences and Mathematics. In Honor of Robert S. Cohen. 1995 ISBN 0-7923-2988-0
164. K. Gavroglu, J. Stachel and M.W. Wartofsky (eds.): *Science, Politics and Social Practice.* Essays on Marxism and Science, Philosophy of Culture and the Social Sciences. In Honor of Robert S. Cohen. 1995 ISBN 0-7923-2989-9
165. K. Gavroglu, J. Stachel and M.W. Wartofsky (eds.): *Science, Mind and Art.* Essays on Science and the Humanistic Understanding in Art, Epistemology, Religion and Ethics. Essays in Honor of Robert S. Cohen. 1995 ISBN 0-7923-2990-2
Set (163–165) ISBN 0-7923-2991-0
166. K.H. Wolff: *Transformation in the Writing.* A Case of Surrender-and-Catch. 1995 ISBN 0-7923-3178-8
167. A.J. Kox and D.M. Siegel (eds.): *No Truth Except in the Details.* Essays in honor of Martin J. Klein. 1995 ISBN 0-7923-3195-8
168. J. Blackmore (ed.): *Ludwig Boltzmann* His Later Life and Philosophy, 1900–1906. 1995 ISBN 0-7923-3231-8
169. R.S. Cohen, R. Hilpinen and Qiu Renzong (eds.): *Realism and Anti-Realism in the Philosophy of Science.* Beijing International Conference, 1992. 1995 (forthcoming) ISBN 0-7923-3233-4
170. I. Kuçuradi and R.S. Cohen (eds.): *The Concept of Knowledge.* The Ankara Seminar. 1995 (forthcoming) ISBN 0-7923-3241-5

9 781402 002526